Using the *Teach Yourself* in 24 Hours Series

Welcome to the *Teach Yourself in 24 Hours* series! You're probably thinking, "What, they want me to stay up all night and learn this stuff?" Well, no, not exactly. This series introduces a new way to teach you about exciting new products: 24 one-hour lessons, designed to keep your interest and keep you learning. Because the learning process is broken into small units, you will not be overwhelmed by the complexity of some of the new technologies that are emerging in today's market. Each hourly lesson has a number of special items, some old, some new, to help you along.

Minutes

The first 10 minutes of each hour lists the topics and skills that you will learn about by the time you finish the hour. You will know exactly what the hour will bring with no surprises.

Minutes

Twenty minutes into the lesson, you will have been introduced to many of the newest features of the software application. In the constantly evolving computer arena, knowing everything a program can do will aid you enormously now and in the future.

Minutes

Before 30 minutes have passed, you will have learned at least one useful task. Many of these tasks take advantage of the newest features of the application. These tasks use a hands-on approach, telling you exactly which menus and commands you need to use to accomplish the goal. This approach is found in each lesson of the *24 Hours* series.

40 Minutes

You will see after 40 minutes that many of the tools you have come to expect from the *Teach Yourself* series are found in the *24 Hours* series as well. Notes and Tips offer special tricks of the trade to make your work faster and more productive. Warnings help you avoid those nasty time-consuming errors.

50 Minutes

By the time you're 50 minutes in, you'll probably run across terms you haven't seen before. Never before has technology thrown so many new words and acronyms into the language. This *Teach Yourself* series will fully explain any confusing or difficult terms.

60 Minutes

At the end of the hour, you may still have questions that need answered. You know the kind—questions on skills or tasks that come up every day for you, but that weren't directly addressed during the lesson. That's where the Q&A section can help. By answering the most frequently asked questions about the topics discussed in the hour, Q&A not only answers your specific question, it provides a succinct review of all that you have learned in the hour.

Teach Yourself
OUTLOOK
in 24 Hours

Teach Yourself
OUTLOOK
in 24 Hours

Kim Spilker
Brian Proffitt

SAMS
PUBLISHING

201 West 103rd Street
Indianapolis, Indiana 46290

To my grandmother, the strongest woman I have ever known. —Brian Proffitt

To Mark, who always supports me no matter what I take on. —Kim Spilker

Copyright © 1997 by Sams Publishing

FIRST EDITION

International Standard Book Number: 0-672-31044-9

Library of Congress Catalog Card Number: 96-72165

2000   99   98   97   4   3   2   1

Interpretation of the printing code: the rightmost double-digit number is the year of the book's printing; the rightmost single-digit, the number of the book's printing. For example, a printing code of 97-1 shows that the first printing of the book occurred in 1997.

Composed in AGaramond and MCPdigital by Macmillan Computer Publishing

Printed in the United States of America

Trademarks

Publisher and President   Richard K. Swadley
Publishing Manager   Dean Miller
Director of Editorial Services   Cindy Morrow
Managing Editor   Kitty Wilson Jarrett
Director of Marketing   Kelli S. Spencer
Assistant Marketing Managers   Kristina Perry, Rachel Wolfe

Acquisitions Editor
Kim Spilker

Development Editor
Jeff Koch

Software Development Specialist
Patty Brooks

Production Editor
Colleen Williams

Indexer
Johnna VanHoose

Technical Reviewer
Robert Bogue

Editorial Coordinator
Katie Wise

Technical Edit Coordinator
Lynette Quinn

Editorial Assistants
Carol Ackerman
Andi Richter
Rhonda Tinch-Mize

Cover Designer
Tim Amrhein

Book Designer
Alyssa Yesh

Copy Writer
Peter Fuller

Production Team Supervisors
Brad Chinn
Charlotte Clapp

Production
Jennifer Dierdorff
Ayanna Lacey
Brad Lenser
Chris Livengood

Overview

Contents

Acknowledgments

We would like to acknowledge everyone at Sams who made it possible to get this book off the ground. Our team leader Dean Miller was instrumental in clearing the bureaucratic path for getting us to write this book (even if we did have to bribe him with a Data Link watch); the Development Editor Jeff Koch, who helped get this to us organized; the Production Editor Colleen Williams, who put up with all our silliness ("I'll be on vacation"), and the Technical Editor Rob Bogue, one of the best. We would also like to thank those who hardly ever get mentioned, but who work damned hard to get Sams books out the door: the layout technicians and the proofreaders. Their dedication to creativity and accuracy makes good books possible.

On a personal note, I would like to thank my wife, Cindy, for taking the family reins while I pounded away at the keyboard. Her strength, love, and dedication is the center of my life and got me through some pretty dark times while this book was being written. (By the way, two of the fictional people in this book, Jamie and Nathan Daniels, are actually me and her—and our new daughter should be arriving at the same time this book hits the stores. Writing a book, we discovered, creates more mood swings than pregnancy!) My oldest daughter Brittany also deserves a big thanks. Only she could make me laugh while I was pulling my hair out.

—Brian Proffitt

I want to thank Brian for agreeing to write this book with me; I thought it would be so easy. Brian was steadfast throughout this entire project, and he kept me going because I didn't want to let him down. I'd also like to thank my husband Mark, who, along with our two dogs, kept me company in our home office as I typed each night into the early morning hours. He kept boosting my morale when it got low. I'd also like to thank my sister Katie and my friend Sanjaya who let me send e-mails, faxes, and tasks to them when I needed examples for my chapters.

—Kim Spilker

About the Authors

Brian Proffitt (bproffitt@sams.mcp.com) is a development editor at Sams Publishing, specializing in operating systems and network servers. He also serves as an independent Internet consultant in central Indiana, getting small businesses out on the Web. A former managing editor of a western Indiana newspaper, Brian has worked for the IEEE, primarily editing the *Transactions on Computer-Aided Design*. Brian is a lifelong resident of Indiana (except for a brief period in New Jersey that he doesn't like to talk about) and lives with his wife, daughter, and daughter-to-be in Indianapolis. This is his first book.

Kim Spilker (kspilker@sams.mcp.com) is an acquisitions editor at Sams Publishing, specializing in operating systems and network servers. Although she has written some freelance articles for magazines, such as *Indiana Business Magazine* and *Indianapolis C.E.O. Magazine*, this is her first endeavor at writing a computer book. (And it's probably her last.) Kim lives in Indianapolis with her husband Mark Bewsey and two dogs, Patti Smith and Tess.

Tell Us What You Think!

As a reader, you are the most important critic and commentator of our books. We value your opinion and want to know what we're doing right, what we could do better, what areas you'd like to see us publish in, and any other words of wisdom you're willing to pass our way. You can help us make strong books that meet your needs and give you the computer guidance you require.

Do you have access to CompuServe or the World Wide Web? Then check out our CompuServe forum by typing GO SAMS at any prompt. If you prefer the World Wide Web, check out our site at http://www.mcp.com.

JUST A MINUTE

If you have a technical question about this book, call the technical support line at 317-581-3833.

As the publishing manager of the group that created this book, I welcome your comments. You can fax, e-mail, or write me directly to let me know what you did or didn't like about this book—as well as what we can do to make our books stronger. Here's the information:

Fax: 317-581-4669

E-mail: opsys_mgr@sams.mcp.com

Mail: Dean Miller
         Sams Publishing
         201 W. 103rd Street
         Indianapolis, IN 46290

Introduction

We all have preconceived notions of how these books are created. I used to think that there were sophisticated market analysis (there is), cutting-edge investigations into the latest technology (there isn't), and the hiring of only the best authors (well… usually).

This whole thing started last fall, when I strolled into Kim's office and saw something really cool running on her computer. In our office, there are few secrets and I'm nosy anyway, so I looked over her shoulder to see what it was. The first thing I noticed was that she had her cc:Mail messages mixed together with messages from her CompuServe account. I was immediately intrigued because I was always forgetting to download my CompuServe mail.

The program, of course, was Outlook, and Kim and I soon became the in-house Outlook gurus.

Outlook, I quickly learned, is Microsoft's first venture into really improving its Exchange Client and Schedule+ programs, as well as entering the world of groupware.

To be sure, Outlook is no Lotus Notes, but it is a start, and it is already compatible with the rest of the Office products. Sometimes it seems like Outlook can hear the other programs *think*. Microsoft also has a way of starting from behind and catching up quickly, so expect to see a lot of power in Outlook now and in the versions to come.

However, this wasn't to be the extent of my association with this program. In a team meeting we had in November, our intrepid leader decided that our team should publish a *Teach Yourself* book on Outlook, and suggested to Kim that she should be the one to find authors for the book because she was so familiar with the program.

Kim then turned around to me with a big grin on her face and said, "You know, Brian, *we* ought to do this book!"

There have been a few times in my life that I have been utterly speechless. When my wife told me about the impending arrivals of our children, when I was asked to start my first job out of college—and now this.

Not quite as scientific as you would think, huh?

Which is not to say this book is just a toss-off. Full of step-by-step explanations of all aspects of Outlook, *Teach Yourself Outlook in 24 Hours* shows you the ins and outs of this great new component of Office 97 and all in short, easy-to-manage hourly sessions.

Other features of this book include the following:

JUST A MINUTE

Notes give you comments and asides about the topic at hand, as well as full explanations.

TIME SAVER

Tips give you great shortcuts and hints on how to get more productivity from Outlook.

CAUTION

Cautions tell you how to make your life miserable if you do something wrong. Heed these, or suffer.

At the end of each hour, frequently asked questions about Outlook are asked and answered in the Q&A section.

You will find Outlook to be one of the best time-managers produced today. And in these hectic days, managing your time is often more important than managing your money. We hope you have as much fun learning about Outlook as we did writing this book.

PART
I

Outlook for Beginners

Hour

Hour 1

Getting Started with Outlook

What Can Outlook Do for You?

In this chapter, you will learn a little bit about how Outlook can help you manage your time, tasks, and e-mail. You will also learn how to install (or modify your installation of) Outlook so that you will have all the components that you need to maximize your benefits from the program.

Defining Outlook can be difficult not only because it is such a multifaceted program, but also because it can be as simple or as complex as you want it to be. You could simply use it as a Personal Information Manager (PIM) to keep track of your calendar and task list, as well as your contacts. If you use Schedule+, which was included in Office 95, you already know how to use Outlook to a certain extent. Outlook can also serve as your universal Inbox, gathering and sending e-mail and fax messages from a number of different services. If you use the Windows Messaging system that ships with Windows 95 and NT, you will easily understand the Inbox feature in Outlook.

On the complex end of the scale, Outlook has the capability of being a full-blown groupware application with the help of an Exchange Server, allowing people to share information in Public Folders, such as schedules, tasks, and contacts. At the same time, Outlook's Personal Folders file allows an individual to store the same kinds of information—tasks, schedules, contacts, and messages—privately.

Outlook is great because it incorporates three programs: Windows Messaging, the Windows Explorer, and Schedule+; it allows all the different features to be interoperable. Forget about copying and pasting information from an e-mail message to your calendar, task list, and contact list. Forget about keeping multiple applications open at all times, which takes up your precious system resources. Outlook is a one-stop shop for

- ☐ Sending and receiving e-mail messages from all your different e-mail accounts
- ☐ Sending and receiving faxes
- ☐ Storing contact information
- ☐ Creating tasks for yourself and others
- ☐ Reminding you when things are due or meetings are scheduled
- ☐ Logging all your electronic activities in a Journal
- ☐ Making electronic sticky notes
- ☐ Keeping track of appointments and special dates in a calendar
- ☐ Viewing and manipulating all the files on your computer by duplicating the Windows Explorer

Best of all, these features work in conjunction with one another. Throughout this book, we will give you tips for using the features together so that you won't have to duplicate your efforts when trying to organize your time and tasks.

Installation

In this chapter, you will learn specifically how to install or change your current installation of Outlook 97. Outlook is available as a program within the Microsoft Office Suite, as well as a stand-alone product. Most likely, you will be installing Outlook as part of your Office 97 installation. If you have not installed Outlook already, Microsoft offers three different ways of installing Office 97:

- ☐ A Typical install, in which Microsoft has made the choices for you. Their software designers pick the most common files and programs to install on your system.
- ☐ A Custom install, in which you can choose which files to install on your computer.
- ☐ Running it from a CD-ROM (as shown in Figure 1.1), which will require that the Office 97 CD is residing in your CD-ROM unit anytime you want to run the Office programs.

1

Figure 1.1.

The initial screen in the Microsoft Office 97 Setup program. Choose the Custom button to install Outlook according to your personal environment.

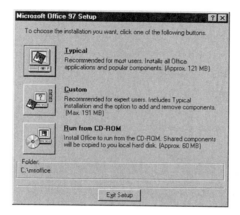

Installation Using the Typical Method

Once you insert the Office 97 CD-ROM, you will be faced with the three choices mentioned previously. If you are not an experienced computer user, you may want to choose the Typical Method option. In this particular option, Microsoft has chosen the most common files that a typical user would want. The following paragraphs discuss the advantages and disadvantages of using the Typical Method, as well as list the size and specific files that will be installed on your computer if you choose this option.

Pros: If you want to install Office the easiest way possible without having to make a lot of decisions, choose this method.

Cons: There may be features that are not added during a typical installation that would be useful to you.

Megabytes of files installed to your hard drive: 121MB

Outlook files that are installed if you choose the Typical method:

☐ Microsoft Outlook program files.

☐ ClipArt and ClipGallery.

☐ Feature for adding holidays to your calendar.

☐ Files for importing information from Schedule+ 1.0 and 95, as well as files that allow you to view other people's information still kept in Schedule+ instead of Outlook.

☐ Find Fast.

☐ Help files.

☐ Office Assistant.

☐ Outlook Form titled While You Were Out (more forms are included in the Microsoft Office 97 ValuPack, which you can add separately.)

☐ Outlook Templates, which are stored in the Templates/Outlook directory and have the extension OFT.

☐ Spell checker.

☐ Word templates for e-mail messages, if your organization uses a Microsoft Exchange Server.

Installation Using the Run from CD-ROM Method

One of the other installation options is running Office from a CD-ROM. This option allows you to do exactly as it seems—run the programs from a CD-ROM. The following paragraphs discuss the advantages and disadvantages of using this method, as well as list the size of the files that will be installed on your computer if you choose this option.

Pros: If you have limited space available on your computer, you might want to choose this method. This method installs the least amount of files to your hard drive.

Cons: You will sacrifice speed and convenience using this method. The Office 97 CD-ROM will have to remain in your CD-ROM drive anytime you want to run an Office application. It will also be slower; it takes more time for the computer to access files from your CD-ROM drive than it does to access them from your hard drive.

Megabytes of files installed to your hard drive: 60MB

Installation Using the Custom Install Method

The third installation option is the Custom Method. This particular option requires that you make all the choices for files to install. For instance, you could choose to install only Outlook 97 on your computer using this method. The following paragraphs discuss the advantages and disadvantages of using the Custom Install Method, as well as list the maximum number of files that could possibly be installed on your computer depending on your choices.

Pros: You get to make all the decisions regarding which files will be installed and where they will be installed on your computer.

Cons: This method is more complicated than the other two installation methods. Because this method can be the most difficult, this chapter covers installing Outlook (not all of Microsoft Office) using the

Custom setup. This will allow you to see what choices are available to you and will ensure that Outlook is set up exactly the way you need it to work in your environment.

Megabytes of files installed to your hard drive: Maximum of 191MB

JUST A MINUTE

If you have already installed Office 97, or it came loaded on your computer at the time of purchase, it's not too late to make changes to your Outlook setup. Insert the Office 97 CD-ROM and double-click on Setup.exe. Choose the option Add/Remove. You will see the setup window, which allows you to remove features you do not want and add those that you need. In the next few pages, you can follow the instructions for performing a custom installation. Review each of the options so that you can make choices that fit your environment.

The Custom Setup Described

Once you choose the Custom option, you will see a screen that offers you the chance to pick and choose which options of Microsoft Office you want to install. Because this book focuses on Outlook, check the box for Outlook if it is not already checked, and click the Change option button located at the bottom of the Description window. You will see the Options list for Outlook (see Figure 1.2).

Figure 1.2.
The Outlook Options list.

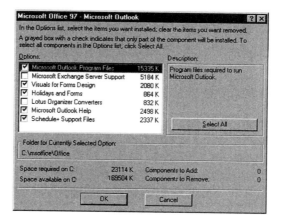

Microsoft Outlook Program Files

The Microsoft Outlook program files are necessary to run Microsoft Outlook. Make sure this box is checked.

Installing Components to Work with an Exchange Server

If you have an Exchange Server in your office, choose Microsoft Exchange Server Support so that you will be able to work in a group environment. This allows you to share Calendar information, set up appointments, create Tasks, and send Notes to other people throughout your network.

Visuals for Forms Design

If you think that you might want to design your own forms to use in Outlook, you will want to install this option. Designing forms is described in Hour 6, "Using and Creating Contact Forms and Templates." It's fairly easy to do, so you don't have to be a programmer or technical user to take advantage of this option.

Holidays and Forms

If you choose the Holiday and Forms option, you can have Outlook automatically add holidays to Calendar. Just choose the option and tell Outlook which country you want holiday information for. The form that will be added is called While You Were Out. Other forms can be added from the ValuPack included on the Office 97 CD-ROM.

Converting Files from Lotus Organizer

If you are switching from Lotus Organizer to Microsoft Outlook and you want to convert an Organizer file to Outlook, choose the option Lotus Organizer Converters. In Hour 3, "Configuring and Exploring Outlook," you will learn how to convert your Organizer file and other files from contact programs, such as Schedule+ and Act!.

Microsoft Outlook Help Files

Install the help files for Outlook unless you simply cannot afford to lose space on your hard drive. They are well-indexed, the explanations are short, and the instructions are easy to follow.

Schedule+ Support Files

Choose this option if you will need to either convert Schedule+ files to Outlook or if you will need to interact with others on your network who are using Schedule+. In Hour 3, you will learn how to convert Schedule+ files to Outlook.

1

Once you have made all your choices regarding Outlook, click the OK button and continue with the rest of the installation.

Extra Programs Offered Through the Office 97 ValuPack

Before you start working in Outlook, you may want to consider installing some of the extra programs that Microsoft offers with the Office 97 CD-ROM. There are two ways to access the ValuPack options. You can allow the Office 97 CD-ROM to Autoplay, and a menu with buttons will appear. Click the button Explore the Office 97 Value Pack to see what kinds of programs are available for installation.

Another way to find the ValuPack list is to view the contents of your Office 97 CD-ROM through the Explorer application. Open the folder named ValuPack on your Office CD-ROM. Double-click on the file named Valupk8.hlp to view the list of programs available (see Figure 1.3).

Figure 1.3.
The Office 97 ValuPack menu. This list can be found by choosing the ValuPack button on the Office 97 CD-ROM.

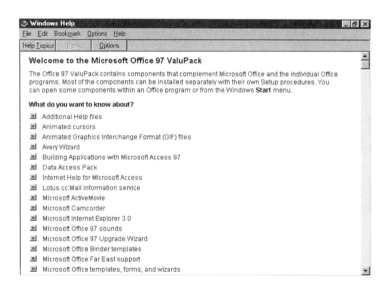

Here are selections from the ValuPack, which specifically apply to Outlook, that you might want to consider installing.

Lotus cc:Mail Information Service

If you have cc:Mail in your office, you will want to install this option to allow you to send and receive all your cc:Mail messages in Outlook. When you install this option, you can use Outlook instead of your cc:Mail client for e-mail messages and cc:Mail bulletin board information. In Hour 3, you will learn how to configure this option in Outlook. For now, simply choose to install this program.

Microsoft Office Templates, Forms, and Wizards

In addition to templates for Word, Excel, and Powerpoint, Microsoft offers a few Outlook templates and forms for you to use. The following is the list of forms and templates that you can install for Outlook:

- ☐ Classified Ads (form)
- ☐ Journal.oft (template)
- ☐ Note.oft (template)
- ☐ Sales Tracking (form)
- ☐ Training Management (form)
- ☐ While You Were Out (form)
- ☐ Vacation Request (form)

Microsoft Outlook Import and Export Converters

The Import and Export Converter option allows you to install converters so that you can import information from other contact programs. Specifically, you can import files from the following:

- ☐ Symantec ACT! 2.0
- ☐ NetManage ECCO Pro 3.0, 3.01, or 3.02
- ☐ Starfish SideKick 1.0/95

This feature also allows you to import or export Outlook Journal entries, Notes, or e-mail messages.

Timex Data Link Watch Wizard

If you purchase the Timex Data Link Watch, you can install this option which allows you to receive information, such as appointments, tasks, and phone numbers from Outlook into

1

your watch. Hour 23, "It Takes a Licking...," describes the Data Link Watch and teaches you how to use it with Outlook.

Once you have completed all the installations, restart your computer and open Microsoft Outlook by double-clicking its icon on your desktop. Begin reading Hour 2, "Becoming Familiar with the Features of Outlook," to learn about Outlook's menus and toolbars.

Summary

In this hour, you learned about what Outlook 97 does and how it can become a good management tool for you and your business. You also learned about the different installation methods available to you, and which ones to choose depending on your situation.

Q&A

Q How many methods does Microsoft offer during the installation process?

A Microsoft offers three installation options: the Typical, Custom, and Run from CD-ROM methods.

Q What are some of the features of Outlook 97?

A Outlook can be a Personal Information Manager (PIM) that keeps track of your Calendar, Task list, and Contacts. Outlook can also be your main mail box, gathering e-mail and faxes from many different services and servers.

Q What do you need to make Outlook a true groupware application?

A An Exchange Server.

Hour **2**

Becoming Familiar with the Features of Outlook

When you open Outlook for the first time, it should look similar to Figure 2.1. You will see the Microsoft Assistant's list of options during each startup of Outlook, offering you help in areas such as adding holidays to your calendar, importing information from Schedule+ and other programs, and setting up an e-mail service. If you do not want to see this list of options each time you open Outlook, just disable it by removing the Show these choices at startup checkmark from the box at the bottom of the list.

Figure 2.1.

*The opening screen of
Outlook. Until you set it
up otherwise, Outlook
defaults to opening in the
Inbox.*

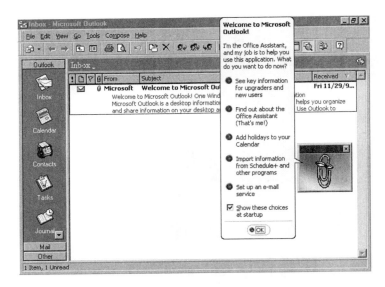

You can choose any option in the list of options, and the Assistant will walk you through the task in a step-by-step manner or give you the detailed information you need to complete the task. For now, click the OK button to make the list disappear until the next time you open Outlook.

Outlook's Features

Outlook has so many features that it can be overwhelming at first. In order to help you understand how each feature works and how practical Outlook is, we have devised a publishing company (not unlike Sams Publishing) called Quantum Ink.

Throughout the proceeding chapters, you can follow examples of how to use Outlook in a business environment from the perspective of an editor at Quantum Ink. The following paragraphs describe briefly the different features of Outlook.

Outlook provides you with seven different tools to work with: Contacts, Inbox, Calendar, Tasks, Notes, Journal, and Explorer. Each of these components is explained in the following paragraphs.

Contacts

Contacts hold all the information you want to store about your co-workers, friends, and other people with whom you communicate. The Contacts form is easy-to-use, and Outlook allows you to view your contacts in a variety of formats, such as address card and table views, as shown in Figure 2.2. Setting up your contacts is probably the first thing you should do when you begin working with Outlook because many of the other features work well with the Contacts database. Working with Contacts is discussed in Part II, "3, 2, 1…Contact."

Figure 2.2.

The Contacts component of Outlook.

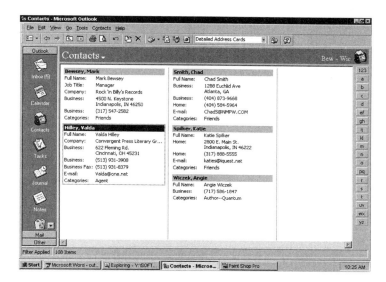

Inbox

The Inbox component is used for e-mail and faxes. You can communicate with co-workers via the network e-mail system and with others through Internet mail and faxes. Outlook uses the Windows Messaging system, which works with any MAPI-compliant mail system. In Figure 2.3, you can see the mail messages that are stored in a subfolder within the Inbox folder. Outlook allows you to create subfolders so that you can organize your mail and fax messages.

JUST A MINUTE

Microsoft At Work fax software is included with Outlook 97. You must install it in order to send and receive faxes in Outlook. If you already have the fax software installed on your computer when you installed Outlook, it will be updated automatically. If you do not have the fax software installed, you can find the fax software driver on your Windows 95 CD-ROM. Do this before installing Outlook.

Figure 2.3.

*The Inbox component
of Outlook, where all
e-mail and fax messages
are stored.*

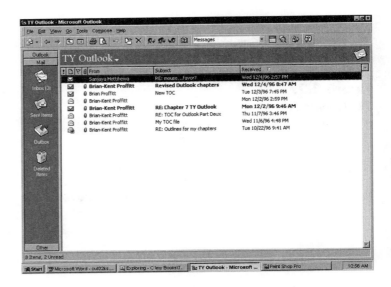

In Part III, "Mail and Fax," you will learn how to send and receive e-mail and faxes. More advanced features of messaging are covered as well. Because many messages contain tasks that you need to complete or meetings that you must attend, you will learn how to drag and drop messages onto the Tasks feature or Calendar feature to start instant reminders for yourself.

Calendar

The Calendar feature is used for setting up appointments, which is discussed in Part IV, "Using the Calendar." You can plan individual appointments or group meetings with the Calendar component (see Figure 2.4). Set alarms in Outlook to alert you when scheduled events are approaching. Using the Calendar feature with a Timex Data Watch is the ultimate way of keeping your appointments when you are away from your computer. See Hour 23, "It Takes a Licking…"

2

Figure 2.4.

The Calendar component of Outlook.

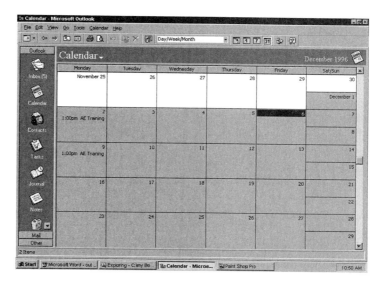

Tasks

You will be able to create tasks for yourself as well as for other people (see Figure 2.5). You can create tasks that you need to complete, and Outlook can send you reminders via onscreen notices and sound alarms. You can also send task requests to other people via e-mail. Keeping track of what you need to do, let alone what someone else owes you, can be difficult; however, Outlook will send reminders to you until you mark the task as 100 percent complete or until you dismiss the reminder.

Figure 2.5.

The Tasks component of Outlook.

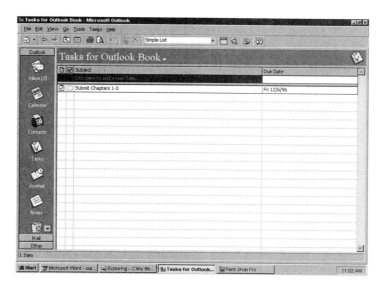

Notes

Notes can replace all the sticky notes that you place all over your desk and on the walls of your office. Whether you store passwords or instructions to which you constantly refer, the Notes feature holds all the information you need to have at your disposal (see Figure 2.6).

Figure 2.6.

The Notes component of Outlook. Instead of placing sticky notes over everything, create electronic notes for yourself in Outlook.

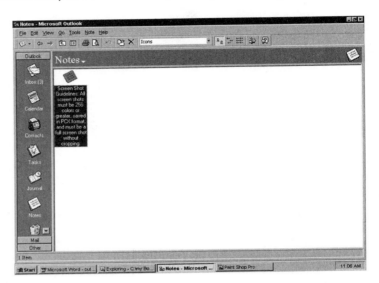

Journal

The Journal in Outlook tracks events for you, both automatically and manually depending on the type of event (see Figure 2.7). The Journal automatically records your electronic activities, such as your usage of Microsoft Word or e-mail messages that you send. You can set the automatic Journal tracking features in the Options box in Outlook. You can also make manual entries into the Journal to keep track of phone calls you make and other things you do throughout the day.

2

Figure 2.7.

The Journal component of Outlook. The Journal will keep track of your daily activities.

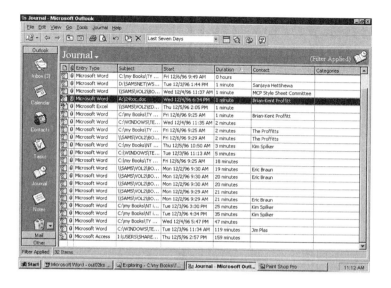

Explorer

Outlook can also be used as the Windows Explorer to view and manage files on your computer. Figure 2.8 shows the different views in Outlook. If you click on the Other tab, you will see that you can view all the folders and files on your computer, just as if you were in the Explorer.

Figure 2.8.

Outlook acts as the Windows Explorer, allowing the user to do all of the same tasks that are available through Explorer.

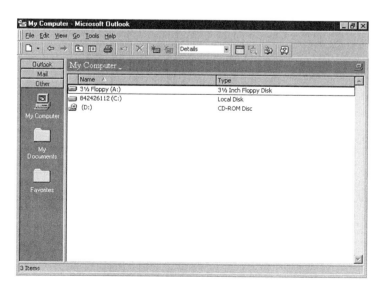

The Personal Folders File and Why It's Important

One important file is created and updated each time you use Outlook—the Personal Folders File (.PST). If you don't have this file set up through the Windows Messaging Service already, Outlook will create it for you. This file contains all the information that you store in Outlook. It can, therefore, grow to be quite large. In Hour 19, "Maintaining Outlook," you will learn how to maintain Outlook by backing up your personal information and using the archive feature.

Your PST file can also be opened by the Windows Messaging System (also known as the Exchange client or Inbox). You won't be able to access all the information in it as you would in Outlook, such as Calendar and Journal, but it's nice to know that you can at least view your e-mail information from another program if you ever need to do so.

Summary

In this chapter, you learned about all the different components that make up Outlook. You learned a little bit about how each feature can be used to help you perform everyday tasks. After reading this chapter, you should be ready to begin configuring Outlook so that it is specifically designed to work in your environment. You should be ready to start exploring each of the different features more in-depth.

Q&A

Q Which component of Outlook keeps track of your activities?

A The Journal.

Q How many different components make up the Outlook program?

A There are seven: Contacts, Journal, Calendar, Notes, Tasks, Inbox, and Explorer.

Q Why is the Personal Folders File important?

A It contains all the information you store in Outlook, such as contacts, mail and faxes, and your calendar information.

Hour 3

Configuring and Exploring Outlook

Before you begin to use Outlook, you will need to customize it to fit the way you plan to work with it. For instance, if you want to use Outlook to handle your e-mail, you will need to configure it to work with your e-mail service. In this chapter, you'll learn how to add and configure any e-mail services, fax services, address books, and other services that you plan to use in Outlook.

Everything you add to Outlook defines your user profile. You most likely will need only one user profile when you work with Outlook. However, if you share a computer with someone else, you each can have your own user profile to keep your personal information private.

Outlook has one place—the Services dialog box—where you can configure new services. Examples in this chapter lead you through setting up an Internet Mail service, a cc:Mail service, and a fax service.

You may also need to convert your files from other contact programs, such as Schedule+, Act!, Lotus Organizer, or an Access database. Outlook's Assistant guides you through the tough decisions to make importing files easier.

Finally, you can customize the look and feel of Outlook, as well as make decisions about how all the components will work. For example, will you use Word as your e-mail editor? Do you want to use AutoArchive? How often will you archive? What do you want the Journal to track? These decisions and many others can be made in one place—the Options dialog box.

Adding Services to Outlook

Outlook has the capability of becoming your fax machine and your only electronic post office. For example, you might have a CompuServe account, Microsoft Mail account, and personal Internet account. Logging on to each one separately and trying to keep track of your mail could be a tremendous burden. With Outlook, you won't have to check each of your online services individually for e-mail; you can set up Outlook to go out to each of your mailboxes and retrieve and deliver mail. Mail accounts are just one type of service you can add to Outlook. You can also store many different contact databases in Outlook. All these services are configured in the Services dialog box.

To open the Services dialog box, go to the Outlook menu and click Tools | Services.

Outlook's Default Services

When you first start Outlook and view the Services dialog box, you will see a window that probably has only three services listed:

- ☐ Outlook Address Book—The address book where Contacts are stored.
- ☐ Personal Address Book—The address book where you store private Contacts that people on your network cannot use.
- ☐ Personal Folders—All the different Outlook folders that you use privately are called the Personal Folders. On a network, you can also use Public Folders to share information with co-workers.

You may have more services that are already visible in the Services dialog box, depending on what you installed if you were previously using Schedule+ or the Windows Messaging System that ships with Windows 95.

First, get to know where the three services listed reside and what their properties are. For instance, if you select the Personal Address Book and then choose Properties, you will see where this file is stored on your computer, as shown in Figure 3.1.

3

Figure 3.1.

The properties window of the Personal Address Book.

Now view the Personal Folders properties, as shown in Figure 3.2. It's a good idea to note the name of the PST file and where it resides on your computer in case you want to back up or transport it.

Figure 3.2.

The properties of the Personal Folders file, which holds all the information for your personal Outlook file.

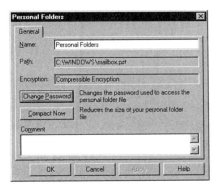

JUST A MINUTE

The PST file and the PAB file can be used by the Windows Messaging System, also known as the Exchange Client. If you transfer these files to another computer that does not have Outlook installed, you can access your messages and Personal Address Book through the Inbox that comes with Windows 95.

A number of other services are available to add to Outlook. Here is a list of the services available after installing Outlook and some of the ValuPack options that were described in Hour 1, "Getting Started with Outlook":

- ☐ Internet Mail
- ☐ Microsoft Fax
- ☐ Outlook Address Book
- ☐ Personal Address Book
- ☐ Personal Folders
- ☐ Microsoft Exchange Server
- ☐ Microsoft Mail
- ☐ Netscape Internet Transport
- ☐ Microsoft Network Online Service
- ☐ cc:Mail

Within the Services dialog box, simply choose the Add button to view the list of available services. Add each one you want to Outlook. In the following paragraphs, you will learn how to add services, including Internet mail, Microsoft Fax, MAPI-compliant e-mail, cc:Mail, and CompuServe, to Outlook.

Configuring Internet Mail for Outlook

Select Internet Mail from the Add Services list and click OK. You will see a form that you must complete with your personal Internet account information. If this is the first time that you have set up an Internet e-mail account on your computer, you may need to contact your Internet service provider (ISP) to obtain some of the requested information. Under the Connection tab in the configuration box, you will have the choice of scheduling automatic dial-ins to your e-mail account or using Remote mail features in Outlook. Remote mail allows you to connect to your e-mail account manually, when it is most convenient for you. You can also download and upload all mail or just check message headers for specific mail to download completely. Figures 3.3 and 3.4 show examples of what kind of information would typically go into the form.

3

Figure 3.3.

A sample Internet e-mail form for adding the Internet Mail service to Outlook.

Figure 3.4.

Configure the connection to the Internet mail server and schedule Outlook to automatically check for new mail at specified intervals.

Adding Microsoft Fax Capabilities to Outlook

All you need to do to add fax services to your Outlook program is choose Microsoft Fax from within the list of available services. If you are using Windows NT Workstation, check the Microsoft Web site at http://www.microsoft.com to download the Personal Fax component, which will work with Outlook. In the configuration dialog box, enter your name, modem number, and information about your modem, as shown in Figure 3.5.

JUST A MINUTE

If you work in a network environment, you can allow other people to use your modem to send faxes from their computers. Find this option within the Microsoft Fax Properties under the Modem tab.

Figure 3.5.

*Microsoft Fax setup
dialog box.*

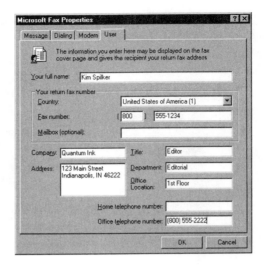

Adding MAPI-Compliant E-mail Services to Outlook

If you get e-mail from services other than Exchange (such as Microsoft Mail, Microsoft
Network, cc:Mail, or CompuServe), you will need to add those services to Outlook through
the Services dialog box. The ValuPack that comes with the Office 97 CD-ROM contains
utilities for cc:Mail, as mentioned in Hour 1. Check with your service provider or go to one
of the many Web pages devoted to Exchange to find utilities designed to work with Outlook.
Here are a few Web sites to visit:

☐ Unofficial Microsoft Exchange Server Internet at hyperlink

  `http://www.anjura.com/exchfaq/ExFAQ09.html`

☐ Slipstick Systems—Exchange Client Issues at hyperlink

  `http://www.slipstick.com/exchange/`

☐ Cool add-ins for Exchange (WinNT & Win95) at hyperlink

  `http://home.istar.ca/~anthony/add-ins.html`

☐ Microsoft's service provider product listing at hyperlink

  `http://www.microsoft.com/isapi/backoffice/exchange/exisv`

☐ Microsoft's free Office software at hyperlink

  `http://www.microsoft.com/officefreestuff/outlook/`

Adding CompuServe Services to Outlook

If you have configured your CompuServe account using CompuServe's software, configuring your account for Outlook will be very similar. You can obtain the CompuServe service

3

add-on for Outlook from CompuServe or from the ValuPack for Windows 95. You should install the add-on first before you add it as a service to Outlook.

To add CompuServe as a service to your Outlook user profile, do the following steps:

1. In the Services dialog box, click the Add button and choose CompuServe from the list.

2. The CompuServe Mail Settings dialog box contains four tabs—General, Connection, Default Send Options, and Advanced. Enter your name, account number, and password into the text boxes in the General tab.

3. In the Connection tab, either enter a local access phone number that you normally use to log on to CompuServe or configure a direct connection or Winsock connection. Figure 3.6 demonstrates how to configure a Winsock connection.

Figure 3.6.

Configuring a Winsock connection to CompuServe mail services.

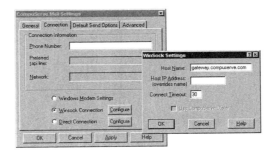

4. In the Default Send Options, choose whether you want mail to be sent in Rich Text Format.

5. The Advanced tab requires that you decide if you want an Event Log created each time you log on and if you want retrieved messages deleted from CompuServe. You can also change the location of your CompuServe directory and set a schedule for Outlook to check your CompuServe mailbox (see Figure 3.7).

Figure 3.7.

Click the Schedule Connect Times button to configure when Outlook will check your CompuServe account for mail.

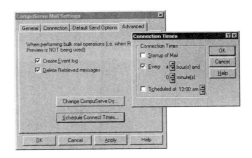

Adding cc:Mail Services to Outlook

If your network uses cc:Mail, you can add the cc:Mail services for Outlook to your Profile. The Office 97 ValuPack offers the software to add cc:Mail services. Refer to Hour 1 to find out how to add the software from the CD-ROM. Once you add cc:Mail as a service to Outlook, your cc:Mail directories will appear in the Address Book list along with the other address books you store, such as Contacts.

To add it as a service, do the following steps:

1. In the Services dialog box, click the Add button and choose cc:Mail from the list.
2. The Configure cc:Mail Services dialog box contains three tabs—Login, Delivery, and Addressing. Enter your Postoffice path, User name, and Password in the Login tab. An example of typical information that would be entered in this window is shown in Figure 3.8. Call your system administrator if you do not know the location of your Postoffice path for cc:Mail.

Figure 3.8.

The Login tab for cc:Mail configuration in Outlook.

3. In the Delivery tab, decide how you want your messages handled, and how often you want Outlook to check cc:Mail for new mail and to deliver your messages to others on your network, as shown in Figure 3.9.

Figure 3.9.

The Delivery tab contains the scheduler for determining how often Outlook will automatically log on to cc:Mail.

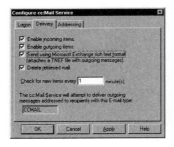

CAUTION

Check with your cc:Mail administrator to find out if there are any scheduled maintenance sessions that take place when you are still logged on to Outlook. Your administrator may ask you to make sure that you use the command File I Exit and Log Off when you want to close Outlook but not log off your company's network. If you simply use the command File I Exit or if you click the × in the upper-right corner to close the program, you will not necessarily be logging off your mail system. A MAPI connection will still exist until you completely log off your network.

Configuring the Delivery Order for the Mail and Fax Services

Once you have installed all the services that you need, you can dictate the order in which the services will be checked by Outlook. Within the Services dialog box, choose the Delivery tab to see the current order. You can move the services up or down the list by selecting them individually and using the arrows to move them in either direction.

TIME SAVER

You may want to move the e-mail services to the top of the list and place the fax service last in line. This may make your remote sessions quicker. In some instances, we found that listing the fax service first caused problems in Outlook.

Using Rules in Outlook

In many e-mail programs, you have the ability to set up rules for your e-mail messages. For instance, you may have a special folder where you store all messages from your co-worker, John. You can create a rule that instructs the application to move John's messages from the Inbox to his folder automatically. In other words, rules are conditions that you set in order for an event to occur.

Unless you have an Exchange Server, creating rules in Outlook requires an add-on, such as the shareware program Exlife, which you can find on the World Wide Web at hyperlink

```
http://www.mokry.cz
```

If you choose to download Exlife and install it on your system, its options will appear in your Options dialog box as an additional tab called Filters, Signature. Exlife can filter messages by the From, To, Cc, Subject and Message fields. You can determine whether you want the messages moved upon arrival, after reading, or after sending them.

See Figure 3.10 for an example of how Exlife works with rules. A rule is being created that will instruct Outlook to look for the substring John Spilker as the sender of a message. If the substring is found, Outlook will move each of those messages from the Inbox to the folder called John's Messages. This event will only occur after the messages from John have been read.

Figure 3.10.

Setting up a rule in Outlook using an add-on program called Exlife.

JUST A MINUTE

Microsoft has created a Rules Wizard that they are offering on their Web site at hyperlink

`http://www.microsoft.com/officefreestuff/outlook/`

Microsoft's Rules Wizard offers natural-language rule options rather than making you type in code to set rules for managing your mail. The Rules Wizard is in beta at the time of this writing.

Converting Files from Other Programs

If you have contact lists that you want to convert to Outlook, you should use the Import command under the File menu. Outlook can import contact databases from such programs and files as Schedule+, Lotus Organizer, a Personal Address Book, a database, or any text file that is set up so that fields are delimited by commas or tabs.

If you have contacts from programs (such as Act!, Ecco, or SideKick), you will need to install specific converters offered on the Office 97 ValuPack before you can import them into Outlook. Refer to Hour 1 if you need information about the ValuPack and how to install programs from it.

Figure 3.11 shows an example of an Access database being imported into Outlook. Notice that a wizard makes the process easy by prompting the user for information about the conversion.

Figure 3.11.

Importing an Access database into Outlook requires that you match the fields from the Access file to the fields in Outlook Contacts database.

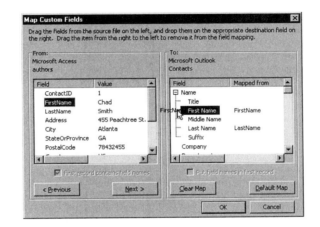

To import a file, such as an Access database, into Outlook, follow these instructions:

1. Choose File | Import and Export.
2. Choose Import from Schedule+ or another program or file.
3. Pick a file type from the list of possible types to import, such as Microsoft Access.
4. State the location of the file you want to import. For example:
   `c:\my documents\authors.mdb`.
5. Choose one of the options regarding duplicate records. If you are afraid of writing over any contacts accidentally, choose Do not import duplicates.
6. Select the destination folder in Outlook, such as Contacts.
7. Map the custom fields, as shown in Figure 3.11.
8. Click the Finish button.

Making Choices about Outlook in the Options Box

If you open the Options dialog box by clicking Tools | Options, you will find an assortment of tabs that contain check boxes and text boxes regarding different features in Outlook, such as e-mail, Calendar, Journal, Forms, and more (see Figure 3.12).

Figure 3.12.

Open the Options dialog box to make choices about how Outlook should look and perform for your environment.

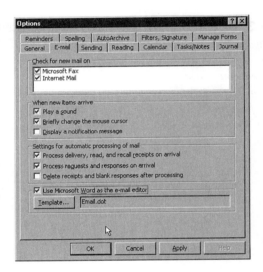

Which options you choose in the different tabs really depends on how you want Outlook to work to suit your needs. Some options might not be easy to understand while reading. Here are a few explanations that might help you when you are making decisions about the options.

Options Under the General Tab

Outlook asks you which profile to use when it starts. If you share your computer with another user, you can each set up your own Profile and ask Outlook to prompt you to choose which profile to use during start up. This way, if you log on and choose your profile, Outlook will appear with your Personal Folders containing your mail, contacts, calendar, and such, instead of your coworker's personal information.

JUST A MINUTE

> If you use Windows NT Workstation, choosing your particular profile from a list of profiles is not necessary because MAPI setup is kept by the user.

3

Options Under the E-mail Tab

Using Word as your e-mail editor is discussed in Part II, "3, 2, 1…Contact." For now, you should know that you can use the Outlook editor or Word as your e-mail editor. You gain a few more formatting options by choosing Word as the editor, but you sacrifice speed upon opening and sending mail messages. You can toggle this option on and off to see which you prefer.

Options Under the Journal Tab

The choices you make in this tab make a big difference in the amount of space that is consumed on your hard drive by your Outlook file. The Journal can automatically record any of your activities with the Office 97 applications as well as record e-mail activity, meeting requests, and task requests and responses. You can pick and choose which individual activities and Office applications that you wish to have the Journal record. The more options you choose, the more hard drive space will be consumed.

Options Under the AutoArchive Tab

AutoArchive is explained in Hour 19, "Maintaining Outlook." In general, archiving is a good thing to do to keep your Outlook file as small as it can be. However, you will still have space on your hard drive taken by the archived files called archive.pst, unless you move them to portable media, such as a floppy disk or a zip drive.

Options Under the Manage Forms Tab

All Outlook items are based on forms—the e-mail form, contacts form, journal entry, appointment form, and so on. Forms can be created by your system administrator or by you. To find out more about forms and creating them, refer to Hour 6, "Using and Creating Contact Forms and Templates." The Manage Forms tab allows you to install and remove forms that you use in Outlook. Sample forms are included on the Office 97 CD-ROM that you must install separately.

Summary

In this chapter, you learned that configuring and setting up Outlook is relatively easy by using the Services and Options dialog boxes. You read about how to set up Outlook to suit your needs. This chapter took you step-by-step into configuring e-mail and fax services for your Outlook user profile. You also learned how to go into the Options dialog box to make specific choices about the features, such as Journal and e-mail.

Q&A

Q What is your user profile?

A Your user profile is made up of the settings and services that you install and configure in Outlook. Your profile may include Internet e-mail and fax services. It may also include information about how you want the Journal to track activities and which address books you have loaded into Outlook.

Q What can you do in the Services dialog box?

A You can add, remove, and configure different services, such as fax, e-mail, and address books in Outlook.

Q What are some mail services that work with Outlook?

A Microsoft Mail, cc:Mail, Microsoft Exchange Server, and CompuServe all work with Outlook.

3

PART
II

3, 2, 1...Contact

Hour

Hour 4

How to Use the Contacts Feature

The Contacts database in Outlook acts as an electronic Rolodex file, holding just about any kind of information you would want to store about someone. The Contacts module is a good place to start when you first begin using Outlook. Entering all your contacts' information should be your first task because so many other features interact with the Contacts database. For instance, you can choose to allow Outlook to automatically record Journal entries whenever you do something involving your contacts, whether you call them, write them letters, or meet with them.

If you want to send an e-mail or fax, schedule a meeting, or send a task request to someone, it will be easier to do if that person has an entry in your Contacts database.

You will be able to view your contacts in a number of different ways, but the most common view is the Detailed Address Card view, shown in Figure 4.1.

Figure 4.1.

*A detailed view of the
Contacts module.*

Autodialer

Delete

Move to Folder

New message to Contact

New meeting with Contact

Explore Web Page

New Contact

Back

Forward

Up one Level

Folder list

Print

Print Preview

Undo

Managing Your Contacts Database

With over 70 different fields for keeping track of Contacts, your biggest challenge in using the Contacts feature in Outlook may be managing and updating your database. Outlook offers the usual Contact fields, such as addresses, phone numbers, and e-mail addresses. It also offers some not-so-predictable fields, such as Government ID Number and ISDN Number. In this hour, you'll learn the basics of using Contacts in Outlook—adding, deleting, opening, and importing Contacts. In later hours in this section, you will learn how to view Contacts in different formats, as well as create your own forms with the Forms Designer.

Adding a New Contact

There are a number of ways that you can add people to your Contacts database. If you prefer to use the menus, go to File, point to New, and then click Contact in the roll-down list; or, if you happen to be in the Contacts folder, go to Contacts on the menu and click on New Contact. If you like to use short-cuts, type Ctrl+N if you happen to be in the Contacts view; otherwise, type Ctrl+Shift+C to call up a new Contact form. A third way of calling up a new Contact form is to click on the icon in the upper-left corner of the toolbar, as shown in Figure 4.2.

4

Figure 4.2.

Calling up a new Contact form using the icon on the toolbar.

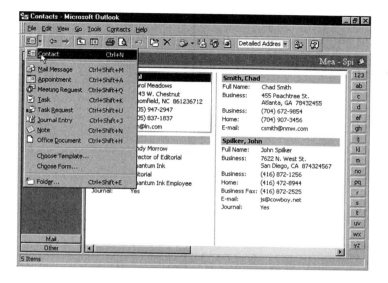

Once you've pulled up a new Contact form, you can enter as much information as you have about that person.

TIME SAVER

If you enter your contacts' birthdays or anniversary dates in their Contact forms, those dates will automatically be entered in the Calendar component of Outlook. No more excuses for missing important dates! They will appear on your calendar as recurring events. If you need to have Outlook remind you to buy a gift or send a card for a contact, just go to the date in the calendar, select and drag it onto the Tasks component. When the Task form appears, you can set an alarm for yourself.

Using Quantum Ink as an example, you will see how to create new Contacts and what purposes the most common fields serve. Mark is an editor at Quantum Ink, and he is starting to enter names of co-workers and authors into his Contacts database. Cindy Morrow is the first name he enters into his database. As you can see in Figure 4.3, there are four tabs on a typical Contact Entry Form: General, Details, Journal, and All Fields. Each of these tabs represents a form for the contact. In the General form, Mark enters her name, title, company, and addresses.

Figure 4.3.

You can enter as many as three different addresses for each contact—Business, Home, and Other.

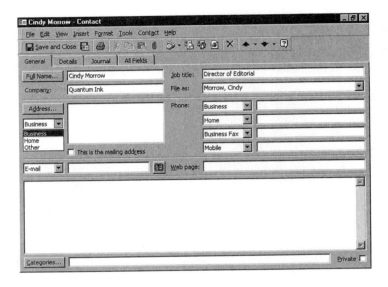

Deleting a Contact

You can delete a Contact in five different ways:

☐ Select the Contact in the Contacts folder, right-click on it, and choose Delete from the drop-down menu.

☐ Select the Contact and choose Edit | Delete.

☐ Select the Contact and type Ctrl+D.

☐ Select the Contact and hit the Delete key.

☐ Drag and drop the Contact onto the Deleted Items Folder.

Opening a Contact

You can also open a Contact in a number of ways:

☐ Simply double-click on it.

☐ Select it in the Contacts folder, right-click on it, and choose Open from the drop-down menu.

☐ Select the Contact and choose File | Open.

☐ Select the Contact and hit the Enter key.

☐ Select the Contact and type Ctrl+O.

4

Importing Contacts from Other Sources

On the File menu, click Import and Export. You can import Contacts from a number of formats, including the following:

> Comma (DOS)
> Comma Separated (Windows)
> dBASE
> Lotus Organizer 1.0, 1.1, 2.1
> Microsoft Access
> Excel
> FoxPro
> Personal Address Book (PAB)
> Schedule+ 1.0 and 7.0
> Tab Separated (DOS)
> Tab Separated (Windows)

To illustrate how to import a Contact database from a file, Mark will import a database of authors that he received from his co-worker, Sharon. The database was created in Microsoft Access. To do this, he follows these steps:

1. He chooses File | Import and Export.

2. He selects Import from Schedule+ or another program or file, and clicks Next.

3. He selects Microsoft Access from the list of possible formats, and clicks Next.

4. He clicks the Browse button to locate the file called Authors.mdb.

5. He chooses the option Do not import duplicates and clicks Next.

6. He selects Contacts as the destination folder.

7. In the next screen, he clicks on the Map Custom Fields to match the field names used in Outlook with the field names that Sharon used when she created her authors' database.

8. In the Map Custom Fields dialog box, he drags each field from Sharon's database onto the matching field in the Contacts database in Outlook, as shown in Figure 4.4.

9. Once he has finished matching the fields, he clicks OK.

10. In the final screen, he clicks the Finish button and waits for the database to be imported.

Figure 4.4.

In the Map Custom Fields dialog box, you can drag-and-drop fields from another database so that when the fields are imported, they are placed in the proper Outlook fields.

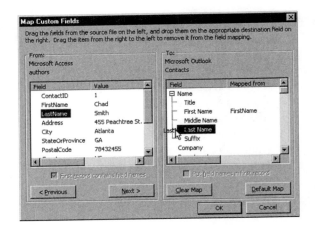

Putting Your Contacts into Categories

At the bottom of the General form, there is a place to list the categories to which this Contact belongs. If you work on many different projects or with many groups of people, the category function is a great tool. Each Contact can belong to many groups or categories. As your Contacts database grows, you can filter your Contacts by categories. Filtering is discussed in Hour 6, "Using and Creating Contact Forms and Templates."

As you can see in Figure 4.5, Mark has clicked the Categories button to get a check list of available categories. He could choose to use the ones that Outlook provides or he could create his own categories by going into the Master Category List at the bottom of the list box and adding his own.

Figure 4.5.

The Categories list box shows a number of typical groups to which a Contact can belong. Use this list or create your own by going into the Master Category List.

4

Filling Out Details About Each of Your Contacts

Mark enters the name of Cindy's department, her office number, her assistant's and manager's names, and other personal information in the Details tab, as shown in Figure 4.6.

Figure 4.6.

By clicking on the Details tab in the Contact entry form, you can enter more personal information about the contact.

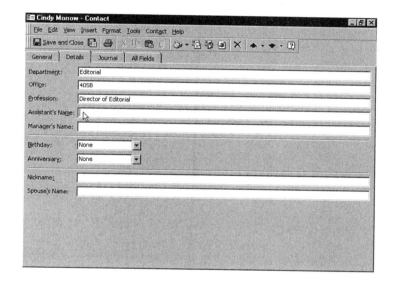

JUST A MINUTE

If you enter a birth date or anniversary date for a contact, an entry is automatically created in the Calendar feature of Outlook to remind you of those special dates.

Recording Journal Entries About a Contact

By clicking on the third tab in the Contact entry form, Mark can add information in the Journal about Cindy. Mark creates an entry for a letter that he sent to her (see Figure 4.7).

Figure 4.7.

Daily activities involving contacts can be recorded in the Outlook Journal.

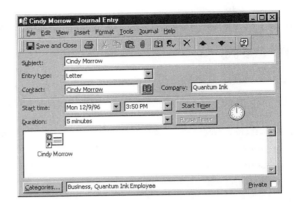

Automatic Journal Entries

Mark can make Journal entries manually, or he could choose to allow Outlook to automatically record Journal entries for him whenever he does an activity regarding one of his contacts, such as sending an e-mail, fax message, or a letter written in Microsoft Word.

To allow Outlook to automatically record Journal entries about a contact, go to the tab marked Journal and enable the Automatically record journal entries for this contact check box.

Outlook can automatically record entries for activities such as e-mail messages, meeting requests, responses, task requests, phone calls (if Outlook dials them for you), and any documents created in Office 97 programs.

CAUTION

The downside to allowing Outlook to automatically record Journal entries is that your Outlook database will increase in size. If you want to save hard drive space, you may want to record most of your entries manually and pick only a few important contacts that you want to record all activities for.

Another way to cut down on the number of automatic Journal entries is to change the options setting in Outlook, as shown in Figure 4.8. Go to Tools on the Outlook menu and choose Options. Click on the tab marked Journal in the dialog box.

Figure 4.8.

You can record as many activities in the Outlook Journal as you want. To save space, choose fewer options.

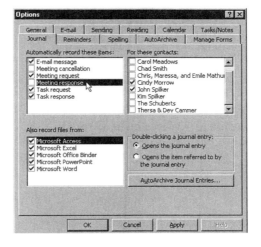

Manual Journal Entries

Some Journal entries need to be recorded manually, such as conversations you have with a contact. In the example, our editor Mark has placed a phone call to one of his authors, John (see Figure 4.9). To place the call, Mark opened the Contact form for John, clicked on the Autodialer icon on the toolbar, and choose the office phone number from the list. Outlook dialed the number, and Mark told Outlook to automatically record the activity and open a Journal entry for the phone call, in which he entered some notes from the conversation.

Figure 4.9.

You can keep track of things said in a conversation by opening a Journal form when you call someone.

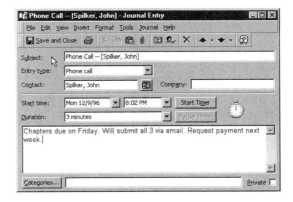

Viewing All Fields

The fourth tab on the Contacts form is All Fields. Within this form, you can choose from a toggle list which fields you would like to view. As you can see in Figure 4.10, the different fields and their corresponding entries are shown in a table format. You can enter information about a contact in this window, and you can select fields and copy information, as well. When you copy cells from this view and paste them into a Word document, for example, the information is separated by tabs.

Figure 4.10.

The Addresses view shows all of the entries in the address fields for this particular contact.

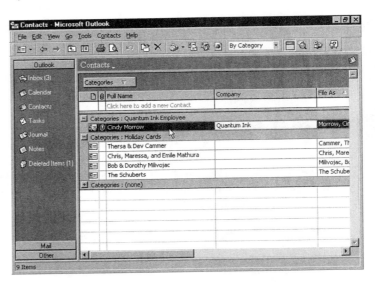

You can also use the All Fields tab to create new fields for a Contact. Click the button marked New at the bottom-right corner of the form. Before you create a new field, remember that Outlook already offers four user fields that you can customize to meet your needs. View the user fields by choosing Miscellaneous fields from the drop-down list.

Summary

In this hour, you learned what the Contacts component can do for you. You read about how to manage Contacts and perform the basic tasks associated with the Contacts feature, such as adding, opening, deleting, and importing Contacts. You also learned about how to place your Contacts into categories so that, as your Contacts database grows, you can easily find groups of people for mailing, faxes, phone calls, and anything else you want to do with Contacts.

Q&A

Q Can you name two different ways to add a Contact?

A Go to the menu and choose File | New | Contact or type the shortcut Ctrl+Shift+C.

Q What happens when you add a birthday or an anniversary date to a Contact?

A The date automatically appears on your Calendar as a recurring event.

Q How many fields are available for keeping track of your Contacts?

A Over 70 different Contact fields are available in Outlook, and you can also define your own fields.

Hour 5

Working with Contacts

Just about everything you do in Outlook will involve one or more of your Contacts. Configuring and organizing your Contacts makes it easier for you to access them, especially if you have a large Contacts database.

Many of the skills you will learn in this chapter about organizing and configuring the Contacts module will apply to the other Outlook modules, as well. Once you become familiar with a module in Outlook, such as Contacts, you will automatically be familiar with the other modules. In fact, Outlook is a very intuitive program as far as using the menus and understanding how features work. The most challenging thing about Outlook is deciding how you want to work with it. You can use as little or as many of the features as you want; it all hinges on your imagination and your ability to organize your work.

Viewing Contacts in Different Formats

The default view for Contacts is the Address Card view, shown in Figure 5.1. Both the Address Card view and the Detailed Address Card view are easy formats to work with, especially if you have many blank fields within each Contact entry. These two views will not show blank fields unless you specify otherwise and modify the views.

Figure 5.1.

The default view in Contacts.

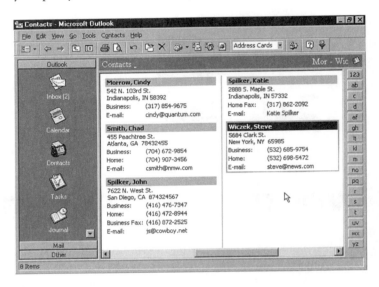

As your Contacts database grows or as you begin to categorize and group your Contacts, you might want to experiment using different views other than the Address Card view so that scanning through the list of names is as efficient as possible.

JUST A MINUTE

The Address Card view is the only format for which you cannot group Contacts. In other views, you can group Contacts by fields, such as State or Category.

Switching Between Views

Besides the two predefined Address Card views, you can switch between different table views, such as the simple phone list, shown in Figure 5.2.

Figure 5.2.

Besides the Address Card views, other Contacts views are formatted as tables, such as the Phone List view.

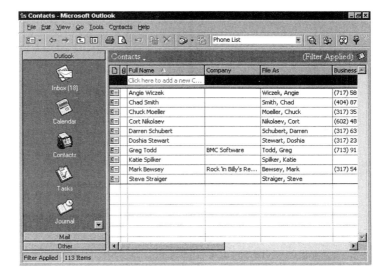

To choose a different view, the easiest way is to click on the Current View list box on the toolbar. You can also choose View | Current View from the menu and pick one of the views in the drop-down list. The list offers different views that have already been defined by the creators of Outlook. So what if you want a different view than the ones that are offered?

Creating a Custom View

If none of the predefined views offer what you need, you can create your own view and save it so that it will appear in the drop-down list of views. To make a new view, you can either modify one of the predefined views or create your own view from scratch. The following example shows you how to create a custom view by the two methods.

Brad is a summer intern at Quantum Ink, and he has been given the task of updating the entire list of authors and agents in the Contacts' database. He wants to create a custom view that will help make his job easier.

He wants to call people to update the list. He wants the following fields to be visible on his screen:

- ☐ Full Name
- ☐ Company
- ☐ Business Phone
- ☐ Home Phone
- ☐ Modified (so that he can easily see which ones have been updated)

He has noticed by scanning the list that many people work for literary agencies. By grouping the contacts by Company, he can update many people with one phone call. In the first example, Brad creates the view he wants by customizing an existing view—the Phone List. In the second example, he creates his new view from scratch using the Define Views command.

Modifying a Current View

The Phone List view is close to meeting Brad's needs. With just a few changes, it will be perfect. Here's how he makes the changes:

1. He begins by right-clicking on each of the columns that he does not want to appear in his new view, and removes them one at a time, as shown in Figure 5.3. He removes the following fields—Icon, Attachment, File As, Business Fax, Mobile Phone, Journal, Categories.

Figure 5.3.

To remove a column from a view, right-click on the column and choose Remove This Column.

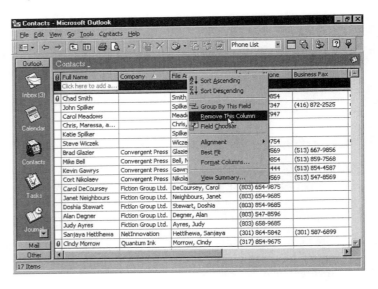

2. He adds the Modified field to the view by clicking View | Field Chooser. From the Field Chooser box, he locates Modified from the list of Frequently-used fields. He drags and drops it into the row of column names until the red arrows appear to indicate placement of the new column, as shown in Figure 5.4.

5

Figure 5.4.

You can drag and drop fields onto the screen to create a new view.

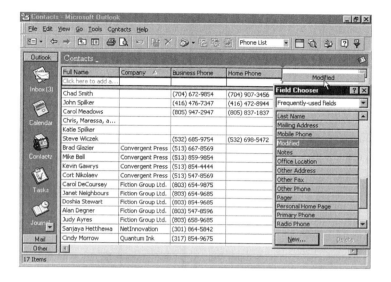

3. He clicks the × at the top of the Field Chooser box to close it.

4. He adjusts the width of the Modified column by moving his cursor near the column until it changes from a pointer to a crossbar with arrows pointing to each side. He clicks and drags the column to the right until all the information is visible.

5. To group the Contacts by Company, he right-clicks on the Company column, and chooses Group by the Field from the drop-down list. The result is shown in Figure 5.5.

Figure 5.5.

The modified Phone List shows the names grouped by Company.

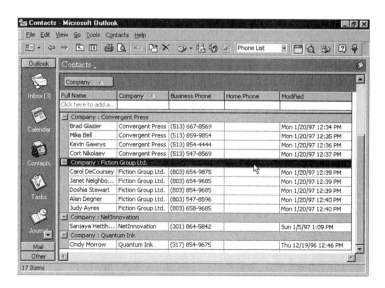

6. Finally, Brad needs to save his new view. To do this, he must choose a different view from the Current View list box on the toolbar. A message box appears on the screen, acknowledging that he has modified the Phone List view. He has to choose one of the three options, shown in Figure 5.6. He chooses the option Save the current view settings as a new view. He names the view Quantum Ink List and chooses to allow it to be visible in all Contact folders.

Figure 5.6.

If you modify a current view, you must save it by a new name or choose to change the current view if you want to use it again.

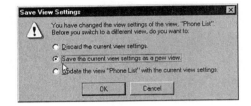

Creating a New View from Scratch

As you'll see in the example, the Define Views command not only allows Brad to create a new view, but it offers options for managing all the views in the Contacts module. To create the same view that he created by modifying the Phone List in the last example, Brad performs the following tasks in the Define Views dialog box:

1. Brad chooses View|Define Views from the menu. A new screen appears that looks like Figure 5.7, in which the list of predefined views are shown in a table with their properties listed below the table.

Figure 5.7.

The Define Views dialog box allows you to manage views.

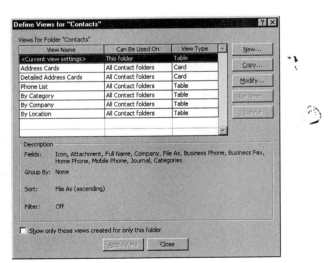

2. He clicks the button marked New and a screen appears, asking him to name his new view and decide which type of view he wants, as shown in Figure 5.8.

Figure 5.8.

Naming the new view and choosing the type—table, timeline, card, and so on.

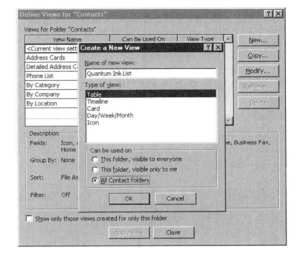

3. He names the new view "Quantum Ink List" and makes it a Table that will be available in all Contacts folders. He clicks OK.
4. The Views Summary box appears next. He clicks each of the buttons—Fields, Group By, Sort, Filter, and Format—to define his new view.
5. He clicks the Fields button first. In the Show Fields dialog box, which appears in Figure 5.9, he removes all of the fields except Full Name, Company, Business Phone, and Home Phone. To remove a field, he selects that field and clicks the Remove button.

Figure 5.9.

The Show Fields dialog box allows you to add and remove fields in a view, and choose the order in which they will appear in the view.

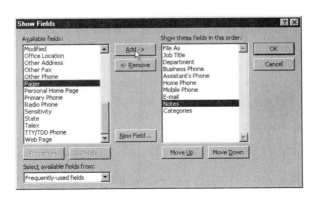

6. He also adds the Modified field by choosing it from the list on the left column and clicking the Add button. He clicks OK.

7. The View Summary box appears again. He clicks the Group By button. In the Group By box, Mark clicks the first drop-down list button and chooses Company from the list, as shown in Figure 5.10. He chooses the option Ascending order and puts a checkmark in the Show field in View box, so that the Company field will appear in the view. Otherwise, if he leaves the box unchecked, the Company field will only appear in the Group items by label. To finish, he clicks OK.

Figure 5.10.

In the Group By box, you can choose to group items by as many as four different fields.

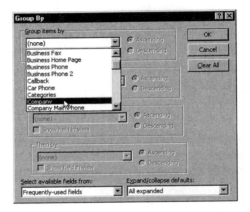

8. Back in the View Summary box, Mark clicks the Sort button. He chooses to sort the names by Full Name field instead of the File As field, which is the default choice. He clicks OK to close the Sort dialog box.

9. In the View Summary box again, he skips the Filter button because he wants to view all the Contacts in the database. He does not want to hide any names.

10. Finally, he clicks the Format button to make choices about fonts and gridlines that will appear in his new view. He keeps the default fonts and sizes. He chooses the options Allow In Cell Editing and Automatic Column Sizing.

11. When he clicks OK in the View Summary box, the new view, Quantum Ink List, appears among the list of saved views in the Define Views table.

12. He clicks the button Apply View to see his newly created view.

Writing a Letter to a Contact

If you have used Schedule+, you know that the Address Book can be accessed from Microsoft Word whenever you need to insert a contact name and address into a document. Outlook turns the task around by allowing you to work in the Contacts module and call up a Letter

5

Wizard to send letters to individual contacts. In the following example, an editor wants to send a letter to Cindy discussing an upcoming editorial meeting:

1. In the Contacts module, she selects Cindy Morrow's entry, and clicks Contacts | New Letter to Contact from the menu.

2. A Letter Wizard appears with four tabs: Letter Format, Recipient Info, Other Elements, and Sender Info. In the Letter Format tab, shown in Figure 5.11, she clicks the Date line box to include the date. Next, she chooses Full Block from the list of letter styles. In the Choose a page design list box, she chooses the current design, although she could have picked from any of the predefined templates that are available with Word 97, such as Contemporary Letter or Elegant Letter. Finally, she checks the Pre-printed letterhead box and enters information about where the letterhead appears on the page and how much space is needed for it.

Figure 5.11.

The Letter Wizard guides you through the steps of creating a letter for a contact.

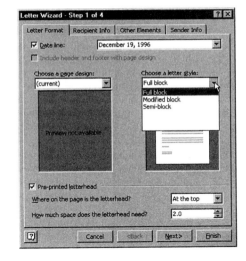

3. In the Recipient Info tab, she confirms that the recipient information is correct and chooses the type of salutation, which she makes informal. She clicks Next.

4. In the Other Elements tab (see Figure 5.12), she includes a reference line and types Editorial Schedule in the text box.

5. Finally, she clicks Next and the Sender Info tab allows her to enter her name and address as the sender, as well as to specify any closing lines.

6. When she clicks Finish, the Letter Wizard closes and the new letter appears in Microsoft Word with the information she entered in the Wizard tabs (see Figure 5.13). From this point forward, she can type the body of the letter, save, and print it.

Figure 5.12.

You can include as many or as few of the elements you want in the Letter Wizard.

Figure 5.13.

After you finish entering the information using the Letter Wizard, Word appears with the new letter ready for you to type the message.

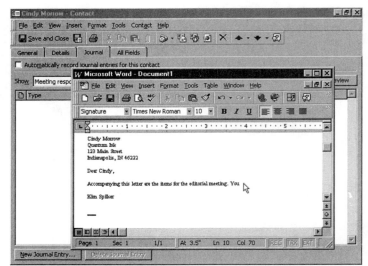

Calling a Contact

If you're like me, you get tired of looking up phone numbers and dialing the phone. In fact, I usually dial the wrong number and have to start over. Outlook can save you a few steps. If you have a modem, you can have Outlook dial phone numbers for you.

The easiest way to have Outlook dial a number is to select the Contact you want to call, click the phone icon (also known as the AutoDialer icon) on the toolbar, and choose from the list of phone numbers for that particular Contact (see Figure 5.14).

Figure 5.14.

The AutoDialer icon offers a drop-down list of phone numbers to choose from, or you can choose a New Call and specify a phone number in the dialog box.

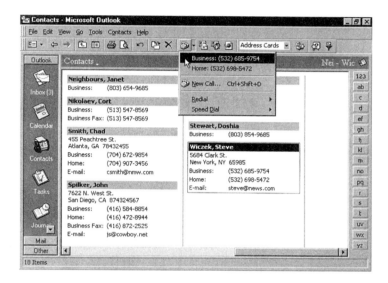

After you have chosen the correct phone number from the drop-down list, a New Call dialog box appears. If you want to record information during the call or the time of the call, click the box to have an automatic Journal entry pop up after the call is placed. Click the button marked Start Call when you are ready for Outlook to dial. When Outlook is dialing the number, a dialog box will appear that will ask you to pick up the receiver and click the Talk button, in that order. When the phone call has ended, hang up the phone, and click End Call and Close in the AutoDialer dialog box.

Printing Your List of Contacts

Outlook offers a lot of great choices for printing your list of Contacts when you open the Print menu:

☐ Card Style—Just like the Address Card view, the Card Style will print your Contacts as address cards in File As order. File As order means that your Contacts will most likely be printed in alphabetical order by last name, unless you chose to have your Contacts filed by first name instead.

☐ Small Booklet Style and Medium Booklet Style—Each of the booklet styles will print your Contacts as address cards, but in a way that you can fold the pages and staple them as you would a book. The pages are numbered so you will easily see how to fold and staple them together.

☐ Memo Style—If you want to print an individual Contact on a sheet, choose memo style.

☐ Phone Directory Style—This style prints your Contact names and all phone numbers listed for each one.

Unless you snoop around the print options, you may not know that Outlook has provided print options for different paper formats, such as Franklin Planners, Day Timers, and Avery labels (see in Figure 5.15). You can also define your own print style in the Print option box.

Figure 5.15.

By choosing Paper under the Print Setup dialog box, you can specify how you want the printed information to be formatted according to a commercial binder or label sheet.

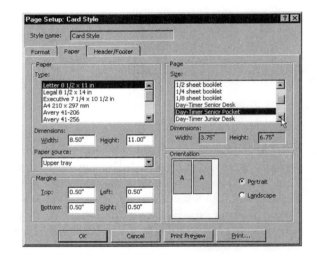

Summary

In this chapter, you worked with the Contacts component, viewing your Contacts in different formats, sending a letter to a Contact, using AutoDialer to call a Contact, and printing your list of Contacts. There are, of course, many other things you can do with your Contacts, such as sending e-mail or setting up an appointment with someone, but those tasks are covered in other parts of this book. You'll find that most everything you do in Outlook involves your Contacts list, so don't be surprised if you learn even more tips and tricks about using the Contacts component in most of the chapters in this book.

Q&A

Q If you want to modify a view of your Contacts, how can you do that?

A You can modify a view in two different ways: using your mouse and using menus. If you are more graphically oriented, you can use your mouse to move elements around on the screen, and then save the new view you created. Another way to modify a view is to click View|Define Views, and make choices in the dialog boxes to modify a view.

Q If you want Outlook to make a phone call for you, what do you have to choose?

A You can select a Contact, click on the AutoDialer icon found on the toolbar, and choose New Call. You can also select a Contact and use the menu by clicking Tools|Dial|New Call.

Q How can you create a letter to a Contact?

A Select a Contact, go to the menu, and click Contacts|New Letter to Contact. When the Letter Wizard appears, it will guide you through the choices for creating a letter. When you click Finish, you will see your letter within a Microsoft Word screen, where you can type the contents of the letter and print and save it.

Hour **6**

Using and Creating Contact Forms and Templates

Outlook already offers a relatively nice Contact form with many of the information fields that you would normally need for people in your database. However, as you begin to work with Outlook and your Contacts, you may find that you want to customize your forms to better meet your needs. Besides, creating your own forms is not as difficult as you might think. Outlook makes it as easy as dragging objects on a form and formatting them, as if you were using a paint program or Microsoft Word.

Why Create a Custom Form?

If you enter a lot of people in your Contacts database, you'll probably find that you don't keep the same kind of information about everyone. For instance, you might need to keep more personal information about your friends than you would your co-workers or other business contacts. If you design your Contact forms correctly, they should help you remember to gather the proper information about the different people in your life.

The standard Contacts form is too complex for entering friends into the Contacts database. For Mark's friends, he needs to keep track of things such as birthdays, anniversaries, names of children, hobbies, and spouses' names. He doesn't use the other fields on the standard form, such as Assistant's Name, Department, and other business-related fields.

In this chapter, Quantum Ink's editor Mark will design a simple Contact form for keeping track of his friends. Read along as he builds his new custom Contact form.

Designing a Custom Contact Form

Mark begins by opening a New Contact form by typing Ctrl+Shift+C, the shortcut for opening a new Contact. Once the new form is opened, he chooses Tools from the menu and clicks on Design Outlook Form. A new screen is opened that looks similar to the normal Contacts form except for the extra tabs marked P.2–P.6, Properties, and Actions (see Figure 6.1).

Figure 6.1.

Designing a New Contact form in Outlook.

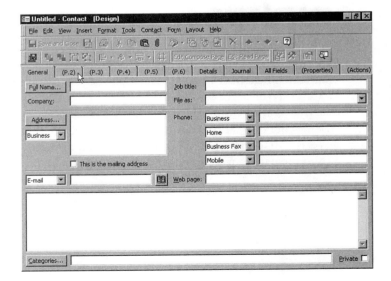

Most of the fields under the General tab are useful for almost any kind of contact, so Mark will keep it for his new Friends Contact form. Next, he clicks on the tab marked P.2 to create a new screen for his friends. In order to start placing fields onto his form, he opens the Field Chooser dialog box by choosing Form from the menu and clicking on Field Chooser. This dialog box offers all the predefined fields that are available in Outlook. They are organized into groups, such as Frequently-used fields, Address fields, and All Contact fields.

Clicking on Personal Fields under the Field Chooser dialog box reveals the kinds of fields that Mark will use for his friends, such as anniversary and birthday. He begins creating the form by dragging the fields one by one onto the blank form, as shown in Figure 6.2.

Figure 6.2.

Creating a new form is as simple as dragging fields from the list onto the blank background.

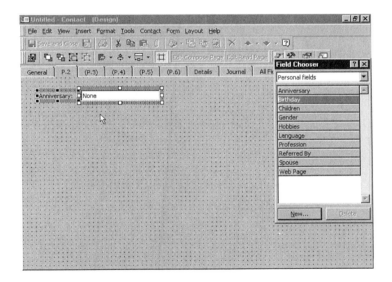

Formatting the Elements on the Form

Once the fields have been placed on the form, Mark begins to format them. By going to Form on the menu and choosing Control Toolbox, he calls up a box of controls like the one in Figure 6.3. With the tools, he can edit the appearance of the fields and labels or add buttons and labels to his form.

The Control Functions

Within the Control Toolbox, there are icons that represent different controls that are available for you when you are building your form. If you have ever designed a form in another Microsoft application, such as Access, these controls will look familiar to you. In the following paragraphs, I will explain the basic 15 controls that appear in the Toolbox by default. If you want to use additional controls, such as ActiveX controls or OLE controls, just right-click on the Toolbox, and choose Custom Controls. A list of available controls will appear for you to load into the existing Toolbox.

Figure 6.3.

The Control Toolbox offers a variety of tools to format labels and add buttons and other controls to a customized form.

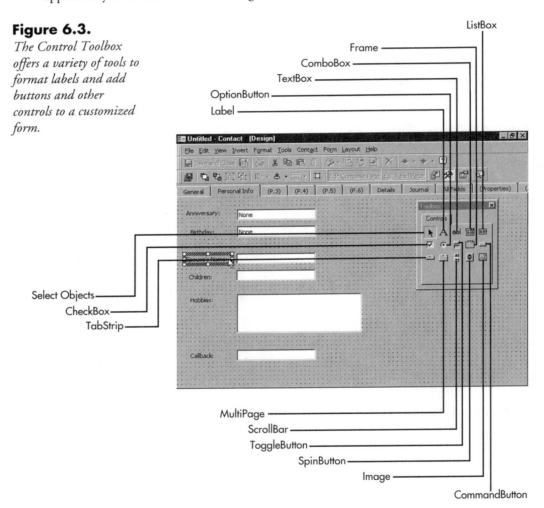

The Select Objects Tool

The Select Objects tool does just what the name implies; it selects objects on the workspace. When an object is selected, handles appear around the edges of the object. You can resize or move the object when it is selected. To select more than one object at a time, hold down the

6

Shift key while you click on each object or hold the mouse button while you drag the pointer across all the objects you want to select. You can also change the type in a text box by clicking the object once to select it and then clicking inside the text to make it available for editing. A cursor appears when you can begin editing.

Label

The Label control allows you to create a label anywhere on your form. If you choose the tool, you can draw a text box with your mouse and click inside the box to type the caption you want. If you click on the Properties icon on the toolbar or right-click on the label, you can set things such as the font, size, and color of the label. In most cases, you will use a label to identify a group of items on your form, such as "Special Dates to Remember," which could be placed above a group of date fields. Labels are also used next to text boxes on forms to instruct users to type the proper information into the text box.

TextBox

The TextBox tool, as previously mentioned, can be used to draw text boxes, which are blank boxes you can enter information into. Whenever you drag a field from the Field Chooser list box onto your workspace, you are pulling over two items: a label and a text box.

ComboBox

The ComboBox allows you to create your own drop-down list on your form so that you can list all possible entries for that particular field in the box. For example, if you create a new field on your contact form for eye color, you could create a ComboBox and specify green, blue, brown, and hazel as the possible values in the drop-down list. Some of Outlook's predefined fields are already set up as ComboBoxes, such as Sensitivity, for which Normal, Personal, Private, and Confidential are predefined choices.

ListBox

The ListBox works similarly to the ComboBox except that instead of a drop-down list, you create a box with values that you can scroll up and down using the scrollbar on the side of the ListBox.

CheckBox

The CheckBox tool could be used for any kind of field for which the answer would be either yes or no, true or false, or on or off. One of Outlook's predefined fields that uses the CheckBox tool is the This is the mailing address check box found within the General tab on the New Contact form.

OptionButton

The OptionButton could be used for situations in which you need the person entering information on your form to make a choice between different items.

ToggleButton

The ToggleButton, like the CheckBox tool, is another way of showing on/off on your form. Depending on the answer, the button appears embossed or debossed onscreen.

Frame

The Frame tool allows you to place a frame around objects on your form, and it allows multiple sets of radio buttons (OptionButtons) on the same form. You can title the frame and size it however you want. It's a good tool to use if you want to separate a field on a form. Maybe you need to provide instructions for the user inside the frame for a particular field entry.

CommandButton

The CommandButton can be used to execute a procedure or function. An example of a CommandButton is the Send button on an e-mail form. When the user hits the Send button, a script is run and the message is sent to the recipient. To use the CommandButton, you need to know how to use Visual Basic for Applications (VBA). If you want to find out more about VBA, see some of the Sams Publishing titles, such as *Visual Basic for Applications Unleashed* by Paul McFedries.

TabStrip

The TabStrip can be used for organizing controls and buttons on tabs. You can create as many tabs as you like by clicking once on the TabStrip to select it and then clicking again until you see the outline change. If you right-click on the TabStrip at this point, you will have four options available to you: Insert, Delete, Rename, and Move.

MultiPage

The MultiPage control essentially allows you to have a form within a form. You can pull a MultiPage control onto your workspace and put fields on each page. Changing the pages works the same way as changing the TabStrip.

ScrollBar

To see an example of a ScrollBar control, all you have to do is open any Microsoft application like Outlook, Word, or Excel, and you will notice that scrollbars can be found at the bottom, side, or both places on the window. ScrollBar controls can be used when there will be more information contained in the box than will be visible. The ScrollBar option can be used to scroll up and down or sideways in a box.

6

SpinButton

The SpinButton control can be used for numbers or anything that you would want to go up or down incrementally. For instance, you could create a number field and let your users enter numbers or dates in the blank box. However, if you create a SpinButton and place it next to the blank box, your users could click on the up and down arrows to increase or decrease the numbers in the box. Like the ControlButton, this control works only if you can program it using VBA.

JUST A MINUTE

To better understand how controls and VBA work together, think of them as a car and gasoline. The controls, such as CommandButton or SpinButton, are similar to a car. The VBA code is the gasoline that makes the car run. The car won't go anywhere without gasoline. The car is dependent on gasoline to run, just as VBA code is needed for a control button to function within a form.

Image

The Image control is essentially a frame in which you can place a picture file. You might place your company's logo in the Image control for company forms.

To illustrate some of the practical uses for controls, see the form pictured in Figure 6.4.

Figure 6.4.

Some of the different controls being used to design a custom form.

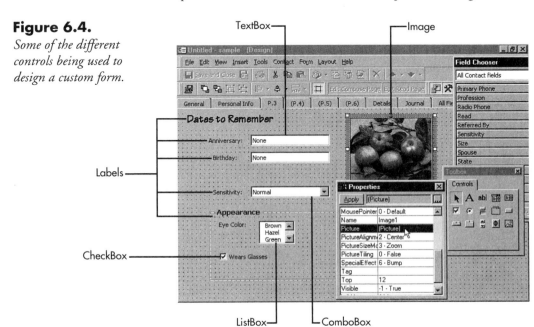

Editing a Label

Sometimes a predefined field does not clearly explain what kind of information should be entered in the text box. You can edit any label to make instructions clearer. Using the Select Objects tool, Mark double-clicks on the field marked Spouse until he gets a cursor, and changes the wording to Spouse's Name so that he will know what type of information to add to this box. He continues to customize the field's labels until he is satisfied with the form. You can see his results in Figure 6.5.

Figure 6.5.

You can edit the text of any label by clicking inside the label until a cursor appears.

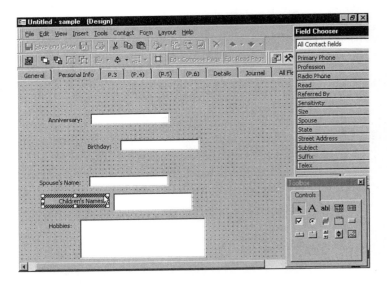

Creating a Label

He also creates a couple of new labels for his form to organize his information. He chooses the Label control and draws a box on the workspace. To change the caption of the label, he has two choices: He can click inside the label until a cursor appears, or he can right-click on the label and choose Properties from the drop-down menu. In the Properties dialog box, Mark can choose the typeface of the text in the label, the color, and the caption all within the same screen. You can see how he edits the label using the Properties menu in Figure 6.6.

TIME SAVER

For multiple changes to a field or a label, it's easier to use the Properties and Advanced Properties dialog boxes as opposed to using the menu. The Properties dialog boxes are simply tables that allow you to go down the list and make many different changes all in one dialog box.

6

Figure 6.6.

You can edit properties of a label by selecting the label, right-clicking, and choosing the Properties and Advanced Properties menus to make changes.

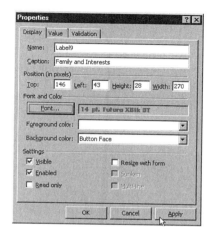

Arranging Objects on a Form

Dragging the fields onto the form is easy, but getting them aligned takes some extra work. Once all the fields are on the form, the Layout options on the menu offer ways to automatically align and space the fields on the form. Each of the following figures shows different ways to format items on a form.

Aligning Objects with One Another

Two or more objects can be aligned by selecting the objects simultaneously and choosing one of the Align options from the Layout menu. To select more than one object at a time, hold down the Ctrl key as you click on each object. In Figure 6.7, Mark has selected two text boxes to align them on the left.

JUST A MINUTE

The order of your selections matters when you are selecting objects to align with each other. Notice that the two selected boxes in Figure 6.7 have different colored handles. The last object selected will always have white handles, and all the other objects will be aligned according to its location. For instance, in Figure 6.7, the box with the black handles will move to the left to align with the box with the white handles.

Making Objects the Same Size

You can size objects so that they are equal in length, width, or both. In Figure 6.8, Mark wants to keep the different boxes' individual heights, but he wants to make them the same length as the longest box. He selects all of the boxes that he wants to size by holding down the Ctrl button on the keyboard while he clicks on each object. He makes sure that he selects the longest box last so that all the other selected boxes will be sized according to it. He clicks on the Layout menu and chooses Make Same Size | Width.

Figure 6.7.

Objects can be aligned with one another in a number of ways: left, right, center, top, middle, bottom, and to the grid.

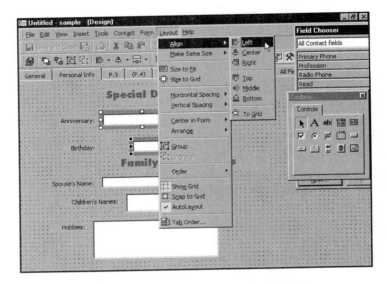

Figure 6.8.

If your objects are all different sizes, you can always make them equal in size by selecting them together and choosing one of the options from the list in Make Same Size under the Layout menu.

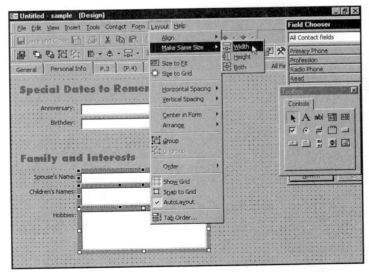

6

Formatting the Space Between Objects

Outlook allows you to space objects vertically and horizontally. Figure 6.9 shows two objects being pulled closer together by using the Horizontal Spacing option under the Layout menu. Because the object marked Birthday has white handles around it, it will remain stationary and the blank text box with the black handles will be pulled toward it.

Figure 6.9.

You can control the spacing between objects both vertically and horizontally in Outlook's Layout screen.

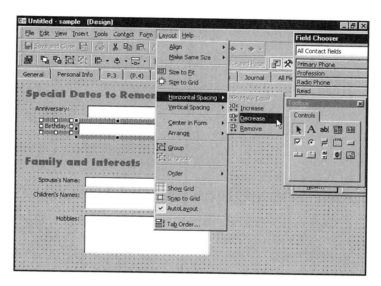

Grouping Objects

Once Mark arranges the spacing between all his labels and text boxes, he groups each of the pairs together so that he can arrange the vertical spacing between the groups, as shown in Figure 6.10. To group objects together, he selects each object and clicks on Group under the Layout menu. Then he selects the two groups of objects and begins spacing them vertically from one another.

TIME SAVER

Don't worry about grouping objects together. You can always choose Ungroup under the Layout menu to separate them into individual objects again.

Figure 6.10.

Grouping objects together can be beneficial when you want to arrange the spacing between objects vertically.

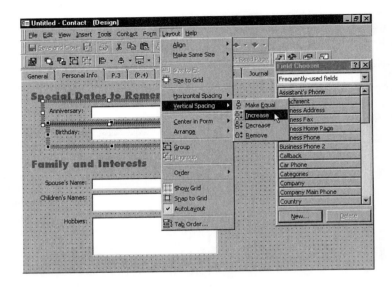

Centering Objects in the Middle of Your Form

In the preceding screen shots, you have seen how you can align and space objects in respect to one another. Outlook also gives you the option of centering your objects exactly in the middle of the form either vertically or horizontally. In Figure 6.11, Mark is putting the final touches to his custom form by centering his objects horizontally. In order to keep the same spacing and alignment of his individual objects, he groups them together and then centers them as one object.

Figure 6.11.

It's a good idea to group your objects together before centering them. Otherwise, all the individual objects will be centered and you will have to realign them and arrange the spacing again.

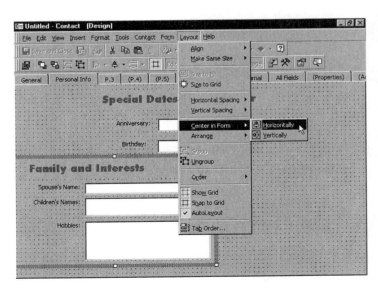

6

Using the Arrange Option

The Arrange option lies within the Layout menu. It works exclusively with CommandButtons. You can select a group of command buttons and arrange them to the right or along the bottom of the form. Because there are so many other alignment and spacing options available to you when you are designing forms, this particular option seems somewhat superfluous, especially because it only works with CommandButtons.

Arranging Stacked Objects

Many times you will want to stack objects on top of each other and arrange their order. In Figure 6.12, Mark wants to place a colored box around his labels and text boxes, but he doesn't want to hide them underneath the box. First he draws the box around the objects, and colors the box using the Properties dialog box. While the box is still selected, he chooses Order from the Layout menu, and clicks on Send to Back, which sends the colored box behind the labels and text boxes.

The Order option offers four different choices: Bring to Front, Send to Back, Bring Forward, and Send Backward. If Mark had multiple layers of objects, he could use the Bring Forward and Send Backward options to send each object backward or forward one layer at a time.

Figure 6.12.

The Order option allows you to dictate the order of objects stacked on top of one another.

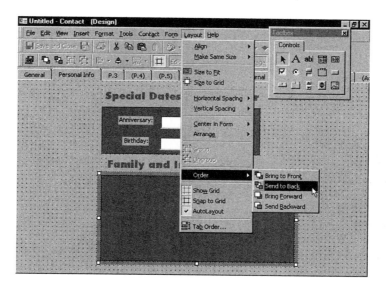

Arranging the Tab Order

Although it might not occur to you when you are first designing your form, the order of your labels and text boxes is important. When you are filling out a form and you hit the Tab key after each entry, you expect your cursor to go to the next blank box on the form. This happens because the person who designed the form dictated the order of the tabs during the design process.

In Figure 6.13, Mark is moving the names of his labels and text boxes up and down the list so that when he uses the form and presses the Tab key, his cursor will move down the form in order of the blank boxes.

Figure 6.13.

Before you save a form, remember to arrange the order of your labels and text boxes using the Tab Order option.

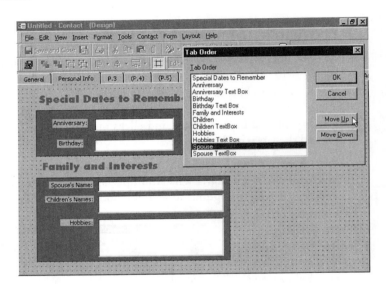

Hiding and Showing Pages

Mark wants the Contact form for his friends to be as simple as possible. He only needs the first two pages, General and Personal Info, when he is entering friends into his database. Therefore, he needs to hide the other pages before he leaves the form design feature. The tab labels at the top of each form page that have parentheses around the words indicate that those pages will not be visible when that form is open. Mark wants to hide the pages marked Details, Journal, and All Fields. Figure 6.14 shows you how he hides pages in a form.

Setting the Properties of a New Form

Although the Properties page is hidden from view whenever Mark pulls up a new Friend Contact form, he still needs to set a few items in the Properties page. Figure 6.15 shows how he describes and categorizes his new form. Because the default Contact form is classified under a category called Standard and a subcategory called Form, he decides to place his new form under those categories for better organization.

He also checks the large and small icons to make sure that they represent a Contact form. More icons can be found in the Forms directory under Microsoft Office.

Figure 6.14.

You can toggle pages on and off by clicking on Display This Page under the Form menu.

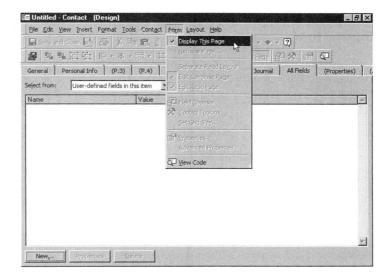

Figure 6.15.

Setting the properties of a form is the last thing to do before publishing it in Outlook.

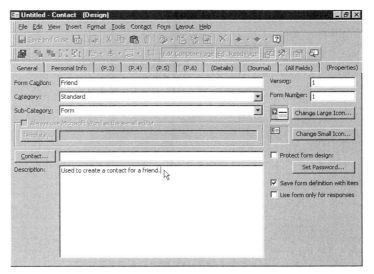

Saving and Publishing a New Form

Now that Mark has finished designing his Friend Contact form, he needs to publish it in order to begin using it to enter his friends in the Contacts database. To do this, he goes to

File | Publish Form As and names the form in the dialog box, as shown in Figure 6.16. Notice that he can also click the Publish In button so that he can indicate the location of the form. He has a choice of publishing it in his Personal Forms Library or in the Folder Forms Library.

Figure 6.16.

Once a form is completed, you need to publish it in order to use it in Outlook.

Managing Forms

Opening a custom form that you have designed depends on where you published it. It could be in either the Folder Forms Library or in your Personal Forms Library. Mark wanted the Friend form to appear under the Contacts menu in Outlook, so he published his form in the Folder Forms Library under the Contacts folder.

If he had published his form in the Personal Forms Library or within a different folder under the Folder Forms Library, he could add it to the Contacts folder by going into the Manage Forms dialog box. To get there, he would have to do the following:

1. Go to Tools | Options.
2. Click on the Manage Forms tab within the Options dialog box.
3. Click the Manage Forms button.
4. Click the Set button on the left and select Personal Forms Library.
5. Click the Set button on the right and select Folder Forms Library | Contacts.
6. Click the plus (+) sign on both sides until the Friend form appears on the left.
7. Click the Copy button to copy the Friend form into the Contacts folder, as shown in Figure 6.17.

Figure 6.17.

In the Forms Manager dialog box, you can copy, update, delete, and view the properties of the forms in Outlook.

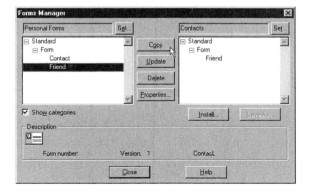

Once the Friend Contact form has been copied to the Contacts folder, it will appear in the drop-down list under the Contacts menu whenever the Contacts module is active. If he wanted to make his new Friend form the default New Contact form in the Contacts component, he could modify the properties of the Contacts folder.

Summary

In this chapter, you learned how to create a custom contact form. All the skills you learned can be applied to making other custom forms in Outlook. If you haven't already figured it out, Outlook is based on forms. Whether you create an e-mail, enter a new contact, or make a journal entry, you're using a form. If you use Outlook on a network that has an Exchange Server, your administrator will most likely distribute custom forms for your organization that you can use, such as personnel, project, or accounting forms.

Q&A

Q If you want to create a custom Contact form, how do you begin?

A Open a New Contact form, and click Tools | Design Outlook Form from the menu.

Q Where you can you publish a form once you have created it?

A You can place it (in other words, publish it) in your Personal Forms Library or on the network in a Folder Forms Library.

Q If you publish a new Contact form in your Personal Forms Library, where will it appear in Outlook so you can use it?

A It will appear under the Contacts menu at the bottom of the list of options. For instance, if you name the form Friend, it will appear as the command New Friend.

PART

III

Mail and Fax

Hour

Hour 7

Introduction to Mail and Fax Messages in Outlook

If you're like most people, sending and receiving e-mail and fax messages has become an important part of your everyday life. E-mail and fax services have provided us with the fastest, cheapest, and most convenient vehicles for sending and receiving documents.

When I first started using e-mail, there were only a handful of people with whom I communicated in this fashion. It was a great way to keep up with old friends who were high-tech enough to belong to an online service. Now, four years later and saddled with an average of 50 e-mail messages a day, I'm wondering if this technology is a curse or a blessing.

If you're feeling the same way as I do, then, hopefully, Outlook can at least help you manage your e-mail and fax messages so that you won't be overwhelmed by the mountains of messages that you send and receive every day.

In this hour, you'll be introduced to the three main features that make up the messaging services in Outlook: Inbox, Sent Items folder, and Outbox. You'll also follow some examples of composing and sending both e-mail and fax messages.

What Is the Inbox?

The Inbox is the folder that stores all incoming e-mail and faxes. You can get to the Inbox in a number of ways:

- [ ] Click on Inbox in the Outlook Bar
- [ ] Click on Mail in the Outlook Bar and then click on Inbox
- [ ] Click on Inbox in the Folder List
- [ ] Using the shortcut, type Ctrl+Shift+I
- [ ] Using the menu, click on Go | Inbox

Figure 7.1 is a snapshot of an Inbox. Notice that there are a number of different icons indicating the status of each message. Each icon is explained in the following paragraphs. Notice also that these messages are sorted in order of the date that they were received. The Inbox messages can be sorted by any of the visible fields by clicking at the top of the preferred column, such as From or Subject.

Figure 7.1.

The Inbox holds all incoming e-mail and faxes.

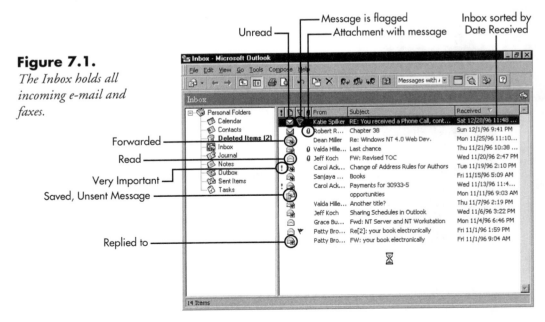

Understanding the Message Symbols in the Inbox

As you can see in Figure 7.1, every message has a status symbol next to it and, in some cases, other symbols, such as flags, attachments, and symbols indicating the importance of a message. After using Outlook for a while, you will begin to remember the meaning of each symbol. Here are the definitions of the symbols and their uses.

Importance of a Message

In Table 7.1, you can see the two symbols that indicate the importance of a message. There are three levels of importance that a message can have: High, Low, and Normal.

Table 7.1. Symbols indicating importance.

Symbol	Meaning
!	High importance
↓	Low importance

A message with Normal importance has no symbol next to it.

The level of a message's importance can be determined by the sender or the receiver. If the sender deems the message to be highly important, the message arrives in the Inbox with the exclamation mark next to it.

If you receive a message and you want to mark the message as high or low in importance, you need to open the message, click the Options tab within the message, and choose the level of importance. When you close the message, a dialog box will appear, asking you if you want to save the changes. Click Yes.

TIME SAVER

Marking your incoming messages as high or low in importance may seem tedious, but if you receive a lot of messages in your Inbox every day, marking messages can help you prioritize your activities. For instance, after you read each of your messages, mark them as high or low in importance. Then sort your Inbox by importance by clicking on the top of the column marked by the exclamation point. If you receive a lot of mail, this activity of marking your messages might help you prioritize answering them.

7

Messages with Attachments

If a message is marked with a paper clip symbol next to it, the message contains one or more attachments. Attachments are embedded files, such as Word documents or Excel spreadsheets. In Figure 7.2, the reader has opened the e-mail message, right-clicked on the attachment, and is about to save the attached Word document to the proper directory on the hard drive.

Figure 7.2.

To save an attachment, open the mail message, right-click on the attachment, and choose Save As from the menu.

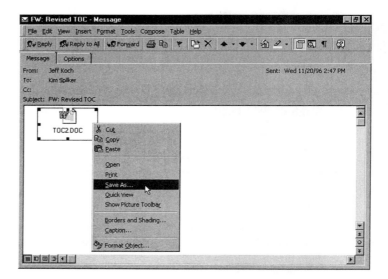

You can do a number of things with an attachment before saving it to your hard drive. You can print, view, or open the attachment by right-clicking on it within the open message. You can save a group of messages at the same time by choosing File | Save Attachments. A dialog box will ask you to specify the directory where you want to place the attachments.

If you want to view the attachment from the Inbox without opening the message, right-click on the message and choose View from the drop-down menu.

CAUTION

Although e-mail messages themselves cannot contain viruses, attachments can. It's a good idea to install virus protection software on your computer to scan all new files, including attachments embedded in e-mail.

7

Flagged Messages

Flagged messages have flag icons next to the messages. The flags are either red or gray, depending on whether they are active or completed. Flagging messages is a way to tag instructions onto your messages. You can flag messages you have received to help you remember to follow up. Simply right-click on the message and choose Flag Message. You can use flags when you send messages to someone else by clicking the Message Flag icon on the toolbar of the New Mail Message window. The shortcut for flagging a message is Ctrl+Shift+G.

If someone sending you an e-mail message wants you to take action, a red flag will appear next to the message in your Inbox. When you open the message, you will see a message at the top of the window, telling you to do one of the following things:

> Call
> Do not forward
> Follow up
> For your information
> Forward
> No response necessary
> Read
> Reply
> Reply to all
> Review

The sender also has the option of sending a due date, as shown in Figure 7.3.

Figure 7.3.

Flagging a message is a way of sending instructions to your recipient.

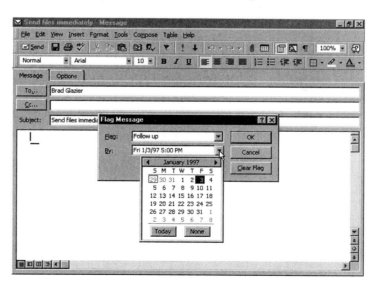

Once a flagged message has been completed, the flag will appear gray instead of red.

Status Symbols Next to Messages

A long list of status symbols for messages are available, although the majority of them will be either Read, Unread, Forwarded, or Replied. Table 7.2 gives you the complete list of icons that can appear next to a message.

Table 7.2. Icons indicating the status of the message.

Symbol	Meaning
	Indicates that the message is read
	Indicates that the message is unread
	Appears after you have forwarded the message
	Appears after you have replied to the message
	Appears if you save a message that you have not sent yet
	Indicates that the message has been sealed using encryption
	Indicates that the message has a digital signature for security measures
	Indicates that the message is a Microsoft Mail 3.x form
	Indicates that the message has been posted in a public folder on the network
	Indicates that an attempt was made to recall the message
	Notifies you of a successful message recall
	Notifies you of an unsuccessful message recall
	Notifies you of a delivered message
	Notifies you of a read message
	Notifies you of a message that was not delivered

7

Symbol	Meaning
	Notifies you of a message that was not read
	Indicates an accepted meeting request
	Indicates a tentatively accepted meeting request
	Indicates a declined meeting request
	Indicates a canceled meeting
	Indicates a task request
	Indicates an accepted task
	Indicates a declined task
	Notifies you of a conflict between messages when synchronizing an offline folder with the online folder

The following three icons can appear when you have remote mail services:

Symbol	Meaning
	Indicates a Remote Mail message header
	Indicates a message marked for download
	Indicates a message marked for copy and download

Composing a Mail Message

To illustrate how to compose and send e-mail messages, let's use Quantum Ink's editor Mark as an example. Mark wants to send a message to his author, Sanjaya, who is already listed in his Contacts database. To call up a new message window, he has the choice of typing Ctrl+Shift+M as a keyboard shortcut, choosing File | New | Mail Message from the Outlook menu, or clicking the Mail Message icon on the far left of the Outlook toolbar. When the new mail message screen opens, he clicks the To: button and chooses the recipient, as shown in Figure 7.4.

7

Figure 7.4.

*When composing a new
message, click the To:
button to pull up drop-
down lists of your
contacts.*

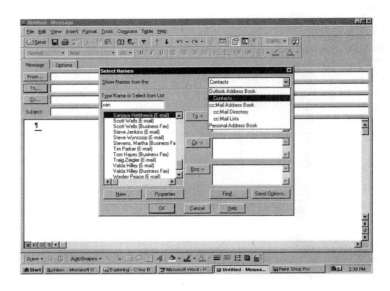

Selecting Recipients from the Address Book

All the different address books appear in the Select Names dialog box. In this case, Mark has a number of different lists that he keeps in Outlook: an Outlook Address Book, a Personal Address Book, and a cc:Mail Address Book from his company's network. He chooses the Contacts list under the Outlook Address Book, picks his recipients, and adds them to the list. Each recipient he adds is automatically separated by a semicolon.

Outlook gives you four recipient fields for any message: From, To, Cc, and Bcc. In addition to Sanjaya, Mark wants to send a copy of this message to his manager Dean, so he picks Dean's name from the address book and enters it into the Cc field. He also wants to send a blind copy to his co-worker, Cindy. The recipient added into the Bcc (blind copy) field will not be visible to the other recipients when they receive the message. Typically, all the header fields will be visible to you when you pull up a new mail message window except Bcc and From. If you want these fields to be visible, click View on the menu and choose the options Bcc Field and From Field from the list of options.

Mark enters the recipient names and leaves the From field blank because his name will automatically be inserted as the sender. Normally, you will not enter anything into the From field unless you are given permission to send messages on behalf of someone else, such as your manager.

7

Entering Names Manually into the Recipient Fields

You can type the names of the recipients directly into the blank boxes next to each field. Outlook will attempt to match the names you type against all of your different address books. If it does not recognize a name from an address book or that the address is a proper Internet address, such as kspilker@sams.mcp.com, it will notify you upon trying to send the message and ask you to select a name from the address lists or enter a new address.

Formatting Your Message

Formatting options in the message editor depends on whether you choose to have Microsoft Word 97 as your e-mail editor. You can see the differences in the menus in Figure 7.5 and 7.6. Using Word as the e-mail editor offers many more formatting choices than the standard Outlook editor, but it will make the response time a little slower when you call up a new mail message.

Figure 7.5.
The Format menu when Microsoft Word is the e-mail editor.

Figure 7.6.
The Format menu without Word as the editor.

Using Word as Your E-mail Editor

Some of the benefits of using Microsoft Word as your e-mail editor include the following:

- ☐ Notification of misspelled words displayed by a red underline
- ☐ Automatic correction of simple typos, such as "the"
- ☐ Extensive formatting options, such as bullets and numbering
- ☐ Ability to format and insert tables into your document

You can turn this option off and on by clicking on Tools | Options, choosing the E-mail tab, and clicking on the check box marked Use Microsoft Word as the E-mail Editor.

Formatted E-mail Messages—What Does the Recipient See on the Other End?

Keep in mind that formatting an e-mail message with typefaces, bullets, colors, and graphics may be in vain unless you are sending the message to someone capable of receiving Rich Text Format messages, such as a person using Exchange, Windows Messaging, or Outlook. To illustrate the differences in formatting from one e-mail recipient to another, my friend Steve Straiger allowed me to send him the same e-mail message to two different e-mail addresses—his Internet address and his address on a cc:Mail network. Figure 7.7 shows how the e-mail message sent to his Internet address, which he received in his Outlook Inbox, retained its formatting. The other e-mail message, shown in Figure 7.8, shows how the message appeared when viewed through his cc:Mail account.

Figure 7.7

The message as viewed through an RTF-capable mail reader.

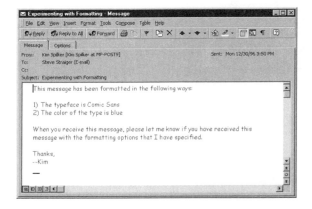

Figure 7.8.

The message as viewed through a non–RTF-capable mail reader.

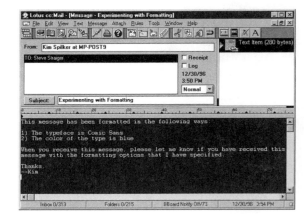

7

TIME SAVER

If your recipient is using an e-mail client, such as Outlook, that can receive messages in Rich Text Format, you must specify this in the e-mail Properties dialog box, as shown in Figure 7.9.

To change the e-mail properties:

1. Open the Contact form for the recipient.
2. Right-click on the person's e-mail address.
3. Choose Properties from the drop-down menu.
4. Check the box Always send to this recipient in Microsoft Exchange rich-text format.

Figure 7.9.

You must specify Rich Text formatting on an individual basis by opening the Properties of each person's e-mail address and clicking on the check box.

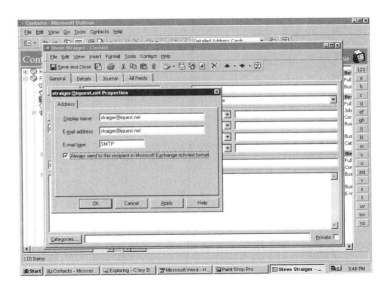

Using the AutoSignature Feature

Instead of typing the same information at the bottom of every message, you could use AutoSignature to automatically add your information to every message. Instructions for setting up AutoSignature depend on whether you use Word as your e-mail editor.

Setting Up AutoSignature if Word Is Your E-mail Editor

To set up AutoSignature if Word is your e-mail editor, complete the following steps:

1. Type Ctrl+Shift+M to bring up a new mail message window.

2. Enter the signature into the message box as you would like it to appear at the end of every message. For example, Mark typed:

```
Mark Bewsey, Editor
Quantum Ink Publishing
(800) 583-5921 ext 4920
mark@quantum_ink.com
http://www.quantum_ink.com
```

3. Select the signature by highlighting all of the text.

4. Go to Tools | AutoSignature.

5. A dialog box will appear that asks you if you want to save the text as your current AutoSignature. Click Yes.

Setting Up AutoSignature if You Are Not Using Word as Your E-mail Editor

To set up AutoSignature if you are not using Word as your e-mail editor, complete the following steps:

1. Make sure you are in the Inbox, and go to Tools | AutoSignature.

2. A dialog box will appear. You can enter your signature into the box. Click the Font or Paragraph buttons to format the text.

3. Click OK.

Spell Checking Your Message

One of the last things to do before sending a message is to use the spell checker. To open the spell check command, click on Tools | Spelling or hit the F7 key to bring up the Spelling feature. The spell checker works the same as it does in Microsoft Word. When the spell checker finds a word in your message that it does not recognize in its dictionary, you have the option of ignoring, changing, or adding the word to your custom dictionary.

TIME SAVER

If you are like me, you may forget to spell check every message you send. If you want Outlook to automatically spell check a message before sending, change the options of the spell checker. When spell checker finds a word that is misspelled, click the Options button at the bottom of the Spelling dialog box. A new dialog box will appear with options for

7

you to choose. Check the box marked Always Check Spelling before sending.

Attaching a File to Your Message

Mark wants to attach two files to his e-mail message to Sanjaya. He needs to send a Word document and a graphic file. Because Sanjaya is not an employee of Quantum Ink, and, therefore, does not have access to the network, Mark sends the complete files in the message. If he just wanted to send the message to his co-workers, he could have attached a shortcut to the files instead of the complete files, in order to keep the size of the e-mail smaller.

To attach the files, Mark performs the following operations:

1. He clicks on the paper clip icon on the New Mail Message toolbar to attach a file.
2. He goes to the directory on his computer where the files are located. In this case, they are located under a directory named Sanjaya.
3. He chooses whether he wants to send each file as an attachment, shortcut, or text only, which appears as plain text in the body of the message. He chooses Attachment.

Figure 7.10 shows how Mark chooses each file, and Figure 7.11 shows how the attachments look in the body of the message.

Figure 7.10.

When adding attachments, you can select more than one file to attach at one time. Just hold the Ctrl key while you select each file.

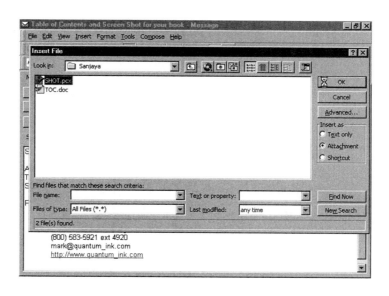

Figure 7.11.

Attached files appear inside the body of a message as labeled icons.

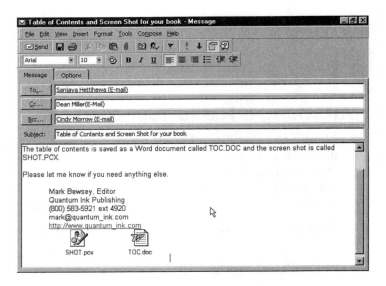

TIME SAVER

Attachments don't always go through the electronic mail system un-scathed. Sometimes you may get attachments that have a name, such as `MIME01.RAW`. This means that the name of the file was lost during transport. It does not necessarily mean that the attachment is corrupt. If you always type the names of the files that you are attaching within the message copy, your recipient will have an easier time recovering your attachments if they lose their names.

If you are on the receiving end of one of these raw attachments and you want to recover the file, save the attachment on your computer. In the Explorer, find the file and rename it with its original name and extension. Open the file. Sometimes renaming it is the only thing you need to do to recover the file.

Sending the Message

Once you have composed a message, click the Send button to deliver the message. The message will automatically be placed in the Outbox. Think of the Outbox as a weigh station for messages. Your messages will remain in the Outbox until the next time you log on to a service or a network to check for new messages and send all outgoing messages. When a message has been delivered, it will be stored in the Sent Items folder unless you specify in the Options dialog box under the Sending tab that you do not want to store sent messages.

7

TIME SAVER

One way to keep your Outlook .PST file smaller in size is to select the Options command under the Tools menu, click on the Sending tab, and turn off the option to Save copies of messages in Sent Items Folder. Then you can specify on a case-by-case basis which e-mail messages you want to store in the Sent Items folder by clicking on the Options tab before sending a message and clicking on the check box marked to store the message.

Troubleshooting Mail Messages

There are a number of things that can go wrong whenever you try to send or receive an e-mail message. In most instances, one of these three things can happen:

☐ A message will sit in the Outbox and not leave, in which case something may be invalid in your Outlook Services setup or network setup. Check the Services setup under the Tools menu. Check the properties of each of the mail services that you have set up in Outlook. Is the phone number or network location correct? Contact your administrator or service provider to ask about the problem.

☐ Outlook will return a message as undeliverable, in which case it could be your setup information. Another explanation may be that the service provider is over-loaded, and you need to try to resend the message.

☐ The Internet returns a message to your Inbox as undeliverable, in which case the recipient's address is probably incorrect or the recipient's system is malfunctioning.

If you have tried these measures but still cannot send or receive mail messages, try exiting Outlook and restarting Windows. Sometimes you will have a MAPI error that can be corrected by simply logging off and logging back on to the system.

Resending a Message

One occasion on which you might want to resend a message is when it has been returned to you as undeliverable. The message will have an undeliverable notification symbol next to it and will have come back from the system administrator. You can open the message by double-clicking it and hitting the Resend button at the top of the message. There will usually be some type of explanation in the message box regarding the problems delivering the message. In the case of an Internet mail message, sometimes you will send a message to a proper address, but when the message gets to its final destination, the recipient's mail server may not be available or the recipient cannot be located by the mail server. If the message states that "no transport was available," you might try resending the message to the recipient.

Recalling a Sent Message

Sometimes you may send a message that has errors or incorrect information. Luckily, there is a way to recall a message that you have already sent. To recall a message, do the following:

1. Go to the Sent Items folder and locate the message that you want to recall.
2. Open the message by double-clicking it.
3. Go to Tools | Recall This Message.
4. A dialog box will appear, and you'll have the choice of recalling all unread copies of the message or replacing all unread copies with another message, as shown in Figure 7.12.

Figure 7.12.

The dialog box for recalling a message.

Keep in mind that recalling a message only works for messages that you have sent to recipients who are logged on and using Outlook, and if the message is still located in their Inbox. The message has to be unread, as well, or there is really no use in recalling it.

Checking for New Messages and Delivering All Outgoing Mail

Receiving and delivering mail is simple if you have configured your mail systems properly, as described in Hour 3, "Configuring and Exploring Outlook." You can schedule automatic logon sessions in Outlook or you can choose to log on to your mail server(s) manually.

Scheduling Automatic Logon

Rather than logging on to an e-mail account manually, you can schedule Outlook to automatically log on to a service. In order to logon, Outlook, or at least the MAPI DLL, needs to be running. To schedule logon sessions, go to the Services command under the Tools menu and perform the following tasks:

7

1. Select the service, such as Internet mail, that you want to schedule logon sessions for and click the Properties button.
2. Click on the Connection tab.
3. At the bottom of the Connection window, deselect the box marked Work off-line and use Remote Mail if there is a check mark in the box.
4. Click the Schedule button.
5. A Schedule dialog box appears. Specify the intervals in minutes that you want Outlook to automatically log on to the service, as shown in Figure 7.13.

Figure 7.13.

Scheduling automatic logon sessions for delivering and checking for new mail.

If you want to keep a log file of your automatic sessions, you can click the Log File button in the Connection window. This button records in text format all the things that happen during each session. Keeping a log file is a good way to understand how mail delivery works and might help you troubleshoot mail problems.

The Log File dialog box gives you three options for logging information:

☐ No Logging.

☐ Basic, which records logon and logoff times and error messages.

☐ Troubleshooting, which records more detailed information, such as transport messages. If you are experiencing problems with e-mail delivery, you might want to turn on Troubleshooting logging so that you can show your system administrator what is happening during your logon sessions.

You also need to pick a location for the log file to be stored on your computer.

Caution

> If you need to save space on your computer, you may want to turn off logging. The log file can become large, especially if you have chosen to log for troubleshooting. If you have problems with mail delivery, choose the troubleshooting log files for a period of time until the problem is resolved. Then turn off logging, and delete the *.LOG file from your computer.

Checking Mail Manually

There could be a number of reasons why you might want to check on mail manually instead of scheduling logons automatically. As an example, Mark at Quantum Ink has three different mail accounts: his company-wide cc:Mail account, a CompuServe account, and an Internet account. He receives most of his mail from co-workers via cc:Mail and about 10 messages each day to his Internet account. He may only get one or two messages sent to his CompuServe account each week. Therefore, he chooses not to schedule automatic logons to his CompuServe account.

When to Use the Check for New Mail Command

Whenever Mark wants to check his CompuServe account, he can click on Tools | Check for New Mail. This command instructs Outlook to check all the services that he has specified in the Options dialog box under the E-mail tab.

He can also choose the other command, Check for New Mail on, under the Tools menu. A dialog box appears, and he is asked to place a check mark next to the service(s) that he wants Outlook to check. With this command, he can choose to log on to only his CompuServe account.

When to Use the Remote Session Commands

If you work on Outlook from a remote location, such as your home, you may want to check for new mail and deliver outgoing messages manually. If you use the Remote Session commands instead of the Check for New Mail command, you will have more choices for your remote session. You can choose any of the following options:

- ☐ Retrieve and Send all new mail.
- ☐ Send only specific mail messages that you designate with a check mark, as shown in Figure 7.14. Let's say you have created three small messages and one large message with an attachment. You know that the large message will take a long time to send

7

and you only have a few minutes to conduct a remote session. Choose only the three small messages during this remote session and send the large message later when you have more time to be online. This option allows you to control the session.

Figure 7.14.

The Remote Connection Wizard allows you to make more specific choices about sending and receiving mail.

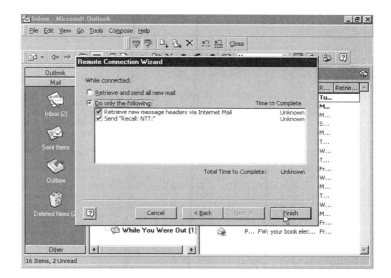

☐ Retrieve new message headers only. You might be on a business trip and need to check your mailbox, but you don't need all of your mail. You want to check the headers and decide which ones you would like to receive at this time. This option allows you to receive only the message headers (From, Subject, and Date). As you read through them, you can use another remote mail tool, the Mark to Retrieve or Mark to Retrieve a Copy, to select which messages you want to retrieve. The unselected messages will remain in your mailbox at the office, waiting for you when you return.

Opening the Mail

Opening and reading a mail message is as simple as double-clicking on the message. What you really need to know about opening a message is what to do with it. You can read it, reply to it, forward it, delete it, print it, or save it as a file. You can even drop it onto other Outlook features, such as Tasks, and start a new Task for yourself based on the message. Most of the time, a mail message that you receive from someone else will ask you to take action in some way. The sender may ask to set up a meeting with you, schedule a phone call, ask you to perform certain tasks, or give you information that you will refer to often. In these cases, Outlook's interoperability makes it easy for you to take a mail message and turn it into something else, such as a Task, Appointment, Journal entry, Contact, or Note.

For now, let's go through each of the easy options, such as printing and saving, and move on to the more complex tasks of taking e-mail messages and making them work with other Outlook features.

Printing a Message

There are two ways to print an e-mail message:

☐ Open the mail message and click on File | Print. In the Print dialog box, you can choose to print not only the message but any attachments, as well. To print the attachments, find the option at the bottom left of the dialog box, and place a check mark in the check box for printing the attachments.

☐ From the Inbox, right-click on any unopened mail message and choose Print from the drop-down list of options.

Saving a Message as a File

There are times when you may want to save an e-mail message as a file. Doing this does not remove the message from Outlook, it simply creates a file with the format you choose in the Save As dialog box. Your choices for formats are Text Only (*.TXT), Rich Text Format (*.RTF), Outlook Template (*.OFT), or Message Format (*.MSG). If you happen to be using Word as your e-mail editor, you may also save any message as a Word document (*.DOC).

You may be wondering what the Outlook Template and Message Format choices mean. If you save an e-mail message as an Outlook Template, you can use it in Outlook as a template for other e-mail messages. In Hours 8, "Viewing the Inbox," and 9, "Making Mail Work for You," you will learn more about templates and custom forms in Outlook. The Message Format is a format that Outlook recognizes. If you double-click on a file with the extension .MSG, it will open as an Outlook message.

Saving an Attachment

There are a few ways to save attachments embedded in e-mail messages:

☐ In the Inbox, right-click on an unopened e-mail message and choose View Attachments from the drop-down list of options.

☐ Open a mail message with an attachment, and choose File | Save Attachments. A dialog box appears, and you will need to specify a location for saving the file or files.

☐ Within the open message, right-click on an attachment and choose either Open or Save As from the drop-down list of options.

Replying and Forwarding Mail Messages

Replying to messages and forwarding them are similar tasks. You would forward a message to someone who wasn't originally listed as a sender or recipient on the message that you want them to see. In all other cases, you would simply use one of the reply options. If you like, you can both forward and reply to an e-mail message. You will have to perform the operations separately, of course.

In an opened mail message, click either the Reply, Reply to All, or Forward buttons on the toolbar. A new mail message window appears with a few blank lines and the original message in the message box separated by a bunch of lines and the words -----Original Message-----. Type your message above the original message or move your cursor down through the original message and reply to specific paragraphs. When you type your reply within the text of the original message, your comments need to be distinguished from the original text. If you use Word as your e-mail editor, your reply will look different than if you use the standard Outlook e-mail editor. Figures 7.15 and 7.16 show the difference between using Word and the standard e-mail editor.

Figure 7.15.

A reply message when the standard Outlook e-mail editor is used.

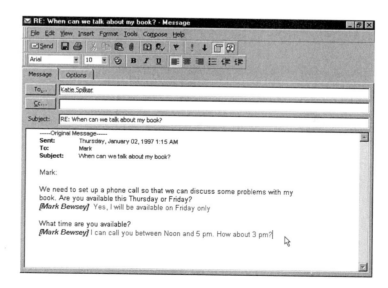

7

Figure 7.16.

*A reply message when
Microsoft Word is the
e-mail editor.*

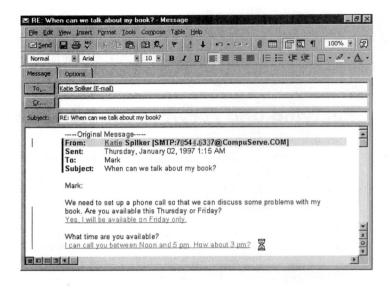

TIME SAVER

The Options dialog box provides you with many ways to customize Outlook to suit your needs. If you open the Options dialog and click on the Reading tab, you will see some options regarding reading and replying to e-mail messages.

When I first started using Outlook, I found it annoying when I replied to an e-mail message, and the original message was still sitting open on my desktop. By placing a check mark in the box marked Close original message on reply or forward, I solved my problem.

Sending a Fax

Sending a fax is similar to sending an e-mail message. Almost all the skills you learned in the preceding section on e-mail will apply to fax messages. Addressing the message involves the same steps; except when you pick the recipient from the Address Book list, you need to choose one with the word "fax" in parentheses next to the name.

Microsoft Fax Service is supplied with Outlook. If you are using Windows NT Workstation, you cannot use the Microsoft Fax software, but, instead, must go to the Microsoft Web site at http://www.microsoft.com to download their fax software called Microsoft Personal Fax. If you choose to add the fax service to your Outlook profile, as described in Hour 3, a few new command options will be added to your drop-down menus, such as Compose | New Fax and Tools | Microsoft Fax Tools.

The following procedure is a step-by-step example of how to send a fax from Outlook:

1. Choose Compose on the menu and click New Fax from the list if you are in the Inbox feature, or choose Contacts | New Fax if you are in the Contacts feature.

2. A Fax Wizard appears and guides you through the process. If you have already set up your fax services properly, you should see Default Location in the text box under the statement I'm dialing from. Otherwise, you may need to click the Dialing Properties button and fill in the information for your location.

3. In the next screen, you are asked to enter the recipient information. If you are sending to a fax number that is already listed in your Contacts database, click the Address Book button to locate the recipient. Otherwise, you can enter the recipient's information manually. You can add as many recipients to the list as you need. Add each one separately.

4. The next screen asks you if you want to use a cover page and what kind of cover you want. You can also click the Options button to set formatting options, dialing instructions, and security.

5. In the next screen, you can enter the subject of the fax message and type a brief note.

6. The next screen asks you if you want to include any files with the fax message, such as a Word document or an Excel spreadsheet. If you choose to add a file, you will need to locate the directory in which the file is stored.

7. The fax is ready to send.

CAUTION

> You can send a fax in the exact same way that you send an e-mail message. Simply choose the recipient's fax address from the Address Book instead of the e-mail address. This process, however, is slower than using the Fax Wizard, and you won't have the option of choosing the cover page and attaching a file, as you do with the Fax Wizard.

Receiving a Fax

All incoming faxes are placed in the Inbox. To set up Outlook to receive a fax, from the Inbox feature, choose Tools from the menu, click on Microsoft Fax Tools | Options. Click on the Modem tab and choose the Properties button. If your Answer Mode properties are set on Don't Answer, choose the Manual option or the option to automatically answer after a specified number of rings. If you choose the Manual option, you need to click Answer on the screen when the sender's fax modem calls.

7

Once a fax has been successfully received, it will appear in your Inbox among your e-mail messages. To open the fax message, just double-click on it as you would to open an e-mail.

Summary

This chapter covers the basic skills related to sending and receiving e-mail and fax messages. You learned what all the different icons associated with messages mean. You also learned about adding elements to messages, such as attachments, flags, and icons that denote the importance of a message. This chapter discusses the difference between using Word and using the Integrated E-mail Editor that is supplied with Outlook. Finally, you learned about formatting messages, and using the Rich Text Format option in cases where the recipient is able to receive formatted messages. The next two chapters delve further into mail-related topics, such as Inbox management and working with mail.

Q&A

Q If you want to send a fax but New Fax Message does not appear on the menu in Outlook, what should you do?

A You should check to make sure you installed the Microsoft Fax Service supplied with Outlook. If you have, you need to add the fax service to Outlook by using the Services dialog box under the Tools menu.

Q What is required if you want to send a message formatted in Rich Text?

A The recipient must be using an e-mail client, such as Outlook, Exchange, or Windows Messaging, that recognizes Rich Text. Otherwise, the fonts, colors, and sizes that you specify in your message will not show the formatting when the recipient has opened the message.

Q How do you set up Outlook to check for messages and send new messages automatically?

A Go to the Services dialog box and open the Properties of each of the services, such as Internet mail or CompuServe, for which you want to schedule logon sessions. Each service will have its own menu options for scheduling logons. Next, go to the Options dialog box under the Tools menu and make sure that logon sessions for each of the services you set are checked under the E-mail tab.

7

Hour **8**

Viewing the Inbox

You might be surprised by all the different ways that you can view your messages. Considering the fact that Outlook is really just a database in which the information is divided into individual fields, such as To, From, Message, and Categories, it makes sense that your data can be manipulated into different views that help you organize your work. The best thing about Outlook is that manipulating the data is easy.

Consider all of the ways that you typically view information. At Quantum Ink, Mark has more than 100 messages stored in his Inbox most of the time. Depending on what he wants to do with his mail, he changes the views of the Inbox accordingly. With Outlook, he can sort, group, filter, and format information so that he can view just the information he wants, in the exact format that he wants it to appear.

Sorting Messages

When Mark logs on to the network every morning and mail starts to arrive in his Inbox, he likes to have the messages sorted in descending order by the date they are received so that all the new mail messages appear at the top of the Inbox.

The default view Messages, shown in Figure 8.1, fits Mark's criteria for working with incoming mail. In this view, the following fields appear: Importance, Icon, Flag Status, Attachment, From, Subject, and Received.

Figure 8.1.

Under the Current View drop-down list on the toolbar, you can choose from 10 different predefined views. If these views aren't designed to suit your needs, you can create your own views with the Define Views command.

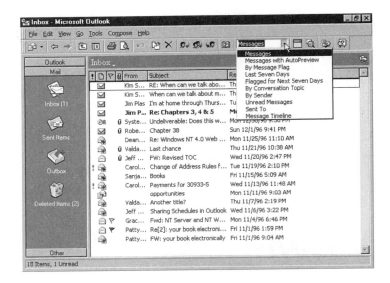

Changing the Sorting Field

Messages can be sorted by almost any of the visible fields in a view. The Categories field is a notable exception: Messages cannot be sorted by it. In the Messages view, if Mark decides to sort his messages by sender instead of the date received, he can click on the column marked From. If he left-clicks on the From column, the default order is ascending order from A–Z. If he clicks on the column a second time, the messages are sorted in descending order. He can specify which way he wants to sort messages if he right-clicks on the column and chooses Sort Ascending or Sort Descending from the drop-down menu.

Adding Preview to a View

Although the Messages view works well enough for Mark, there are a couple of things that he would like to add to make it work even better. As you'll see, modifying a view is relatively simple.

Being able to see the first few lines of every unopened e-mail message would give Mark a little more information about the message than the Subject field could provide. Outlook offers users a way to preview snippets of a message before opening it. To preview unread messages, Mark chooses View | Format View from the menu. In the Format Table View dialog box, he clicks the Preview Unread Items button in the AutoPreview frame.

Examples of messages with previews are shown in Figure 8.2. In this view, it's easy to tell which messages Mark still needs to open. If he wants to mark read messages as unread so that he can see the preview, he can right-click on the message and choose Mark as Unread. Mark can also preview all messages by going back into the Format Table View dialog box and choosing Preview all items, or he can choose View | AutoPreview from the menu.

Figure 8.2.

In this view, the first few lines of unread messages can be previewed before opening.

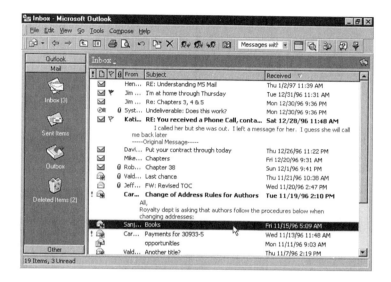

JUST A MINUTE

Previewing complete messages is still not available in Outlook at the time of this writing, but many shareware developers and software companies are currently developing products that work with Microsoft Exchange, Windows Messaging, and Outlook. By the time you read this book, there may be a third-party product that allows full previewing of messages. To find products related to Outlook, visit the Microsoft Web site at or go to a search engine, such as Yahoo! at http://www.yahoo.com, and search for the terms *Microsoft Exchange, Microsoft Outlook*, and *Windows Messaging*. You might be amazed at the amount of cool products that are available to enhance Outlook.

Adding a Field to a View

Quantum Ink frequently has e-mail problems, and Mark has to look at the properties of his e-mail messages to see when they were sent and compare those dates to the dates when he received them. Because the Messages view contains all the fields except the Sent field, he decides to modify the view slightly. There are two different ways to add fields to a view: using the Define Views command and using the Field Chooser.

Adding a Field Using the Define Views Command

To modify the Messages view, Mark has to do the following things:

1. From the Inbox, he clicks on View | Define Views.
2. He selects Messages and clicks the Modify button.
3. In the Views Summary dialog box, he clicks the Fields button.
4. In the Show Fields dialog box, he chooses Date/Time fields from the list box at the bottom.
5. He adds the Sent field to the list of fields already being used in this view, as shown in Figure 8.3.

Figure 8.3.

Modifying the Messages view by adding a field.

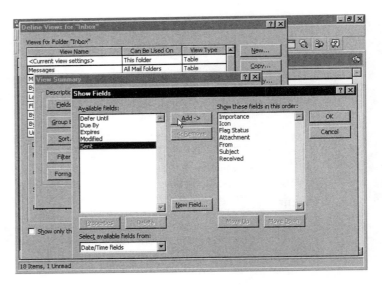

6. He moves the Sent field above the Received field so that they will appear in that order in the Inbox view.
7. He clicks OK on every dialog box until the Define Views dialog box is uncovered and then he clicks the Apply View button.
8. A Save View Settings dialog box appears, asking him if he wants to Discard the current view settings, Save the current view settings as a new view, or Update the view "Messages" with the current view settings. Mark is choosing to discard the current Messages view to replace it with the one he just created. If he had made

radical changes to the Messages view and had wanted to save the original settings, he would have chosen to save the current settings as a new view.

Adding a Field Using the Field Chooser ControlBox

The exact same task of modifying a view can be accomplished with the Field Chooser ControlBox. In fact, this method seems even a bit easier if all you want to do is add and drop fields from a view. However, if you plan to change multiple features at one time, the first method is probably easier.

To modify the Messages view using the Field Chooser, Mark does the following tasks:

1. From the Inbox, he clicks on View | Field Chooser.

2. He chooses one of the field groups from the drop-down list in the Field Chooser ControlBox.

3. He drags the Sent field over to the columns in the Messages view. Arrows appear on the columns indicating where the field will be placed in conjunction with the other columns, as shown in Figure 8.4.

Figure 8.4.

Open the Field Chooser ControlBox and drag fields onto the columns to modify a view.

4. Once he has added the new field in the view, he clicks on another view and a Save View Settings dialog box appears. The message says You have changed the view settings of the view Messages. He can choose one of three options: Discard the current view settings, Save the current view settings as a new view, or Update the view "Messages" with the current view settings. Mark chooses the third option to update the view.

Filtering Information

Although you may prefer all of your messages to be visible most of the time, there might be times when you want to view only the messages that meet certain criteria by using filters.

Outlook offers three predefined filters that you can access by choosing View | Current View and choosing either Unread Messages, Last Seven Days, or Flagged for Next Seven Days. As shown in Figure 8.5, switching to the Unread Messages view allows only unread messages to appear through the filter.

Figure 8.5.

Filtering the Inbox by showing only unread messages.

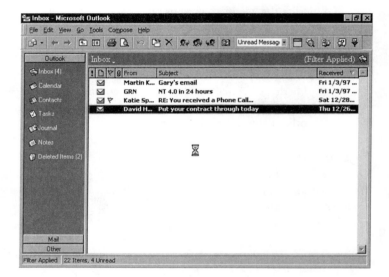

Defining Filters

There are 33 individual fields that apply to mail messages. You can design a filter to match criteria from one mail field or narrow the filter by making the messages match information in a combination of fields. To define a filter, open the Filter dialog box under the View menu. The dialog box has three tabs in which you can enter information to find messages that match certain conditions, as shown in Figure 8.6.

The first two tabs, Messages and More Choices, help you define your criteria by offering ways of categorizing information. The third tab, Advanced, is the most flexible as far as defining exactly what you want to filter, but it is also the most difficult to construct.

8

Figure 8.6.

The first tab in the Filter dialog box.

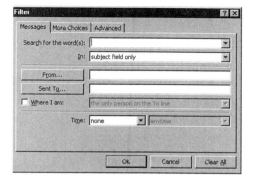

The fields related to the e-mail feature are listed here. You can sort, filter, or group messages by any of these fields:

Attachment	Message Class
BCC	Message Flag
Billing Information	Mileage
Categories	Modified
CC	Outlook Internal Version
Conversation	Outlook Version
Created	Read
Defer Until	Received
Do Not AutoArchive	Remote Status
Due By	Retrieval Time
Expires	Sensitivity
Flag Status	Sent
From	Size
Have Replies Sent To	Subject
Importance	To
In Folder	Tracking Status
Message	

Example of a Simple Filter

Mark wants to set up a filter so that the only messages showing are those sent by co-workers. Here's how he does it:

1. He opens the Filter dialog box by clicking on View | Filter.
2. He chooses the second tab in the dialog box marked More Choices.
3. He clicks the Categories button and chooses Quantum Ink Employee from the list of categories, as shown in Figure 8.7.

Figure 8.7.

Filtering the Inbox by messages matching a specified category.

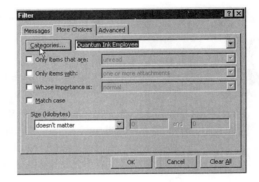

4. He clicks the OK button on the Filter dialog box, and the filter is applied to the view. The results are shown in Figure 8.8.

Figure 8.8.

When a filter has been applied to a view, a Filter Applied tag appears above the messages in the upper-right corner.

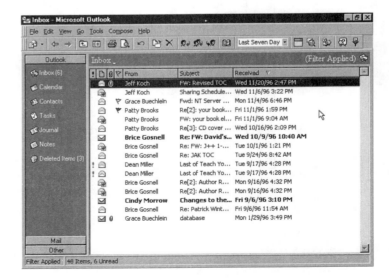

8

JUST A MINUTE

You may wonder how the messages in the example had been entered into a category called Quantum Ink Employees. Messages, such as Contacts or any other item in Outlook, can be categorized. You can use the pre-defined list of categories that is provided in Outlook or you can create your own categories by adding them to the Master Category List. You can choose to place a message in one or more categories while the message is open or closed. When the message is open, click on the Options tab in the message window and choose one or more categories from the list after you click the Categories button, as shown in Figure 8.9.

If a message is closed, right-click on the message and choose Categories from the drop-down menu. Follow these instructions if you want to categorize a group of messages at the same time:

1. Select the messages you want to categorize by holding down the Ctrl key as you click on each message.

2. When all the messages have been selected, right-click within the highlighted area and choose Categories from the drop-down menu.

3. Choose categories for the group and click OK.

Figure 8.9.

The Categories box under the Options tab in an open message.

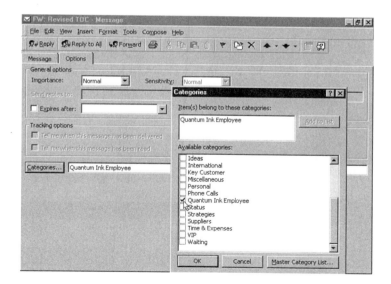

Example of a Complex Filter

The results of the first filter left 16 messages showing in Mark's Inbox. He wants to narrow his filter to display only those messages in which questions have been asked that he needs to answer. To do this, he performs the following operations:

1. He opens the Filter dialog box under the View menu.

2. He leaves the Categories box as it is because he still wants to see only messages from his co-workers.

3. He clicks on the Advanced tab.

4. In the Define More Criteria frame, he scans through the list of field groups until he sees one that includes the Message field.

5. He has to set the Condition next. In the list box, he is given the choices of contains, is (exactly), doesn't contain, is empty, and is not empty. He wants to look for messages that have a question mark (?) anywhere within the text of the message. He chooses the condition contains.

6. He types a ? symbol in the blank box next to the Condition and clicks the Add to List button.

7. He clicks OK, and the result of his new filter leaves him with only seven messages showing in his Inbox.

8. If he clicks on the icon column, he can sort the messages by their status—read, unread, replied to, forwarded, and so on. This is shown in Figure 8.10. He will assume that the messages marked with a replied to or forwarded icon have already been answered or sent to someone else to be answered.

TIME SAVER

If you create a filter that you want to reuse from time to time, save it as a view. After you have created the filter, choose another view. When the Save View Settings dialog appears, choose the option to Save the current view settings as a new view. Another dialog box, shown in Figure 8.11, will appear in which you have to name the new view and pick how the view can be used.

Figure 8.10.

The results of a filter and sort by message status.

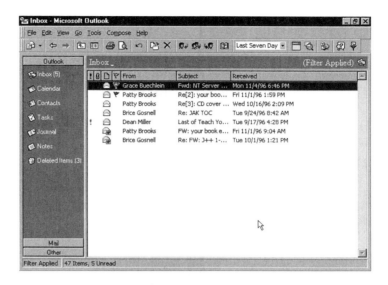

Figure 8.11.

Naming a new view.

Grouping Messages

Grouping messages by topic is another way to view them. To see a few examples of messages that have been grouped by one or more fields, choose one of the views By Messages Flag, By Conversation Topic, or By Sender (see Figure 8.12).

Figure 8.12.

Messages grouped by sender. Some groups are expanded, revealing the messages, while others are collapsed, showing only the name of the group.

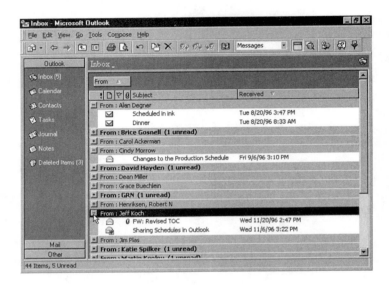

Using the Mouse to Make a Group

An easy way to group messages by a mail field is to simply right-click on the column that you want to group messages by, and choose Group By This Field, which is demonstrated in Figure 8.13.

You can also group by more than one field. You could group by name and then by date or subject.

Grouping by More than One Field

If you really want to organize messages, you can group them by multiple fields. As an example, Mark wants to view the messages he has already sent by category, such as all messages in reference to Peter's Book or Sanjaya's Book. Within each category group he wants the messages to be grouped by recipient. Finally, he wants the messages to be sorted in the order that they were sent. This process involves quite a few steps, such as creating categories, placing messages into categories, grouping messages, and sorting messages. Follow along as Mark organizes his Sent Items folder:

Figure 8.13.

You can group messages by any field, such as From, by right-clicking at the top of the column.

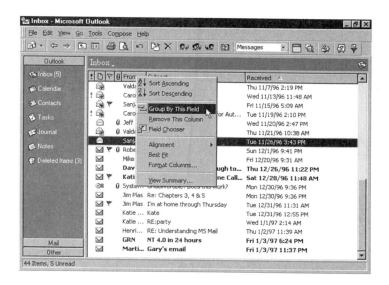

1. Mark opens the Sent Items folder.
2. He clicks on the column marked To and sorts the messages in ascending order.
3. He scans down the list of recipients and places each recipient into a category, making new categories as he makes his way down the list. Figures 8.14 and 8.15 illustrate how he selects a group of messages and places them into a new category that he creates.

Figure 8.14.

You can place multiple messages into a category by selecting them, right-clicking within the highlighted area, and choosing Categories from the drop-down menu.

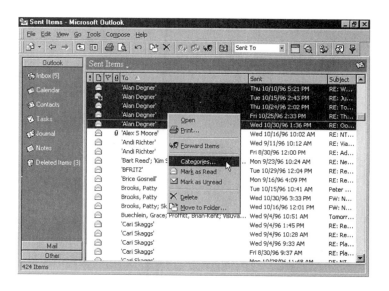

Figure 8.15.

To create you own categories, click the Master Category button and add new categories to the Master Category List. You can also delete categories from this dialog box.

4. After he has organized all his messages into categories, it's time to group them by fields. In Figure 8.16, Mark has clicked on the Group By command under the View menu. He chooses to group primarily by Categories and secondly by the To field.

Figure 8.16.

The Group By dialog box allows you to specify how you want items to be grouped.

5. After the messages have been grouped by category and recipient, he clicks on the Sent column to sort the messages by the date that they were sent. The result of his grouping and sorting is shown in Figure 8.17.

Figure 8.17.

The Sent Items folder after messages have been grouped by the fields Category and To, then sorted by the Sent field.

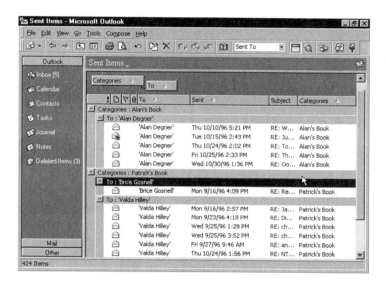

Managing Views

If you want to see the master list of all the views that have been saved, click on the View | Define Views command. From this dialog box, shown in Figure 8.18, you can

☐ Create new views

☐ Copy views

☐ Modify existing views

☐ Rename views

☐ Delete views

Figure 8.18.

The Define Views dialog box helps you maintain your list of views by allowing you to see their properties in one view. You can see how grouping, sorting, and filtering define each view and which fields are visible.

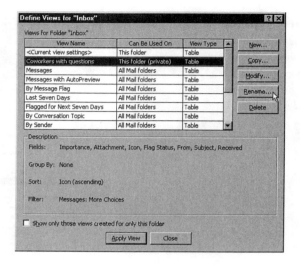

Summary

Because Outlook is so flexible and provides you with many options to view information, the most difficult thing about using it is deciding how you want items to look and be organized. If you begin using Outlook without a clear plan for organizing and sorting your messages, you may find yourself experimenting with different ways of grouping, sorting, and filtering messages until you find formats in which you like to work.

Q&A

Q How can you sort your messages?

A There are a number of ways to sort messages. One way is to click on the column that you want to sort by. Another way is to right-click on the preferred column and choose either Sort Ascending or Sort Descending. You can also use the menu, click on View | Sort, and use the Sort dialog box to pick the columns you want to sort by.

Q If you only wanted to see messages that were about a certain project, such as Marilyn's Book, what would you do?

A You could go to the menu and click View | Filter. In the Filter dialog box, type in the word Marilyn and specify the location as Subject field only. You could expand the search later to Subject field and message body if you think there may be more messages that did not make it through the first filter.

Hour 9

Making Mail Work for You

I have to admit that writing these chapters about e-mail messages and working with the Inbox has made me realize that my e-mail isn't as organized as it could be, and that I reopen and search for messages constantly because I don't have a well-planned system. Maybe you feel the same way about your Inbox. So the question for this chapter is "How should I organize my messages to help me work more efficiently?"

Start by analyzing how you work. Do you work on projects? Do you work with accounts, such as customers or suppliers? Think of ways that you can divide your messages into groups to organize them.

Next, think about the kinds of repetitive activities that you do with each account or project. When people write messages to you, what do they usually discuss? Contracts? Payments? Due dates? The answers to these kinds of questions should help you categorize your e-mail messages.

As you read how Mark analyzes his job as an editor at Quantum Ink and organizes his system, it might spark ideas that will help you organize your own system.

Organizing Your Mail

Mark works on book projects, sometimes as many as 20 at the same time. These projects all have life cycles of four to six months, and they are all in different stages of completeness; some are just beginning as others are being finished. For this example, let's focus on five books, each named after the author.

Creating Subfolders

To organize his book projects, Mark creates a folder for each project to store all messages related to it. When a project is complete, he can archive its folder and all the contents to make room for new projects. Archiving is explained in Hour 19, "Maintaining Outlook."

Mark creates folders for each of these projects:

- ☐ Alan's Book
- ☐ Katie's Book
- ☐ Patrick's Book
- ☐ Robert's Book
- ☐ Sanjaya's Book

To create each new folder, he clicks on File | Folder and chooses Create Subfolder from the drop-down list of options. A shortcut to creating a new subfolder is Ctrl+Shift+E. In the Create New Folder dialog box, he chooses the name of the folder and its location within his Personal Folders, and then gives a brief description of the folder, as shown in Figure 9.1.

Figure 9.1.

Create New Folder dialog box.

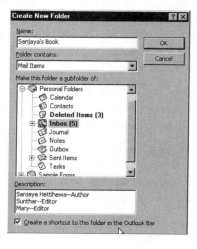

If you create many subfolders that have shortcuts to them in the Outlook Bar, you may notice that your Outlook Bar is getting crowded. You might want to consider turning off the Outlook Bar and turning on the Folder List. To turn the views off and on, click on View|Folder List and View|Outlook Bar. You can expand or collapse the subfolders by clicking on the plus (+) or minus (–) signs next to each folder that contains subfolders.

Creating New Categories

Mark wants his messages organized by categories within each project folder. He decides that there are five main subjects that can be found throughout his e-mail messages. He creates categories for each one of them. An Outlook item can belong to more than one category; therefore, if an e-mail message covers more than one of the topics in the category list, he can mark the message as belonging to both category listings. These are the topics he adds:

- ☐ Chapters and Content
- ☐ Due Dates
- ☐ Author Contracts and Payments
- ☐ Author Contact and Bios
- ☐ Marketing Information

To add these topics to the Master Category List, Mark chooses Edit|Categories, and clicks the Master Category List button. Because he will use these topics frequently, he numbers them so that they will appear at the top of the Master Category List, as shown in Figure 9.2.

Figure 9.2.

If you want categories you create to appear at the top of the list, number them.

Spring Cleaning—Moving E-mail to Folders and Categorizing Messages

When Mark has finished creating the folders and categories, it's time to move his e-mail messages into their proper locations and mark them as belonging to appropriate categories. Because he has always kept messages only in the Inbox, he has many to move into folders. He will be able to identify where a message belongs by looking at the sender, so he sorts the Inbox messages by the From field. (Refer to Hour 8, "Viewing the Inbox," to refresh your memory on sorting, grouping, and filtering messages.)

Moving Messages

Mark can select all the messages from the same sender and move them as a group into their proper folder. To select multiple messages, he clicks on the first message in the list, holds down the Shift key, and clicks on the last message in the list. Once the messages are highlighted, he drags them to their new location.

Categorizing Messages

Once the messages have been placed in their individual folders, Mark begins to categorize them. Instead of opening all the e-mail messages again, he tries to judge by the Subject field which categories would be fitting for each message. To place an e-mail into one or more categories, he right-clicks on the message and chooses Categories from the drop-down list. In the Categories dialog box, he can add as many categories as he thinks he needs for each message. From now on, whenever new messages arrive in the Inbox, he can designate categories after reading them, while they are still open.

Setting the View

Creating a new view by grouping and sorting puts the final touches on an organized message system. Compare the two views in Figures 9.3 and 9.4. The first view simply shows the message fields without special formatting. No message is visually distinguishable from any other. The second view, by contrast, has been grouped by category and sorted by date received. If Mark saves this view, he can scan his messages and quickly narrow his search if he is looking for a message that falls in a particular topic area, such as contract discussions.

9

Figure 9.3.

Messages in the Inbox that have not been organized in any way, such as sorting and grouping.

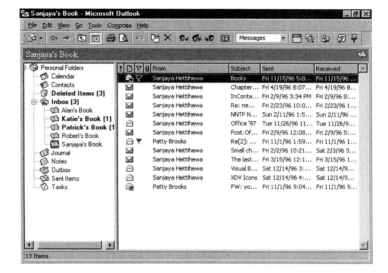

Figure 9.4.

The same messages shown in Figure 9.3. have been grouped by category and sorted by the date each message was received.

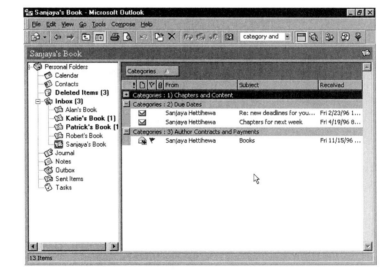

Working with Mail

If you analyze the e-mail messages that you receive, you will probably discover that the form of communication falls into three categories:

- ☐ Questions
- ☐ Requests/orders
- ☐ Information/facts

Likewise, if you analyze what you do with e-mail messages, you probably do these three things:

- ☐ Reply back to the sender(s), answering questions
- ☐ Reply back to the sender(s), confirming that you will (or will not) do whatever has been requested of you
- ☐ Store the information

In Outlook, the modules work well with one another so that you can drag and drop items onto another item instead of typing the same information into many different areas. Here is an example to illustrate this point.

Accomplishing Two Things with One E-mail Message

My friend, Carol, sent me an e-mail message, asking me to have dinner with her and notifying me that she had moved to a new address, as shown in Figure 9.5.

Figure 9.5.

An e-mail message.

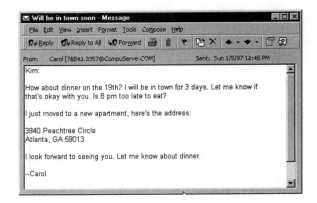

Three things need to be done with this message:

☐ I need to reply to her, confirming that I can have dinner on the 19th.

☐ I need to schedule the dinner in Calendar.

☐ I need to add her new address to the Contacts database.

Flagging a New Message for Follow Up

Carol sent me this message from her CompuServe account, which came to me via the Internet. She didn't have the option of flagging the message for me, but I can flag it when the message is open. By clicking on the Flag icon on the toolbar, I can flag the message, reminding me to reply to my friend within two days, as shown in Figure 9.6. After I set the flag, I can close the message and click Yes to save the changes.

Figure 9.6.

Flagging a message to remind the user to reply within a certain period of time.

Turning a Message into an Appointment or Meeting

The next thing to do is set the appointment in my calendar. Instead of opening a new appointment and trying to remember what the e-mail message contained, I can simply drag and drop the message into the Calendar folder to set the appointment in Calendar, as shown in Figure 9.7.

Figure 9.7.

Dragging an e-mail message onto the Calendar folder automatically calls up a new appointment.

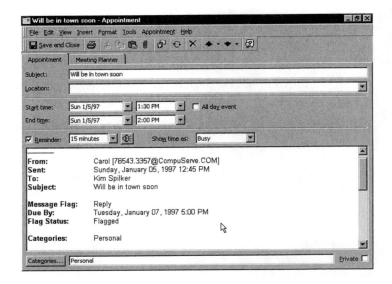

Notice that some of the blanks have been automatically filled in based on the information from the e-mail message. The body of the e-mail message appears in the text box so that all the information is available in the appointment. Otherwise, I would have had to switch back and forth between the appointment and the message to find the information. Here are the things I set:

> Subject: Dinner with Carol
>
> Location: I leave it blank until we decide where to eat
>
> Start time: Sunday, 1/19/97, 8:00 PM
>
> End time: Sunday, 1/19/97, 10:30 PM
>
> Reminder: 30 minutes before the scheduled appointment

Once I click the Save and Close button in the upper-left corner, the appointment is automatically entered into my calendar, as shown in Figure 9.8.

Turning a Message into a Contact

I still need to enter Carol into my Contact database. If I go back to the Inbox, I can drag and drop her e-mail message into the Contacts folder. When the new Contact is generated, it looks like Figure 9.9.

Figure 9.8.

Appointments are entered automatically into Calendar. The bell icon signals that an alarm has been set for this appointment.

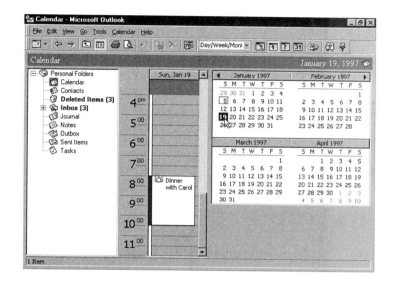

9

Figure 9.9.

Dragging and dropping an e-mail message into the Contacts folder opens a new Contact form.

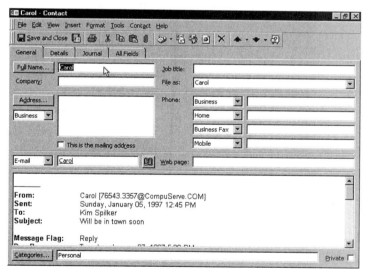

Some of the information, such as the name field and e-mail field, has already been completed because of the dynamic linking of information between the e-mail message fields and the Contacts form fields. Like the appointment, her e-mail message appears in the text box in the Contact form. All I have to do is scroll down to her new address, select it, copy it, and paste it into the Address text box.

Summary

This chapter shows you how to make e-mail work for you. In every e-mail message there is usually an instruction, request, question, or something that you must respond to after reading it. By showing you how to drag and drop your messages into other Outlook components (such as Calendar, Contacts, or Tasks), you can avoid retyping information in different places so that you can work more efficiently.

Q&A

Q **If someone sends you an e-mail message and asks to meet with you, what should you do with the message?**

A Drag and drop the message onto the Calendar to set an appointment.

Q **What are the message flag categories?**

A The categories are Follow up, Call, Do not Forward, Forward, Reply, Read, For Your Information, No Response Necessary, Reply to All, and Review.

Q **If you wanted to create your own custom category for a message, how would you do it?**

A Right-click on the message and choose Categories. In the Master Category dialog box, click the Master Category List. Type the new category, click the Add button, and click OK to save.

9

PART
IV

Using the Calendar

Hour

Hour 10

Keeping Track of Your Life

In this hour, you're going to take a look at what is, for some of you, Outlook's most attractive feature: the Calendar.

Calendars have been around for quite some time. Humankind has always been interested in keeping track of the days and minutes for agricultural and religious reasons—not to mention starting the odd war or two. Early time-keeping devices were slightly cumbersome. No one really used Stonehenge as a personal information manager. Sundials were more portable, but getting the time on a cloudy day became quite a chore.

It wasn't until 46 B.C. that Julius Caesar said enough, and set up the 365-day Julian calendar. Now those clever Romans knew how many shopping days there were until Christmas (after Christmas was invented, of course.) It worked pretty well, too—until some people started noticing that the Spring Equinox, always March 21, was slipping earlier and earlier into the year. This was upsetting to a lot of Catholics. Easter was tied directly to the Jewish Passover, and it was moving farther and farther away.

In 1582, Pope Gregory XIII took the advice of his calendar commission and came up with a calendar that more accurately stayed with the 365.25 day solar year (and more importantly to him, kept the Christian holidays straight). In order to make the switch, the day after October 4, 1582 became October 15.

Today, we in the Western world are used to everyone using this Gregorian calendar. However, it was only as international commerce expanded that people started adopting the Gregorian version as their civic calendar. Greece held out until 1923, and there are still many different calendars in use today, mostly for religious reasons.

JUST A MINUTE

Think you know what day it is? Think again. As I write this, it's November 27, 1996 by the ol' Gregorian calendar. In other calendars it's quite different:

Julian	14 November 1996
Hebrew	16 Kislev 5757
Islamic	16 Rajab 1417
Chinese	Cycle 78, year 13 (Bing-Zi), month 10 (Ren-Xu), day 17 (Wu-Chen)
French	Décade I, Septidi de Frimaire de l'Année 205 de la Révolution
Mayan (my personal calendar)	Long count: 12.19.3.12.10; tzolkin: 10 Oc; haab: 13Ceh

The Gregorian calendar is still not perfect. Because the solar year is not exactly 365.25 days long, another error of one day every 2,500 years is present. Sounds like there may be another sale day at the mall.

For the purposes of this book, let's stick with the Gregorian calendar, the one that Outlook uses. Also in keeping consistent with Outlook, let's use the seven-day week, and the 24-hour day, but only if you're good; otherwise, it's right back to Mayan.

Overview of Features

Besides its ability to show us the nifty calendar put together by Pope Gregory XIII, Outlook's Calendar tool also helps you keep track of your time by setting appointments, holidays, and meeting dates. Calendar can

☐ Set detailed appointments for any time of day. These appointments can be categorized by whatever criteria you create (business meeting, school event, in-law interaction). They easily can be set to remind you of their impending arrival with an onscreen message and any sound you choose.

10

☐ Create all-day events on your schedule. Similar to appointments, scheduling events allows you to quickly block out days of time, rather than just hours. You can indicate how reachable you are (free, busy, or out of the office) and if the time and date is firm or tentative.

☐ Plan meetings with anyone in your office who owns or uses Outlook. Calendar's Meeting Planner can show you who's busy when, automatically set a meeting time and place for you, and notify everyone who needs to attend. This feature will be discussed in Hour 11, "Getting Together with Calendar."

☐ Enhance your déjà vu by making recurring appointments, meetings, and events a snap. If you have to go to the gym every Monday at noon, except in December, Calendar can set that up for you in just a few clicks.

Starting Calendar

Like so much of the Microsoft get-there-from-anywhere paradigm, there is more than one way to get into Calendar. You can even enter data into the Calendar without starting Outlook. Choose your path, grasshopper.

The main way to start Calendar is within Outlook itself. From any part of Outlook, you can start Calendar by clicking the Calendar icon in the Outlook bar (see Figure 10.1) or the Calendar folder in the Folder list (see Figure 10.2), depending on which view you choose. If you are a menu-oriented person, you can get to Calendar by clicking the Go|Calendar command.

Figure 10.1.

The Outlook Bar's Calendar icon.

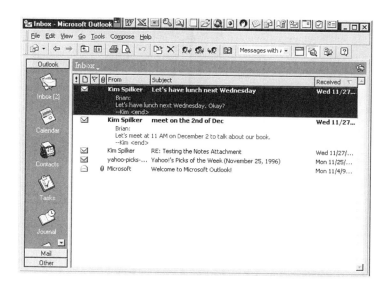

Figure 10.2.
The Folder list's Calendar folder.

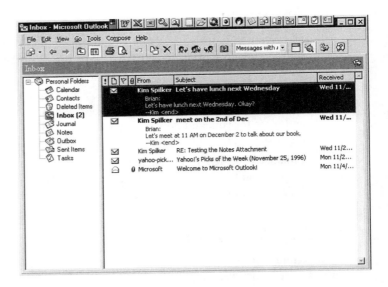

Going Through the Grand Tour

Once you get the Calendar tool open in Outlook, you will be presented with the default Calendar screen, shown in Figure 10.3.

Figure 10.3.
The default Calendar screen.

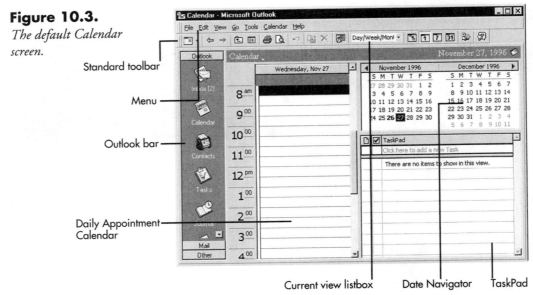

If you are paying close attention to the figure, stop right now. You will find out quickly that you've just wasted some time. This is because Calendar, like all the other Outlook tools, has dynamic menus and toolbars. As the situation changes, so do the tools available in the toolbars and menus. The "situation" is actually dictated by two criteria: first, which Outlook tool you are using, and second, which view you have in that tool. In Calendar, there are eight possible views, with slightly different toolbars in each. This hour exclusively covers the Day/Week/ Month view. Hour 12, "Configuring Calendar," has a discussion on the other Calendar views and how to customize them to your needs.

In the Day/Week/Month view, the Information Viewer has three panes: the Daily Appointment Calendar, a view of the current and next month called the Date Navigator, and the TaskPad. For now, let's skip the TaskPad, saving that until Part V, "Working with Tasks."

Before we look at Calendar through these different views, let's first get something in Calendar for us to look at!

Appointments

In the old days, setting an appointment was fairly straightforward. If you were important enough to need appointments, you most likely had a secretary to handle that for you.

In these politically enlightened times, we now have support personnel to make appointments, but there is never enough to go around. More and more it's the Average Joes and Josephines who are making appointments, trying to get the work done in the "group mentality," which is so pervasive in Western business.

Sometimes making appointments and tracking dates yourself is a challenge. The old standby of writing it down on a slip of paper is good—until you lose the paper. Desk calendars are better, and day planners even better than them. Unfortunately, they both have the drawback of being hard to update, especially for recurring meetings. They also can't show much detail and block out time for you.

These are the things Calendar can do for you easily. Let's get to it!

Creating a New Appointment

There is (naturally) more than one way to begin the process to set an appointment. However, all roads lead to the same place—the Appointment tool.

The easiest way to start the Appointment tool is to click the New Appointment button on the far-left side of the Standard Toolbar when you are in Calendar. The menu command to get there is Calendar | New Appointment. If you like shortcut keys, Ctrl+N activates the New Appointment tool.

TIME SAVER

Ctrl+N gets you the main tool in whatever part of Outlook you are in at that moment. For instance, if you are in the Inbox, Ctrl+N activates the New Message tool. If you are in Contacts, the same command activates the New Contact tool.

What is important to remember is that if you want to create some new item in a part of Outlook you are not currently in, *another shortcut key* is used to activate the New... tool you need.

If you are in Outlook, but *not* in Calendar and you need to set up an appointment, you can select the Appointment command in the Standard Toolbar's New Items drop-down box, as shown in Figure 10.4. As you can see, an even faster way to enter a new appointment or meeting is to use shortcut keys. Type Ctrl+Shift+A to activate the New Appointment tool.

Figure 10.4.

The Outlook Shortcuts.

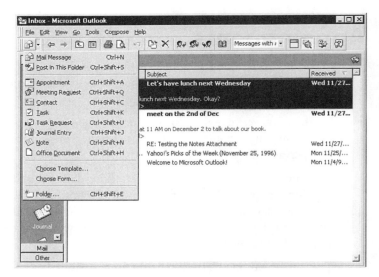

If you are not in Outlook (shame on you) and you need to quickly set up an appointment, you can do so without opening the Outlook program. When you installed Office 97, you had the option of creating the Office Shortcut Bar. If you created it, then besides putting up buttons to all your Office 97 programs, the installation also placed a button—you guessed it—to create a new appointment (see Figure 10.5).

10

New Appointment button

Figure 10.5.

The Office 97 way to a new appointment.

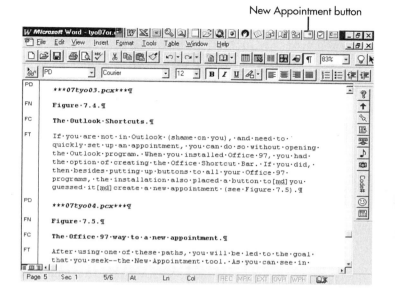

After using one of these paths, you will be led to the goal that you seek—the New Appointment tool. As you can see in Figure 10.6, it is a little application unto itself, with plenty of menu commands and toolbar functions to give your appointments as much flexibility as needed.

Figure 10.6.

The New Appointment tool.

For simplicity's sake, let's go through setting up an appointment to surprise one of your office workers, Andy, with a 40th birthday party. The party is today at 2 p.m. in the cafeteria, and you need to be the one who gets Andy there.

The first thing you need to enter into the Appointment tool is the Subject. What is it you will need to do? Attend the big sales meeting? Make your flight to Clinton, IA? Get the kids to soccer practice? These are the types of things that fit well into the Subject field. In this case, enter Andy's birthday party, which should be sufficient. You can be as detailed as you want, but I would recommend just a quick one-liner, saving more detail for the note box near the bottom of the Appointment tool.

Location is pretty self-explanatory. If you have a large office building, it is always good to note where meetings and events will be held. This field is especially helpful for off-site events. Here, it's the cafeteria. The nice thing about the Location field is that it is actually a drop-down list box that remembers the last seven locations you have entered into this field. This is great for office appointments, as invariably these tend to occur in the same places.

The next two lines are very important—when is the event? Calendar allows you to enter not only the start time of the appointment, but the end time as well. This is important for blocking out your overall schedule.

JUST A MINUTE

As you can see in Figure 10.6, when you first call up an appointment using a toolbar, key, or menu command, Calendar defaults to 8:00 a.m. today. The This appointment occurs in the past message at the top of the Appointment tool will disappear as soon as you enter a time later than the moment you are entering the new appointment. This is a nice feature to have because very few people (save H. G. Wells) really have a need to set appointments yesterday.

And, to help prevent you from typing in lots of dates and times, Calendar's drop-down boxes in these fields enable you to use the mouse to set up the appointment's time. Click the drop-down arrow next to the date field in the Start time line. You will see a nice little calendar of the current month (see Figure 10.7). You can click on any day in the month showing, and that will become the day for your appointment. The current date always appears enclosed in a little red box. If you want to move into another month, click the back (left) or forward (right) arrows in the top corners of the calendar. And, if you want to move quickly back to your present position in the space-time continuum, simply click the Today button on the bottom of the calendar. Because the party is today, leave this field be, as well as the companion field in the End time line just below.

10

Figure 10.7.

Entering dates with a calendar.

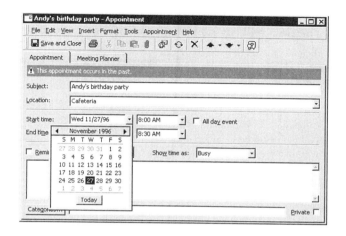

Next, enter the time. If you click the drop-down control next to the time field, you will see a list of half-hour times. By clicking on the appropriate time, this sets up the start time (see Figure 10.8). As soon as you do this, notice that in the End time fields, the date and time immediately change to the same date and a half-hour later than your time in the Start time fields. This saves steps setting up the end time. If the party is going to be only a half-hour long, this appointment's times would be set now. However, Andy and his co-workers are a bit more fun than that, and the plan is to have the party last about an hour and a half.

Figure 10.8.

A faster way to enter a time.

Skipping the End time date field for now (corporate parties usually only last less than one day), click the drop-down tool for the time field of End time. You will see a similar list of half-hour times, but now they have duration notations next to them (see Figure 10.9). If you are thinking of a specific time, you can click that, or if you are just thinking of a duration, you can search for that without doing the mental calculations of determining the actual end time. This party will last 1.5 hours, so let's click that duration. You'll get the end time of 3:30.

Figure 10.9.

Setting the end time.

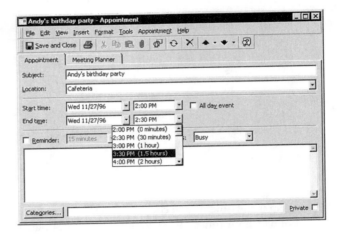

TIME SAVER

There are other ways to set your times and to create a new appointment. I call them the backdoor methods. Instead of using the Appointment tool to set the dates and times, you can use Calendar itself. To do this, follow these steps:

1. Move to the day and time you wish to set up the appointment.

2. Double-click the half-hour block of time in the daily calendar when the appointment will begin.

3. The New Appointment tool will pop up with the correct date and time for a half-hour appointment already entered.

The second backdoor method is done by selecting the complete time you want for the appointment on the Calendar. Then right-click on the selected time, and click New Appointment on the pop-up menu. This fills in the beginning AND ending time in the new Appointment tool.

If you have more specific times to enter, or you do not want to mess around with calendars to enter dates, you can directly enter the information you need into the Start time and End time fields. To save steps, enter the date and time in the Start time fields first. The End time fields will automatically adjust to the information in the Start time fields.

10

Time Saver

Outlook defaults the work day to 8 a.m. to 5 p.m., Monday–Friday. But what do you do if your work day is 7 a.m. to 4 p.m.? Or third shift Sunday–Thursday from 11 p.m. to 7 a.m.? Not a problem. Calendar lets you define when your work day and week begins and ends.

To change the work day times, click the Tools | Options menu command. (If you do this from another part of Outlook than Calendar, click the Calendar tab.)

In the Calendar working hours section, enter the start and end times of your day with either the drop-down lists or through direct entry into the fields.

In the * work week section, click the appropriate days' check boxes to match your work week.

Now your subject, location, and times are set. This is the minimal amount of information you need to set up an appointment. However, being the complete and thorough person you are, you will want to add more information to this appointment so you will not forget it later.

Reminders

Below the Start and End time fields is the Reminder section of the Appointment tool. Reminders are, in my opinion, the greatest invention since sliced bread. By setting a Reminder for your appointment, you will have little chance to forget about it, no matter how busy you get. They are very easy to create, too.

Click on the Reminder check box, and the time list box next to it will activate. The times in this list range from 0 minutes to 2 days. The default is 15 minutes before the appointment, and we'll keep that for the party appointment.

Time Saver

Do you have a certain time of day you would like to be reminded about appointments? You can set the default reminder duration in Calendar.

First, click the Tools | Options command. (If you do this from another part of Outlook than Calendar, click the Calendar tab in the Options dialog.)

In the Reminder field in the Appointment defaults section, use the drop-down list to set your preferred Reminder duration.

Next to the time list is a little button with a speaker icon on it. If you click this button, you will get the Reminder Sound dialog (see Figure 10.10). This contains the path to the sound file (usually in WAV format) that will activate when the Reminder time begins. It can be any sound you like, from a Tarzan yell to a baby crying. Windows 95 and Office 97 have default sounds, but the silly ones you have to get from an outside source, such as the Internet. If you're in an office (particularly one with cubicles), try to keep the sound from being too obnoxious.

Figure 10.10.

The Reminder Sound dialog.

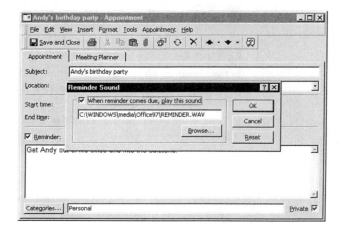

TIME SAVER

For a really good index to sound sites on the Web, try surfing to this site:

`http://www.yahoo.com/Computers_and_Internet/Multimedia/Sound/`
`Archives/WAV/`

Once you set up a Reminder, a dialog box, similar to the one in Figure 10.11, will appear at the appropriate time. (If you are using Office Assistant, a dialog balloon with the same information appears.) There are three buttons in this dialog that you can use.

The Dismiss button does just that—dismisses the Reminder so it never appears again. Use this only when you are ready to start, because once you dismiss a Reminder, it won't be able to help you anymore.

The Postpone button turns the Reminder off temporarily, to return at a time you determine. The drop-down list that appears (see Figure 10.11) shows some of the choices for delay time available. The default is 5 minutes. You should choose a time shorter than the amount of time left to the actual appointment, so another Reminder will go off before the event.

The Open Item button opens the Appointment tool to show all the information associated with the item.

10

Figure 10.11.
The Reminder dialog with the drop-down list for Postpone times selected.

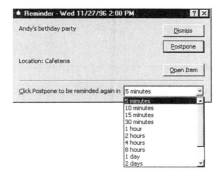

Rating the Appointment

Next to the Reminder field is the field Show time as. This field is a drop-down list box with four choices: Free, Tentative, Busy, and Out of Office. Selecting one of these choices allows the people who can view your schedule to see when you are available. This is handy when someone is setting up a meeting and wants you there. If your appointment is tentative, or is something that can be interrupted and is marked "Free," then the meeting organizer will be able to count you as a potential attendee.

Each one of these choices is graphically shown in the daily calendar by color-coded status bars that surround the items. Busy time is marked by dark blue, tentative appointments by light blue, free time by white, and out of the office by purple.

One other field in the Appointment tool is used to set your availability—and keep your privacy. The Private check box in the lower-right corner of the toolbox makes an appointment's contents invisible to those looking at your schedule. The time, however, is still blocked off, so people will know you are busy doing *something*. Because you don't want Andy to know what's going to happen at 2 p.m., it would be a good idea to mark this appointment as private.

Notes and Attachments

The big empty box in the lower part of the Appointment tool is for writing important notes about the appointment and attaching any computer files associated with the event. In this case, simply write a note to get Andy into the cafeteria. What if there was a birthday card being passed around electronically, and you were the one who had to print it out and bring it? This card, card.doc, could be attached to the appointment as a reminder to print it before the party.

10

JUST A MINUTE

Please remember that to share and view others' Appointments, you must be running Outlook with Microsoft Exchange Server.

To attach a document to an appointment, follow these steps:

1. Click the Insert File button on the Standard toolbar, or click the File command on the Insert menu. The Insert File dialog box, shown in Figure 10.12, appears.

2. The Insert File dialog box functions like a standard Open File dialog—with one exception. In the far right of the dialog is an Insert as section. This section allows you to insert the file as a text file in the appointment item, an attached file, or a shortcut to the file's location. Choose the option you want.

   Inserting a text file will take the document in question and place it as part of the message. Inserting an attachment actually sticks the document (as an icon) to the Appointment and will follow along with that Appointment until it is deleted. Attaching a shortcut places a shortcut icon in the Appointment. If the shortcut is double-clicked, the single version of the document is opened, even if it is on another computer. This last option is useful to prevent multiple copies of a document from floating around the Exchange network, hogging disk space.

TIME SAVER

If you are a standalone user of Outlook, you can attach shortcuts to appointments, Contacts, Tasks, or messages to someone on your local network. Attaching the entire file merely increases the size of the Outlook file. This is silly if the file you need is right there on your local computer.

When you e-mail an attached file to someone not on your network, send the actual file, not the shortcut. A shortcut would be useless to someone on the other end.

3. After navigating to the appropriate directory, highlight the file you wish to insert, and click OK.

Figure 10.12.
The Insert File dialog.

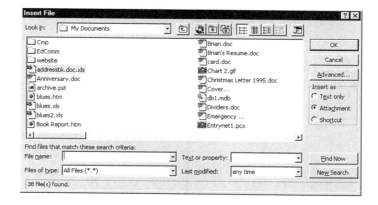

The Categories Tool

A lot of things in Outlook subtly change from tool to tool—and a lot of things remain constant. One constant is the Categories tool, accessed by clicking the Categories button at the bottom of the Appointment tool. Do this, and you will get the Categories dialog, shown in Figure 10.13.

Figure 10.13.
The Categories dialog.

The list of categories you see are accessible from *all parts of Outlook*, not just the Calendar. So, the same category can apply to an e-mail message, a Contact item, or a Task. And, to give it even more power, you can quickly add your own custom categories. For instance, there isn't really a good category to describe this event, so we can create one: Birthdays. To do so, follow these steps:

1. Click the Master Category List button. The Master Category List dialog, shown in Figure 10.14, appears.

Figure 10.14.

The Master Category List dialog.

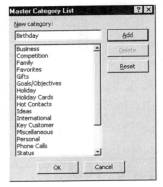

2. In the New category field at the top of the box, type in the new category you want. Once complete, click the Add button.

3. Your category is added. If you want to remove a category, highlight that category, and click the Delete button.

Once you find or create the appropriate category for your appointment, simply click as many category check boxes that will apply in the Categories dialog. When finished, click OK.

Now the appointment is complete (see Figure 10.15). Click the Save and Close button in the Standard toolbar to enter it into the daily calendar. In this view, it will look like Figure 10.16. The little key on the left side of the appointment item indicates a private item. The little bell indicates that there is a Reminder associated with this appointment.

Figure 10.15.

The finished appointment.

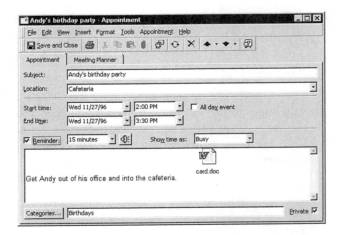

10

Figure 10.16.

The appointment in the daily calendar.

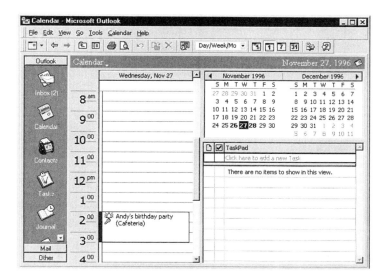

AutoCreating an Appointment

Outlook's AutoCreate function is really nifty. If you have received an e-mail message requesting or confirming a time for an appointment, follow these steps to make an appointment item from the message itself:

1. In the Inbox, click on the message containing the information for the appointment.

2. Drag the message over to the Calendar icon in the Outlook bar or to the Calendar folder in the Folder list.

3. Immediately, a New Appointment tool appears (see Figure 10.17), with the message in the notebox and the message subject in the appointment subject field. All that remains is to complete the date and time information.

Using AutoCreate, you can also create Appointments from Tasks, Journal entries, and Notes.

Figure 10.17.

The AutoCreated appointment.

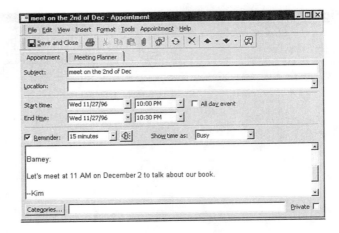

Editing an Appointment

In a perfect world, once you set up an appointment, that would be it. No changes, no conflicts, nothing to disturb your inner harmony. But, call it Murphy's Law, entropy, or whatever, we all know this will never happen. Look at Figure 10.18 for a case in point.

Figure 10.18.

Jammed worse than Times Square at rush hour.

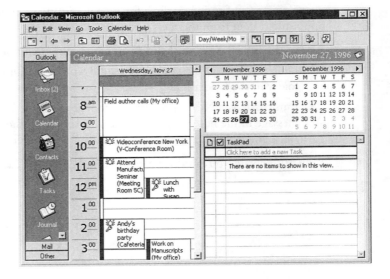

This schedule, which easily could be made over a number of different days, has some conflicts that need to be resolved. If the user, the harried Quantum Ink editor Barney, had been paying attention as these appointments were created, this might have never happened. When an appointment is created, Calendar warns you if the appointment conflicts with another, or is immediately adjacent to another (see Figure 10.19).

Figure 10.19.

Conflicting appointments give this warning message.

The warning message

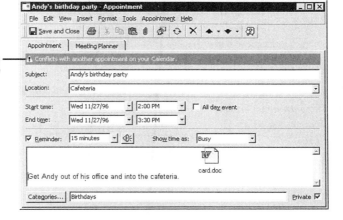

However, the damage is done, and your schedule needs to be fixed.

TIME SAVER

If you want, you can select and open more than one item at a time. For items that are consecutive, hold down the Shift key while clicking the items with the mouse. To select nonconsecutive items, hold down the Ctrl key.

Once all items are selected, right-click the mouse and select Open from the pop-up menu.

Changing Times

You must first determine which appointment can be moved and which can't. The first is easy: the 3–5 p.m. block of time spent in the office editing manuscripts can be adjusted because it is Barney's time alone to work. There are two ways to go about this:

☐ Double-click the item's move handle to open its Appointment tool and change the time.

JUST A MINUTE

> The *move handle* is the colored bar that always appears on the left of the appointment item. If you click the item once, move handles on the top and bottom of the item appear as well.

☐ Change the time by resizing the appointment item. This is done by moving the cursor to the top or bottom edge of the appointment. When the cursor changes to a double-headed arrow, click and hold the mouse button to drag the item's edge to the new time. In this case, Barney would move the appointment to 3:30, just after Andy's birthday party (see Figure 10.20).

Figure 10.20.

Resizing an appointment to change its start and end times.

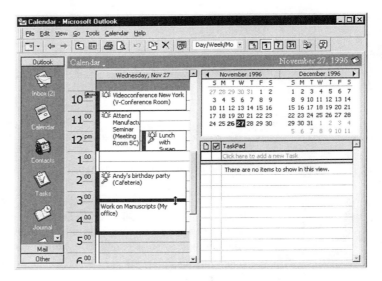

Changing Dates

The conflict between the seminar and the lunch date cannot be resolved so easily. The seminar is mandatory, and Susan cannot move the lunch time. She can, however, have lunch at the same time tomorrow. Again, there are two ways to do this:

☐ Double-click the item's move handle to open its Appointment tool and change the date.

☐ Change the date by dragging and dropping the appointment item to another day. Click and hold the mouse button on the appointment item, then drag it to the new date in the Date Navigator on the right side of Calendar. In this case, Barney would move the appointment to Nov. 28. The lunch date automatically drops into the same time it was set for Nov. 27 (see Figure 10.21).

10

Figure 10.21.

Dragging and dropping an appointment to another day.

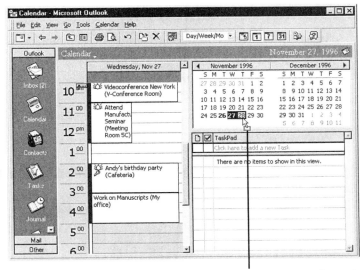

This symbol indicates an item is being dragged.

Changing Subjects

During the course of rechecking his schedule, Barney became aware of another goof: the videoconference call is to London, not New York. This is good to know because Barney has to bring a completely different set of notes to the London meeting. To change this, he can either

☐ Double-click the item's move handle to open its Appointment tool and change the subject.

☐ Change the subject clicking once on the appointment item. All but the subject information disappears, allowing a direct edit. As soon as any other part of the screen is clicked, the new information is saved.

Changing Locations

It's a good thing Barney had to rethink his schedule, because he found yet another goof: the seminar is in conference room 4C, not 5C. There is only one method to change the location of an appointment: double-click the item's move handle to open its Appointment tool and re-enter the new location information.

Deleting Appointments

If Barney decides that he does not have to hang around his office in the morning to wait for authors to call, he can delete the appointment altogether. He has two choices:

☐ Double-click the item's move handle, open its Appointment tool, and click the Delete button on the Appointment's toolbar.

☐ Single-click the item, and then click the Delete button on the Calendar toolbar.

November 27 is now a much smoother day for Barney (see Figure 10.22).

Figure 10.22.

A calmer, gentler day.

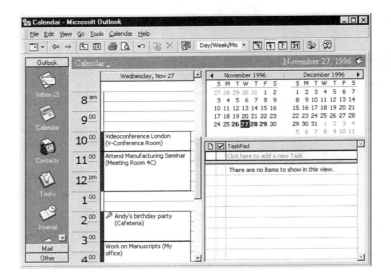

Handling Events

Outlook calls any appointment that lasts 24 or more hours an event. Handling events is much the same as handling appointments. In fact, the procedures involved are virtually identical, except for one thing.

In the Appointment tool, just to the right of the Start and End time fields, you see the check box All day event. Once this is checked, the Start and End times immediately disappear, because the event now stretches over the entire day. Figure 10.23 shows how the event looks in the Appointment tool, and Figure 10.24 shows how it looks in the daily calendar. Notice that the event is displayed as a fixed banner at the top of the daily calendar.

10

Figure 10.23.

An event in the Appointment tool.

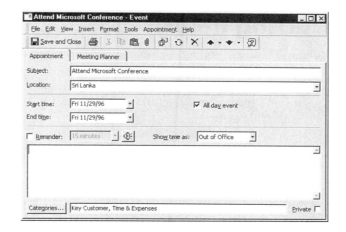

Figure 10.24.

An event in the daily calendar.

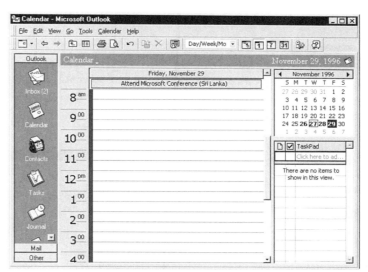

To edit, move, or delete an event, use the same techniques used for appointments. See? Wasn't that easy?

Recurring Items

Often in business, you will find that certain events happen over and over again, such as that pesky Friday afternoon team meeting or the quarterly staff meeting. If your events are always tied to a certain date (the second Thursday of the month, for example), you can make them recurring. Let's create two recurring events: a weekly team meeting and an annual half-day Fourth of July party.

Creating a New Recurring Appointment

Unlike all the myriad ways of creating a new appointment, there is only one way to create a new recurring appointment from scratch. The New Recurring Appointment command is in the Calendar menu. After highlighting the first block of time in the daily calendar in which the recurring event will take place, click this command and the New Appointment tool will open, along with the Appointment Recurrence dialog, shown in Figure 10.25.

JUST A MINUTE

> When creating a recurring appointment, you need to set the time and date information first. Once you finish this, you can enter the subject, location, and reminder information, just as you would a regular appointment.

Figure 10.25.
The Appointment Recurrence dialog.

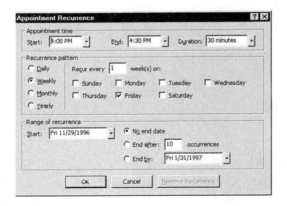

The Appointment time section is at the top of the box. Set the beginning and ending times for the recurring appointment, just as you would a regular appointment. For the weekly meeting, set the times from 2–3 p.m. For the Fourth party, set the times for 12 noon–6 p.m.

At the bottom of the dialog is the Range of recurrence section. This sets the length of time an appointment will recur. The start date defaults to the date you first entered this appointment. This can easily be changed through the calendar method or through direct data entry. The end date is variable. If the appointment recurs indefinitely, then the No end date radio button should be active. If a specific number of recurrences is known, this value can be entered in the End after: *x* occurrences field. If a specific end date is known, enter this value in the End by field.

The center section, Recurrence pattern, is the heart of the Appointment Recurrence dialog. There are four view settings for this section, controlled by the Daily, Weekly, Monthly, and Yearly radio buttons on the left side of the dialog. Figure 10.25 shows you the Weekly view of this section, which is the default.

The Weekly Pattern (Default)

At the top of the Weekly section is the Recur every *x* week(s) on field. The number in the middle of the sentence refers to the frequency you want the appointment to recur. If you wanted to set an appointment every third week, you would set the number to 3. For a meeting every week, the value should be 1.

The rest of the section contains check boxes for every day of the week. Check the appropriate days. If you have an appointment that happens every business day but Wednesday, you would check off Monday, Tuesday, Thursday, and Friday.

Daily Pattern

The Daily pattern view (see Figure 10.26) has only two options. The first, Every *x* day(s), lets you indicate what repetition pattern the appointment should take. If it's every day, the value is 1. If it's every fourth day, the value should be 4.

The other option, Every weekday, is set when you need an appointment to occur every day within the Monday–Friday period.

Figure 10.26.

The Daily recurrence pattern section.

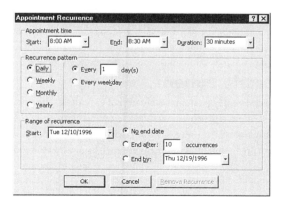

CAUTION

Even if you have changed your work week to something other then Monday–Friday, the Every weekday option still sets recurring appointments from Monday–Friday.

Monthly Pattern

The Monthly pattern section also has two options (see Figure 10.27). The first option, Day *x* of every *x* month(s), is used if your appointment happens on a specific date in a month *and* indicates how often it occurs. If it's every month on the 10th, the values would be Day 10 of every 1 month(s). If it's every other month on the 20th, then the values would appear as Day 25 of every 2 month(s).

The second option is used when the appointment recurs on a specific day of the week. The *x x* of every *x* month(s) option has two drop-down lists and a data value field. The first drop-down list has the values first, second, third, fourth, and last. The second list has the values of the days of the week, as well as day, weekday, and weekend day. The data value indicates the frequency of months, just as in the first option. For example, say you wanted to have the appointment recur on every third Wednesday of every second month. The option should appear as The third Wednesday of every 2 month(s).

Figure 10.27.

The Monthly recurrence pattern section.

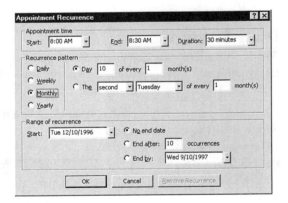

Yearly Pattern

In the yearly pattern section, you can set up the annual Fourth of July party (see Figure 10.28). The first option is perfect for this: Every *x x*. The first value, a drop-down list, offers the months of the year. The second value is the specific date. For the Fourth party, this option would be active and should read Every July 4.

10

The second option allows the user to set a certain day of the week within a given month once a year. For an appointment that occurs on the fourth Thursday of November, the value of the second option would be The fourth Thursday of November. The subject for this particular appointment could be Date with Turkey.

Figure 10.28.

The Yearly recurrence pattern section.

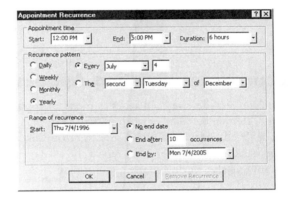

Creating a New Recurring Event

Like creating a new recurring appointment, there is only one way of starting a new recurring event—by clicking the Calendar | New Recurring Event menu command.

Every option in creating a recurring event is identical to that of creating a new appointment. The only difference is that the Start and End times default to Midnight to Midnight, thus making the appointment an all-day event.

One form of recurring event is holidays. Adding them to your Calendar is a snap:

1. Click the Tools | Options menu command. Make sure you click the Calendar tab in the Options dialog.

2. Click the Add Holidays button. The Add Holidays to Calendar dialog appears (see Figure 10.29).

3. Find the country or countries you want to mark holidays for, and click OK. Calendar will import all the holidays for the countries you selected.

10

Figure 10.29.
*The Add Holidays to
Calendar dialog.*

Recurring an Existing Appointment or Event

Once in a while, the need arises to make an appointment repeat indefinitely or for a short time. Remember Barney's trip to Sri Lanka that was in his mixed-up schedule earlier this hour? Well, unless he's a strange visitor from another planet, there's no way he can get there and back in one day. So, let's repeat the all-day event and stretch out his travel time. This technique also works for any appointment.

Open the Appointment tool for the Sri Lanka trip by double-clicking the event item's move handle. In the Standard toolbar, click the Recurrence button. This opens the Appointment Recurrence dialog. Click the Daily Recurrence pattern radio button and then the Every 1 day(s) radio button. In the Range of recurrence section, set the End by: date to be one week after his departure date (in this case Dec. 6). The settings should match those in Figure 10.30.

Figure 10.30.
The Sri Lanka odyssey.

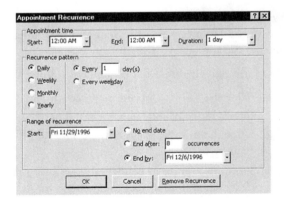

Editing a Recurrence

Editing a recurring item is much the same as editing any item in Calendar. But, when you first double-click the item's move handle in the daily calendar, you get the exclamation dialog, shown in Figure 10.31, asking you if you want to edit the entire series or just that item. Use caution here because if you only want to edit one occurrence of the appointment, you could inadvertently change the entire series' information.

10

Figure 10.31.
The Open Recurring Item dialog.

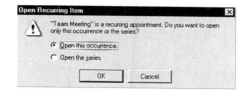

From here on, proceed to edit the item or series as you normally would edit a single item.

Removing a Recurrence

When an appointment that was supposed to repeat changes to a one-time only event, Calendar gives you a way to make this change. For the earlier example, the regular Friday team meeting was met with open revolt and will now just occur once.

Enter the instance of a single recurring appointment that you wish to remain in the Calendar by double-clicking the item's move handle. When Calendar asks you if you want to edit just this item or the entire recurring series, choose the Open the series option.

Once the Appointment tool is open, click the Recurrence button once more. At the bottom of the Appointment Recurrence dialog is the Remove Recurrence button. If you click this, all other occurrences of this series, except the one you are currently in, will be dropped.

CAUTION

> Be careful when removing an occurrence; there is no undo command for this action.

Deleting a Recurring Item

If you want to get rid of all or one occurrence of a recurring series, do the following:

- ☐ Double-click the item's move handle, open its Appointment tool, and click the Delete button on the Appointment's toolbar.
- ☐ Single-click the item, and then click the Delete button on the Calendar toolbar.

Whichever way you choose, you will immediately see a Confirm Delete dialog box (see Figure 10.32). This dialog gives you two options: to delete either the one item of the series you are currently in or all the items in the series. Use great care, so you don't delete too much.

Figure 10.32.
The Confirm Delete dialog.

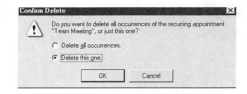

Summary

By now, you should be clued in on just how easy it is to set up and edit appointments and events. Recurring appointments and events, the bane of anyone with an electron-challenged day planner, are simple to create as well.

But wait, there's more!

Calendar also gives you the ability to set up meetings. As you'll see in the next hour, Calendar can let you view other people's schedules, choose the best time for everyone to meet, and even invite the attendees to the meeting using Outlook's messaging tools.

Q&A

Q My weekly status report was scheduled to be turned in every Tuesday. Now it's every Monday. How do I quickly change this in Calendar?

A Use the Date Navigator to find the next occurrence of the report's deadline. When you double-click the item's move handle, you will get a dialog asking you if you want to edit just that item or all the items in the series. Choose the Open the series option and make your changes in the Appointment Recurrence dialog. All the report deadlines will shift from Tuesday to Monday.

Q I would like to use Calendar to remind me of things I have to do tonight when I go home. How can I do this?

A There are two ways. You could print out a schedule of the entire day and take that home with you. Or, if you just need a reminder and don't want to kill more trees, try setting Reminders for your after-work appointments to go off 30 minutes before you leave.

Q My company just closed its Luxembourg office, and I don't really need to track those holidays anymore. How do I remove these from Calendar?

A Click Events in the Current View list box. Calendar will display the holiday's country in the Location column. Select the Luxembourgian holidays you want to remove, using multiple selection techniques, then hit the Delete button on the toolbar. However, what kind of person are you for not wanting to send Quinquagesima Sunday cards to your old colleagues? Shame on you!

10

Hour **11**

Getting Together with Calendar

The first meeting on record was between God and Adam. "Go ahead, go live over in Eden," God said. "But mind you, if you eat from that big tree over there, you will be in such trouble!"

This meeting was typical, because not much was accomplished by it. After the introduction of animals and Eve, Adam still managed to goof up the instructions. This led to the second meeting, which like most second meetings, was typically disciplinary. The gist of it was basically this:

"Out!"

Or so the story goes.

Meetings have gone on in pretty much the same way ever since. People come, people share ideas, someone doesn't get it, and the process starts over again. Of course, some meeting topics do take hold. If they didn't, we'd still be hanging out in caves.

It is that glimmer of hope that keeps the business world always coming back for more. These days meetings occur in record numbers. Everyone wants to meet. One can actually be employed as a meeting coordinator—the person who sets up the room, gets the slide projector ready, and orders the bagels.

Like most offices, however, you don't have the money to keep a meeting coordinator on staff, so you have to make do on your own. It will come as no big surprise that Calendar can give you a lot of help with meetings—from setting them up to inviting the attendees. Calendar can even make sure there's a room available.

After you pass the meeting process, I'll show you more advanced Calendar manipulation: how to view, print, and find items in your schedule.

Planning a Meeting

At Quantum Ink, planning a meeting used to be as simple as Lynn calling Andy, Linda, and Nathan and saying, "Let's meet at three to discuss the new Fulson book." Simple, unless Andy had a training seminar from 2–4 p.m., Linda was in another meeting that started at 3, and Nathan was out on vacation.

JUST A MINUTE

> Before we start, a word about Exchange server. Many of the group capabilities in Outlook can be accomplished only if the users are connected to Microsoft Exchange Server. The Meeting Planner definitely falls into this category. So, the next few sections are split into doing the task both with and without Exchange. You will quickly see that having Exchange is a good thing. If your office doesn't have it, go pester your Information Service (IS) person.

Today, Andy needs to meet with Lynn and Brittany to talk about a new hang-up with one of the more touchy authors at Quantum Ink. Let's try this with Calendar and see what happens.

Setting the Meeting with Exchange Server

The first thing to do when you want to plan a meeting is to open the Meeting Planner. There are two quick ways to do this. The first way is to click the Plan a Meeting button on the Standard Toolbar. If you like menus, the Calendar | Plan a Meeting command will get you to the same place.

When Andy does this, he gets the Plan a Meeting dialog, shown in Figure 11.1. It reflects his schedule for the day he wants to call the meeting.

Figure 11.1.

The Plan a Meeting dialog.

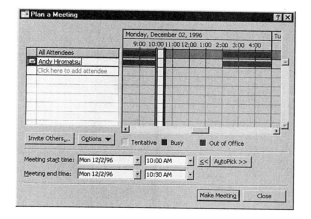

The next thing Andy must do is invite Lynn and Brittany to the meeting. The Invite Others button starts that process. When clicked, it shows the Select Attendees and Resources dialog, shown in Figure 11.2. Andy, because he is setting up the meeting, is already in the Required field. To place more people in the Required or Optional fields, merely select the person to invite, then click the Required or Optional button. If Andy wanted to have this meeting in a certain meeting room, he would highlight that resource, then click the Resource button. This resource would appear in the Location field after the meeting was set.

Figure 11.2.

The Select Attendees and Resources dialog.

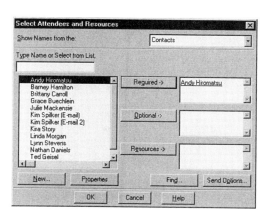

Once Lynn and Brittany are in the Required field, Andy clicks OK. Now back in the Plan a Meeting dialog, Andy clicks the AutoPick button, and Calendar selects 10 a.m. as the first available start time. This sounds good to him, although the half-hour default time may not be enough to go over all the nuances of dealing with that author. Andy could re-enter 11 a.m. in the End Time field below, but instead takes the easier route of clicking on the vertical red End Time bar and moving it to the right until it is even with the 11:00 time line. Now his dialog looks like the one in Figure 11.3.

Figure 11.3.

The Plan a Meeting dialog with attendees' schedules.

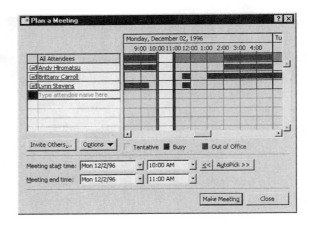

Now that the time has been set, everyone needs to be invited. Andy starts this process by clicking the Make Meeting button. This brings up a modified Appointment tool, with Lynn and Brittany in a new To field at the top. The other change to the Appointment tool is in the toolbar. As seen in Figure 11.4, the Save and Close button has been replaced with a Send button. Once Andy fills in the pertinent information in the Appointment tool, he will click the Send button. This automatically notifies his two colleagues that he is requesting this meeting.

Figure 11.4.

The modified Appointment tool.

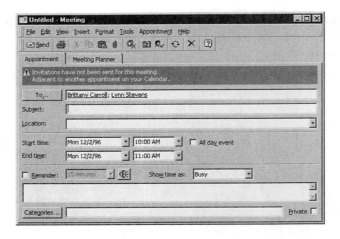

There is another way of setting up a meeting—by creating a new meeting request. Using the Calendar|New Meeting Request command activates the Meeting Appointment tool, with the Appointment tab open by default. The same steps are followed to create the meeting, except instead of using the Plan a Meeting dialog, the tools on the Meeting Planner tab (which are identical) are used. Why did Microsoft create such a redundant method? Probably in an effort to give users as many choices as possible.

11

Setting the Meeting

Setting up meeting times *without* Exchange can be done—really! But, without the ability to see others' schedule files, you will not be able to time your meeting when others are free.

Imagine, if you will, that Quantum Ink is in a parallel universe where the publisher opted not to fork over the dough for Exchange Server. Can Andy still get the meeting set?

Again, his first step is to activate the Plan a Meeting dialog. This time when he Invites Others, he sees that all the people in the Select Attendees and Resources dialog (see Figure 11.5) now have (e-mail) after them. This is because the only way Outlook can contact these people without Exchange is through e-mail.

CAUTION

This entire hour is based on the requirement that your office or organization has e-mail access through Outlook. If it does not, the Meeting Planner functions simply will not work, and you'll be forced to contact people the old-fashioned way—start dialing.

Figure 11.5.
Adding attendees without Exchange.

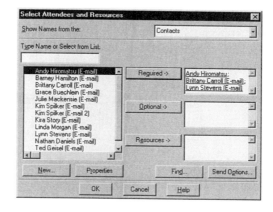

When Andy finishes this task, the Plan a Meeting dialog will not show him any times but his own (see Figure 11.6). Brittany and Lynn's rows now appear as slashed lines. Andy will have to pick the meeting time based only on his schedule. So, what good is this tool?

Plenty. Even though you are still using the old-fashioned method of throwing the party and hoping everyone will come, using Calendar still saves you the hassle of calling everyone up, confirming a time, then calling them back if it's unworkable. With Calendar, you e-mail everyone at once automatically, and if there is a conflict, you can make the change and resend the meeting request to all the attendees. You might be saying to yourself that you could use e-mail alone to accomplish this same thing, but using the Meeting Planner addresses everyone for you and updates your schedule.

Figure 11.6.

Ouija method: picking a time without Exchange.

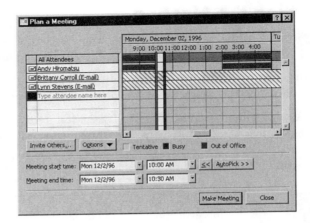

Andy takes the chance that 10–11 a.m. will work (perhaps he's in tune with his counterpart in the parallel universe), and clicks Make Meeting. The Appointment tool comes up, and after filling in the subject and location information, Andy should write a note repeating his request in the note box. When Exchange sends a request, it sends a meeting object that, if accepted, an Outlook recipient automatically becomes a new appointment. In case one of his attendees does not have Outlook as his or her mail tool (hey, you never know), Andy should send a plain-text note detailing his request. After he does this, he will be ready to click Send (see Figure 11.7).

Figure 11.7.

Ready to get the meeting going.

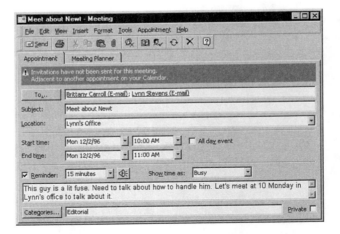

Changing the Meeting

Even when using Calendar and Exchange to organize a meeting, sometimes things come up. Other things arise that need to be handled or perhaps someone was inadvertently left off the guest list.

Changing Information

To change some information within a meeting, double-click the meeting item's move handle to open its Appointment tool. After making your modifications, ask yourself one question: Does what I just changed need to be known by the rest of the attendees? If the answer to this question is yes, click the Send Updates to Attendees and Close button (which looks like a little envelope). If your changes do not need to be passed along, click the Save and Close button.

Changing the Attendees

Sometimes you discover that more (or fewer) people need to be invited to a meeting, or your resources have changed because you need a larger meeting room. Not to worry. Try this:

1. Open the meeting item by double-clicking on its move handle.
2. Click open the Meeting Planner tab.
3. Click the Invite Others button. After selecting or removing the appropriate attendees or resources, click OK.
4. Click the Send Updates to Attendees and Close button to be sure all concerned are aware of the changes.

Canceling the Meeting

If you want to cancel a meeting, simply open the meeting item and then click the Appointment|Cancel Meeting menu command. Before you close the window, be sure to click the Send button, so that the attendees will know the meeting is canceled.

Creating a Meeting from an Appointment

Let's say you have an appointment that really needs to have some other people there as well. Calendar can easily set up a meeting from within the Appointment tool. In the Appointment tool, click the Meeting Planner tab. Follow the preceding steps to set up the meeting time and to invite attendees. After you invite your first attendee, the Save and Close button changes to the Send button on the toolbar. You can now click the Send button and get the invitations out.

Creating a Meeting from a Contact

Outlook's AutoCreate feature allows you to create a meeting from a Contact listing. There are two ways to begin this action:

☐ In an open Contact item, click the New Meeting with Contact button (see Figure 11.8).

☐ In Contact, drag-and-drop a Contact item onto the Calendar icon in the Outlook bar or the Calendar folder in the Folder List.

Either of these actions will immediately open an Appointment tool with the contact already invited as an attendee. Invite others, set times, and send the meeting request just as you would for any other meeting.

Figure 11.8.

Creating a meeting from a Contact listing.

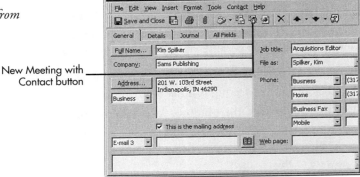

New Meeting with
Contact button

Creating a Recurrent Meeting

If you are creating a recurrent meeting from scratch, follow these steps:

1. Click the Calendar | New Recurring Meeting command. An Appointment tool appears, quickly covered up by the Appointment Recurrence dialog.

2. Using the techniques for setting recurring appointments that you learned in Hour 10, "Keeping Track of Your Life," set the recurrence pattern for this meeting. Click OK when finished.

3. Fill in all the pertinent information in the Appointment and Meeting Planner tabs. Click Send.

If you want to make an existing meeting recurrent, follow these steps:

1. Open the meeting item by double-clicking its move handle.

2. Click either the Recurrence button on the toolbar or the Appointment | Recurrence menu command. Complete the Appointment | Recurrence dialog and click OK.

3. Click the Send Updates to Attendees and Close button to be sure all concerned are aware of the changes.

Getting Meeting Requests

By now you should be a real pro at creating a meeting. But what if you're on the receiving end of one of those meeting requests?

Meeting requests come in the form of messages in your Inbox. Once they are opened, they look like Figure 11.9.

Figure 11.9.

A received message request.

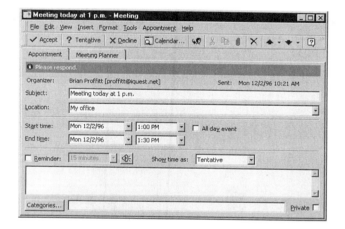

Like many choices in life, you have the option of saying yes (Accept), no (Decline), or being wishy-washy (Tentative). Before you decide, you may want to click the Calendar button to see how the appointment fits into your schedule. As an extra help, if the meeting conflicts with an existing appointment, the message request will tell you so (see Figure 11.10).

Figure 11.10.

A conflicting message request.

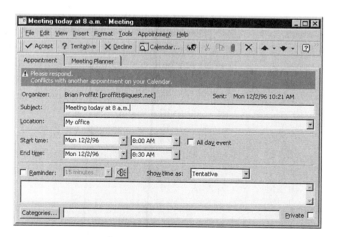

Once you pick a choice, a message is returned back to the meeting's organizer informing him or her of your decision.

If you should happen to receive a meeting cancellation notice, as seen in Figure 11.11, the most helpful button on the toolbar is now the Remove from Calendar button. By clicking this, you remove the meeting from your schedule and acknowledge the message's receipt to the meeting organizer in one fell swoop.

Figure 11.11.

A cancellation notification.

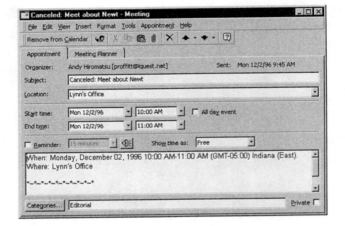

TIME SAVER

There is a way to automatically process such cancellation requests. Click the Tools | Options dialog and then the Advanced Scheduling button. Choose one or more of the following options as needed:

☐ If you are an easy-going individual and would like to automatically accept nonconflicting meeting requests and remove canceled meetings from your schedule, check the Automatically accept meeting requests and process cancellations check box.

☐ If you hate conflict and don't even want to mess with it, click the Automatically decline conflicting meeting requests check box.

☐ If you hate repetition and redundancy, click the Automatically decline recurring meeting request check box.

11

Summary

The next hour also shows you the many different ways Calendar can view your schedule, and how to customize the look to what you want. You'll also learn how to find Appointment and Meeting items in Calendar.

Q&A

Q Will Calendar notify me if no one responds to my meeting requests?

A Not actively. You can check on attendee status by clicking the Show attendee status radio button in the Meeting Planner tab of the Appointment tool. This will show you who has *not* responded yet.

Q What if some of my attendees don't have e-mail? Should I still bother with the Meeting Planner?

A If a few of your attendees will get a benefit from using Meeting Planner, you should certainly do so. Besides, Calendar still will help you keep track of who's coming.

Hour 12

Configuring Calendar

On a recent trip to Disney World, I told my three-year-old daughter that the ride we were about to go on was the scariest in the park. It was, of course, the dreaded "It's a Small World." Despite my warnings, she wanted to ride it over and over. Fear, it seems, is a matter of perception.

It is in this spirit that I introduce the most frightening term in the book. Are you sitting down?

Calendar is just one big *database*.

Scary, isn't it? Unwittingly, you have been playing around with one of the most intimidating concepts in computers today. It's just been well-disguised.

In this hour, we're going to start treating Calendar like the big naughty database it is by examining new ways of viewing, finding, and printing Calendar items.

Looking at Calendar a Whole New Way

Back in Hour 10, "Keeping Track of Your Life," I mentioned that there were several different views that come with Calendar. Actually, I said eight, in case you weren't paying attention.

These eight views are packaged with Calendar. You can change them by adding or subtracting the amount of information shown, removing the view altogether, or creating your own view from scratch. We will look at the procedures to do this later in this hour.

Daily/Weekly/Monthly

The first three views are grouped into one category, the Daily/Weekly/Monthly (D/W/M) view set.

So far, all the work we have done in Calendar has been completed in the Daily view (see Figure 12.1). There are, however, two more variations of the Daily view we haven't seen: the addition of time zone information and reformatting of the time intervals.

Figure 12.1.

The Daily view.

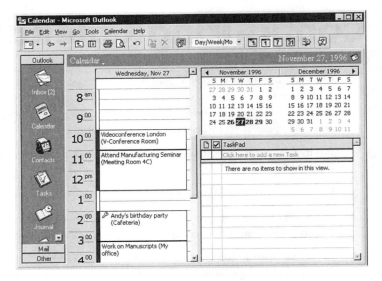

Just to the left of the daily calendar box are time intervals. Calendar defaults these intervals to 30 minutes. However, when you right-click anywhere in the time interval area, a pop-up menu appears that gives you a choice to set the intervals anywhere from 5 to 60 minutes (see Figure 12.2).

12

Figure 12.2.

Resetting your time intervals.

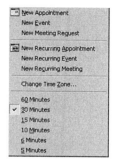

Changing our adding time zone information is a little more involved. By default, Calendar displays times based on the time zone you specified way back when you first installed Windows 95 (or when you last moved). To change the zone, click the Tools|Options menu command, and click the Time Zone button toward the bottom of the Options dialog. In the Time Zone dialog that appears (see Figure 12.3), you can apply a label to your current time zone or change your time zone location. After checking the Show an additional time zone check box, you can also add and label a second time zone. The results of the setting in Figure 12.3 are shown in Figure 12.4.

Figure 12.3.

The Time Zone dialog.

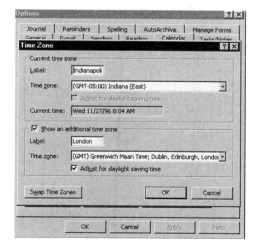

Figure 12.4.

*Now you can be sure
meetings don't intrude on
tea time.*

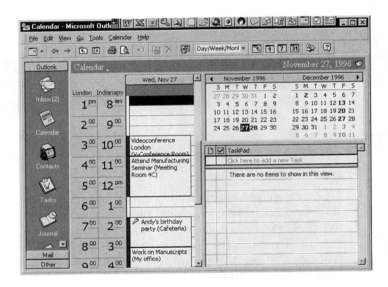

The next view in the D/W/M set is the Week view. By clicking the Week button in the toolbar, we get a screen much like Figure 12.5. Note that not much has changed. The toolbar is the same, as is the TaskPad and Date Navigator. The biggest change is in the information viewer. The daily calendar has been replaced with the weekly calendar. Each appointment is still marked by times and reminder and privacy symbols, but gone are the color-coded appointment status bars.

Figure 12.5.

The Week view.

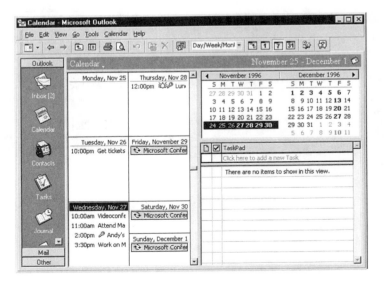

12

When the Month button is clicked, the Calendar page gets a more dramatic makeover (see Figure 12.6). Now, only the current month is visible. Each day that has appointments shows only the subject of each appointment or event. No times, locations, or symbols are used. If the appointments don't fit entirely within a single day's cell, a tiny yellow arrow/ellipsis symbol (shown in the margin) is used to indicate a continuation of the day's appointments. Clicking on this icon immediately takes you back to the Daily view of that day.

Figure 12.6.

The Month view.

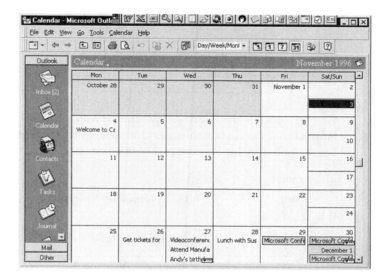

Active Appointments

The next view in Calendar to examine is the Active Appointments view. Instead of using a toolbar button to activate this view, though, you must use either the View drop-down list box in the toolbar or the View|Current View|Active Appointments menu command.

You can see that this type of view is different from the D/W/M view set. Calendar refers to this type of view as a table view. In table views, all pertinent information is shown and appointments are now grouped by recurrence group first, then by chronology. Four of the remaining five table views are just variations of this theme—same view with different filters applied.

12

JUST A MINUTE

A filter is a database term used to describe a certain set of criteria that's applied to how data is viewed.

Now, in plain English, filters are just rules that dictate what data you can see and in what order. People do this all the time. If you want celery, you sort through all your possible store choices first: hardware, department, deli, grocery. Then, at the grocery store, you sort (filter) through the aisles: snacks, frozen foods, meats, produce. In the produce aisle, you apply a more specific filter: You are looking for a pale-green, long-stalked item with leaves on top. You scan the displays, mentally filtering through the produce: lettuce (too round), tomatoes (wrong color)...until you see celery.

That is filtering.

Getting back to the Active Appointment view, Figure 12.7 shows eight columns of information. The first column uses icons to represent the type of appointment or event listed. See the following list for examples of the icons available.

Icon	Definition
	This icon represents an appointment or event.
	This icon represents a meeting.
	This icon represents a recurring appointment or event.
	This icon represents a recurring meeting.

The second column indicates whether an appointment has an attached file or item associated with it by the presence of the Attachment icon, which resembles a paper clip. The remaining columns contain information you've seen before: Subject, Location, Start time, End time, Recurrence pattern, and Categories.

12

Figure 12.7.

The Active Appointment view.

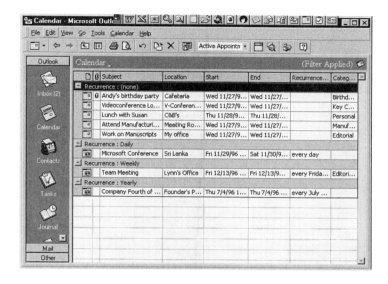

Events and Annual Events

The Events view shows you just the appointments Calendar classifies as Events, sorted by recurrence group (see Figure 12.8). The information columns in this view include Appointment Type, Attachments, Subject, Location, Recurrence Range Start, Duration, Recurrence Pattern, and Categories.

Figure 12.8.

The Events view.

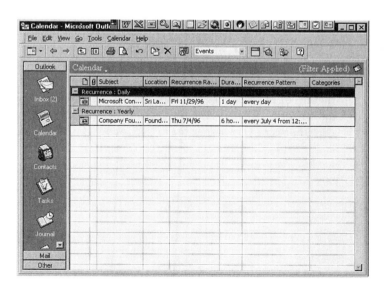

As you can see in Figure 12.9, the Annual Events view shows the exact same kind of information; only now it shows just the events that have an annual recurrence pattern.

Figure 12.9.

The Annual Events view.

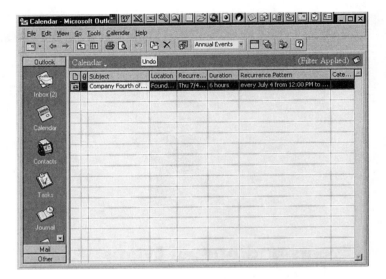

Note the small boxes with minus signs in the recurrence group headings. When clicked, these boxes will collapse the recurrence group until only the heading (now with a plus sign in the box) is visible. This tool is available in all of the table views.

Recurring Appointments

Of all the table views, I find that the Recurring Appointments view is the second most helpful. By listing any item (appointment, meeting, event) that recurs, I can quickly memorize the rhythm of my meetings and plan my days accordingly (see Figure 12.10). The columnar information includes Appointment Type, Attachments, Subject, Location, Recurrence Pattern, Recurrence Range Start, Recurrence Range End, and Categories.

12

Figure 12.10.

The Recurring Appointments view.

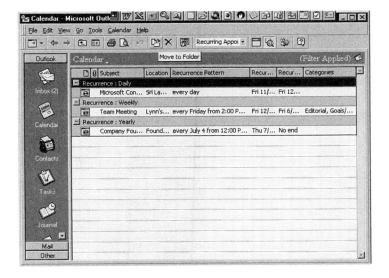

By Category

The By Category view is the last of the pre-set Calendar views. Instead of grouping items by recurrence pattern, items are now grouped by categories (see Figure 12.11). This, in case you were really curious, is my favorite table view. It's great when you can see all the items associated with one category in one place.

TIME SAVER

> To really make full use of this view, go ahead and categorize your items as detailed as you can. For example, I categorize all my work on a project level.

12

Figure 12.11.

The By Category view.

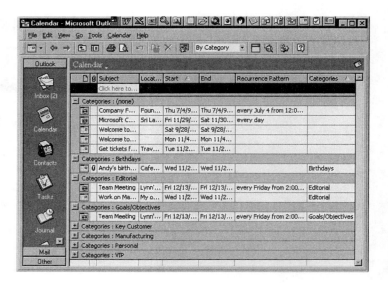

Creating Your Own Views

Hey, you're not one of those lemmings that just blindly follows the beaten path, are you? No! You set your own rules! Set your own pace!

No, it's not a beer commercial. It's just a melodramatic way of introducing another Calendar function: the capability to make your own views.

Grouping Items

The first way to create your own view is to modify an existing group. Let's start out easy and change the way one of the table views sorts items. When you are in any of the table views, click the View | Group By menu command. This opens the Group By dialog, shown in Figure 12.12. There are four nearly identical sections containing a drop-down list box, and ascending and descending radio buttons.

12

Figure 12.12.

The Group By dialog.

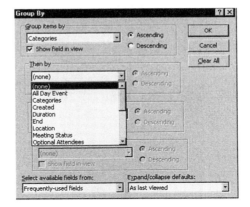

In the Group items by section, you see the current grouping criteria for the view you are in. Because this is the By Category view, items are being grouped by, well, categories in ascending order. The Show field in view check box tells Calendar to do just that: show the sort field in the group heading and the information columns.

JUST A MINUTE

> Ascending order means items are sorted from A to Z or 1 to 10. Descending order means items are sorted from Z to A or 10 to 1.

The Then by list box, which is expanded in Figure 12.12, allows you to establish a second level of grouping criteria. For instance, if you regularly deal with more than one office in your company, you could sort by category in the first level, then by location (or vice versa).

The remainder of the sections let you sort down to a fourth grouping level, if you wish. At the bottom of the dialog is the Select available fields from list box, which lets you choose which field set you can pick your grouping fields from. Next to this is the Expand/collapse defaults list box, which will set the default view for any expandable group heading.

Defining Views

What if you don't like the information fields you are seeing? Can you drop some of them or add more? Yes, indeed. If you click the View | Define Views menu command, the great and powerful Define Views for "Calendar" dialog appears (see Figure 12.13). I write this only with a touch of facetiousness because this really is a powerful tool. From here, you can modify the look of every Calendar view—right down to the font color used.

Figure 12.13.

The Define Views dialog.

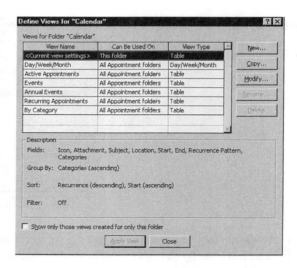

To change a current view, click the Modify button on the right side of the dialog. This brings up the View Summary dialog (see Figure 12.14). This shows all the current settings for the view you are in right now and has five buttons that serve as jump-points to other dialogs that can modify these settings.

Figure 12.14.

The View Summary dialog.

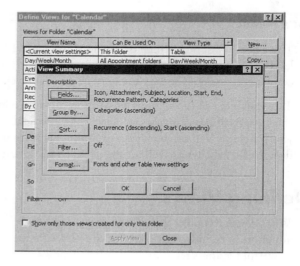

12

If you click the Fields button in the View Summary dialog, you see the Show Fields dialog (see Figure 12.15). With this tool, you can choose what information will be visible in this view. To add a field to the list Show fields in this order, highlight it in the left column, then click the Add button. The field will appear on the bottom of the list. If you wish to change the order of the fields, highlight the field you wish to move, then click the Move Up or Move Down buttons until the field name is in the right place.

Figure 12.15.
The Show Fields dialog.

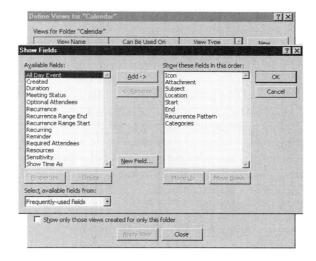

Returning to the View Summary dialog, if you click the Group By button, you will get the Group By dialog (see Figure 12.12). Similarly, clicking the Sort button activates the Sort dialog, which is almost identical to the Group By dialog. This dialog, however, sorts the information within the columns, not the group headings.

Clicking the Filter button, you get the Filter dialog, shown in Figure 12.16.

JUST A MINUTE

It is important that you distinguish the difference between grouping, sorting, and filtering.

Grouping items places them into groups where the items share some information fields in common.

Sorting items shuffles the order of items within a group, based on values of a common information field.

Filtering adjusts which items you will even see, based on certain values contained in any information field.

Figure 12.16.

The Filter dialog.

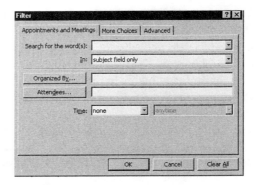

To use the Filter dialog, enter the information value you want Calendar to show. For instance, if I wanted to just view any item associated with a trip to Los Angeles, I would search for Los Angeles in frequently used text fields. After clicking OK, my schedule, no matter how it was formatted, would only show those items. All of my appointments to the dentist, the business lunches, my mother's birthday...everything else is rendered invisible. Not to worry. To get things back, re-enter the Filter dialog (you can get there in a more direct fashion with the View | Filter menu command) and click the Clear All button. All data in your schedule will be made visible again.

Format, the last button to click in the View Summary dialog, brings up the Format Table View (shown in Figure 12.17) or the Format Day/Week/Month View dialog, depending on which type of view you are formatting. The settings in these dialogs are fairly self-explanatory and give you a wide range of options in modifying the cosmetic look of Calendar.

Figure 12.17.

The Format Table View dialog.

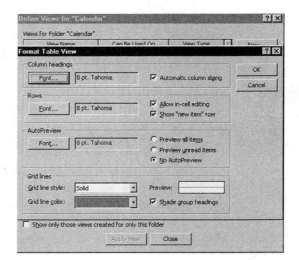

Creating a New View

Creating a new view is much like modifying a current view. If you click the New button in the Define Views for "Calendar" dialog, the first thing you will see is the Create a New View dialog, shown in Figure 12.18. It allows you to give the new view a name, and set what view type on which you want to base your view. The radio buttons at the bottom choose who gets to see this new view and to which folder the view will apply. After you click OK, a blank View Summary dialog appears, which you can modify just as you've learned in the last section.

Figure 12.18.

The Create a New View dialog.

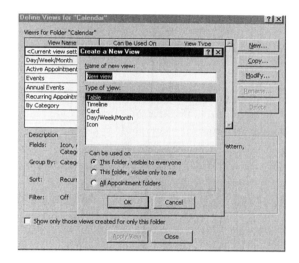

Finding What You've Got

Sometimes too much functionality can be a bad thing. With all of these clever ways of viewing your schedule, a certain appointment could get lost in the shuffle. Did I sort that by category? Lunar phase? Where is it?

Take a deep breath, then click the Find Items button in the toolbar. Doesn't the appearance of the Find dialog, shown in Figure 12.19, send a wave of relaxation over you? Ahhh…

Figure 12.19.
The Find dialog.

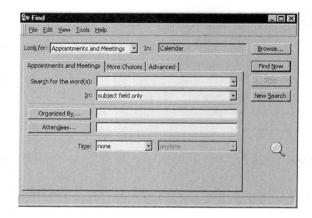

Now, all you need to do is enter the word you are looking for and choose the field in which you want to search. If you cannot find the right field in the Appointments and Meetings tab, click on the More Choices tab. Use the Advanced tab to really narrow your search down.

It's better than yoga.

Printing What You've Got

Throughout all of this, you may be getting the urge to get this information down on paper so you can carry it around with you. This can be done by clicking the Print button in the toolbar. The Print dialog that appears (see Figure 12.20) is very similar to the standard Windows Print dialog, although you are given a choice of which style (Daily, Weekly, Monthly, or Table) you want to print in.

Figure 12.20.
The Print dialog.

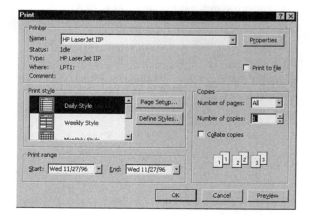

12

If you're feeling really aesthetic, click the Define Styles button. You can get really artsy with your hard copy.

Summary

Now you are done with this hour's look at Calendar. You can see that it can be a simple or very complex tool. What shapes Calendar's functionality, like any other part of Outlook, is how you want to use it. Gone are the days of just living with what you get. Now, you can change every aspect of Calendar to meet your needs and even your wants.

In Hour 13, "Things to Do with Tasks," you'll start organizing your work as well as your time using Outlook's Task tool.

Q&A

Q How often will I really need to filter my schedule?

A I have found it's useful to just view the appointments I need to keep on a trip. By filtering out all but the trip stuff, I can easily print out just this information or export the data to my laptop.

Q I don't like having all of these views. Can't I get rid of some?

A You can only get rid of customized views you have made. The eight standard views in Calendar are there to stay. To delete a custom view, click the View | Define Views menu command, highlight the custom view, then click Delete.

12

PART V

Working with Tasks

Hour

Hour 13

Things to Do with Tasks

My fourth grade teacher, Mrs. Lindsey, once told me this truism about procrastinating: "Always do the hardest thing first. If you do the easy things first, you'll be too tired to do the hard thing." Works, too.

The problem is, today we are beset by so many things to do, it's difficult to figure out which is hardest, or more important, or (if you're feeling a bit lazy) can be done in the shortest amount of time. This is because our jobs, like our computers, have a lot more multitasking. I don't just go to work and berate authors all day to make a book. My colleagues and I have to find them, get them started, tell our salespeople what's going on, tell our boss what's going on—*then* I get to berate the authors. This computer technology we praise so highly has enabled us to talk to anyone on the planet, but talking to all those people takes time. So does answering all those e-mails, faxing all those reports—well, you get the idea.

Outlook's Tasks function makes the jobs of time and task management a lot easier by allowing you to create and monitor your old "things to do" list quickly. Tasks is the focus of this hour, so let's get ready to, umm, work!

Time Management and You

A brief interlude before we start.

While I like to function by Mrs. Lindsey's creed, obviously you might have different methods or techniques to use. There are many tried-and-true methods out there, as well as a lot of new ones. Just wander over to the Business section of the bookstore and you will see what I mean.

While I am not here to recommend a certain time management method, here are some ideas that seem to work:

- ☐ Do the Tasks that accomplish the most with the least energy.
- ☐ Be accessible, but don't let a lot of interruptions drag you down.
- ☐ Set aside a little time at the beginning of each day (or the end of the previous day) to set goals. They don't have to be big, just some things you can manage.
- ☐ This is the most important: *Make sure you always, always make time for yourself and your loved ones.* No matter how much you love your job, it's only one part of your life. If it becomes all of your life, you're missing out. If you haven't talked to your spouse, parent, kids, whomever today, put this book down right now and go do that.

A Look at Outlook's Tasks

If you are among the many skeptics of time management and personal organizers, Tasks will make a believer of you by

- ☐ Allowing you to create and maintain lists of things to do, as well as track Tasks by project, by people involved, and by priority.
- ☐ Letting you maintain lists of recurring Tasks that occur either on set dates, or a certain time after the previous occurrence of the Task is completed.
- ☐ Allowing delegation of Tasks and Task management to other people, for those times when you're too busy to do it yourself.
- ☐ Accepting Task assignments from others. This is certainly not fun, but at least Tasks makes the pill a little easier to swallow by enabling you to easily integrate a new incoming Task into your list of things to do easily.

Starting Tasks

Getting to the Tasks screen in Outlook is done much the same as with any of the other tools.

The first way to start Tasks is from within Outlook itself. From any part of Outlook, you can start Tasks by clicking the Tasks icon in the Outlook bar (see Figure 13.1) or the Tasks folder

13

in the Personal Folders list (see Figure 13.2), depending on which view you choose. If you like menus, you can get to Tasks by clicking the Go|Tasks command.

Figure 13.1.

The Outlook bar's Tasks icon.

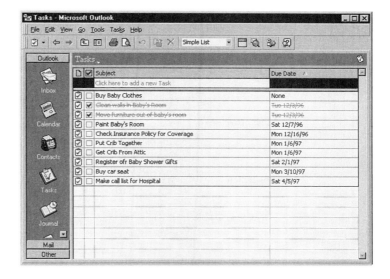

Figure 13.2.

The Personal Folders list's Tasks folder.

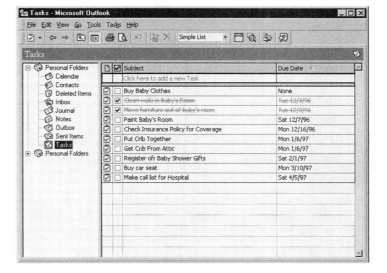

And on Your Left, You Can See...

The Tasks screen is not flashy. As you can see in Figure 13.3, the Information Viewer section of the Outlook screen is filled with a simple-looking, four-column table. But, you know by now that such things are never quite as simple as they seem. If they were, this book would be very short.

Figure 13.3.

The Tasks screen.

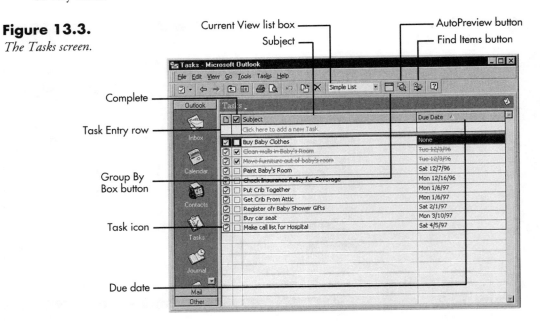

This particular view of Tasks is the Simple List view. Actually, there is one view more compact than this—the TaskPad seen in the Calendar, which we will examine with the other nine views in Hour 15, "Configuring Tasks." For now, let's stick with this view as we try out all of Tasks' functions. In the Simple List, the four columns of information are Icon, Complete, Subject, and Due Date.

The Icon column shows the user what kind of Outlook item this is. Most of the time, just the Tasks icon will be present here, although, as you saw in Figure 13.3, assigned Tasks are symbolized in this column as well. We'll take a closer look at assigning Tasks in Hour 14, "Project Management with Tasks."

The Complete column is merely a check box that indicates when a Task is complete. It can be used as a proactive tool or reactive symbol, depending on how the Task is actually marked complete.

The Subject column is what the Task is. Take out the trash. Get Dave the Top Ten List by 5:30. Launch the Mars probe. These are all good examples of Task subjects.

Finally, the Date Due column displays the date the Task should be completed. Not all Tasks need due dates (my favorite Task, "earn a million dollars," is pretty much an ongoing Task). Those that do not have due dates are indicated by None.

Creating a Task

Okay, I'll 'fess up. There's a theme in this chapter's Tasks. Yes, it's care and feeding of a dog. Well, maybe not. Sometimes Tasks can help you out with things around the house—especially if your home is about to be invaded.

One of the employees at Quantum Ink, Nathan Daniels, is going to have a baby in a few months. Actually, his wife Jamie is. They both are going to be extremely busy in the ensuing months, preparing for the new arrival. Nathan is a man who knows his own limits; he can be very scatterbrained. To combat this, he has been using Tasks at work religiously. It helps, and when confronted with this new project, he installed Outlook at home. With Jamie's help, they started creating a list of things that had to be accomplished before the baby's arrival.

After reviewing the list they made so far, Jamie remembered a big Task to complete: settling on the baby's name.

To add this Task, she can choose from several different ways to activate the New Task tool.

In Tasks, a new Task can be started by (see Figure 13.4):

☐ Clicking the New Task button on the far-left end of the Standard Toolbar

☐ Typing the shortcut keys Ctrl+N

☐ Clicking on the Tasks|New Task menu command

☐ Single- or double-clicking the button Click here to add a new Task in the Task Entry row

Figure 13.4.

The ways to begin creating a Task in Tasks.

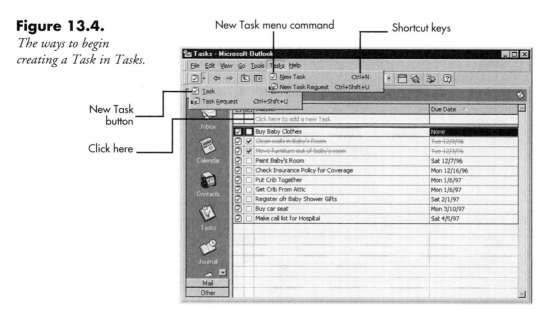

If Jamie was not in Tasks but still in Outlook, she could create a new Task by clicking the New Task command in the Create New drop-down list in the Standard Toolbar or by using the shortcut keys Ctrl+Shift+K.

You can still create a Task and not even have Outlook running. If you have installed the Microsoft Office Shortcut Bar, click the New Task button to start the New Task tool (see Figure 13.5).

Figure 13.5.

The ways to begin creating a Task from outside Tasks.

Shortcut keys

New Task command

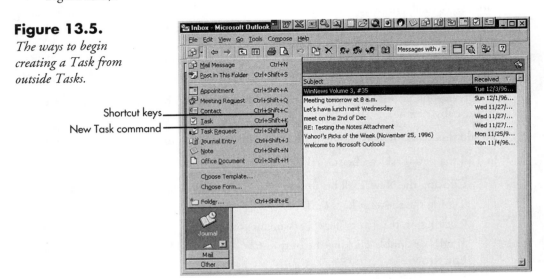

After choosing one of these methods, where does Jamie end up? In the New Task tool, shown in Figure 13.6.

Besides its similarity in style to all of Outlook's other tools, you should also notice the small number of fields to fill out. There is a perfectly logical reason for this, in that if there were too many pieces of information to fill out, creating Tasks would be far too slow to be useful.

The first field to enter data into is the Subject field. This should be a brief description of the Task. Don't go crazy with detail here. You can always fill in extra information in the note box at the bottom of the Task tool. Jamie will enter, "Decide on baby's name!" in this field.

The next information group is the Due date fields. The None and Due radio buttons enable you to denote if you have a deadline or if this is an ongoing Task that does not need to be done at a determined time. If you have a due date in mind, click the Due radio button. Immediately, a due date of today appears in the adjacent date field, and a Due Today message appears near the top of the Task tool. If you want another date, click the drop-down control to the right of the date field, and you will see a Date Navigator (see Figure 13.7). With this

13

Navigator, you can click on the appropriate date. If you do not want to use the Date Navigator, highlight the current date in the date field, and type in the correct date directly over it. Jamie's choice is easy: She enters the *baby's* due date.

Figure 13.6.

The New Task tool.

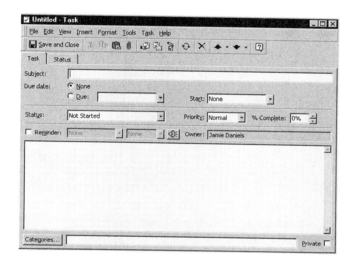

JUST A MINUTE

Typing any date in the Due date field will automatically change the due date status from None to Due.

The Start date field works in much the same way as the Due date field. It is used to establish a date work on the Task will begin. Sometimes this will be the present time or it will be put off to the near future. If the Task is in progress, it could be in the past. Jamie opts to make the Start date today, although she and Nathan have been discussing this for awhile, mostly because tracking the start time for this Task is unnecessary.

The next section begins with the Status field. How is the project going? Has it begun? This is what we mean by status. In the Status field, there are five choices:

☐ Not Started

☐ In Progress

☐ Completed

☐ Waiting on someone else

☐ Deferred

Figure 13.7.

The Date Navigator.

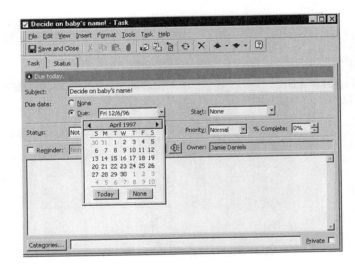

Jamie clicks the In Progress choice and moves to the next field, Priority. Here, another drop-down list box presents her with three priority choices: High, Normal, and Low. Because she does not want to call the baby "hey, you" all of its life, she decides to make this a High priority.

The next field, % Complete, is optional. There are certain situations, such as Jamie's, where pinning down a percentage value is tricky. When the Task is more segmented or can be more easily measured, then it's helpful to use this field. For instance, when writing a set number of chapters in a book, an author could change the percentage of chapters completed and submitted to the editor through either directly entering or using the spin buttons to the right of the field to increase or decrease the value to the one needed. Because there are other ways of marking a Task complete, Jamie will skip this field.

For those of you who were paying attention in Part IV, "Using the Calendar," the next section should look familiar to you. As in Calendar, Tasks allows you to set Reminders for any Task you wish. However, there are some differences between Reminders in Tasks and Reminders in Calendar.

When you click the Reminder check box, the date field next to it will activate, and the default data value will be the due date of the Task. If there is no due date, the date field will default to today. The next field is the Reminder time field. The default is 8:00 AM.

JUST A MINUTE

At this point, you may be asking yourself, what's the difference between Calendar and Task items? On the surface, not much. They handle different things in a similar way.

13

> What makes Tasks different is that it does not focus on a certain point in time—once you set a Reminder and that date is reached, Tasks will keep reminding you every day until the Task is complete. Tasks also lets you manage projects, something we'll cover in Hour 14.

Next to the time field is a little button with a speaker icon on it. If you click this button, you will get the Reminder Sound dialog. This contains the path to the sound file (usually in WAV format) that will sound when the Reminder time begins. Jamie decides to set the Reminder to start one month before the big day, at 7 p.m., when the home computer is almost always on.

TIME SAVER

> If a certain time of day would be better for you to receive Task Reminders, you can change the default time. To do so, complete the following steps:
>
> 1. In Tasks, click the Tools | Options menu command. Be sure the Tasks/Notes tab is in front.
> 2. In the Reminder time field, either directly enter or use the list box to set a new daily time.
> 3. Click OK.

The Owner field is not editable, because it shows the user who has created the Task and therefore who "owns" it. This information comes in handy when Tasks are assigned and delegated.

The large note box that dominates the lower third of the screen lets you enter as many details about the Task as you need. To help keep track of the names she and Nathan have narrowed the choices to, Jamie puts the top six candidate names in the note box.

The final section of the New Task tool starts with the Categories field. A close examination of how to use this field and add new categories is found in Hour 10, "Keeping Track of Your Life."

The final field in the New Task tool is the Private check box. This is used when a Task is created that not everyone needs to know about, such as if your personal folder is being shared across a network.

Once Jamie completes the field entries, her New Task tool should look like Figure 13.8. At this point, all she needs to do is click the Save and Close button on the toolbar, and this new Task will be placed in the Tasks information viewer.

13

Figure 13.8.

The new Task: What's in a name?

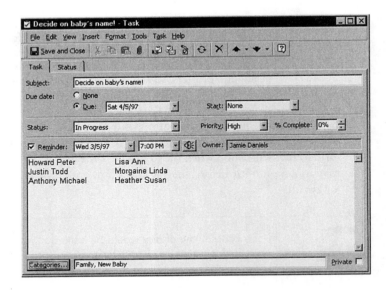

AutoCreating a Task

If you are like me (and you really should hope you aren't), you get a lot of e-mail that contains matters that you must deal with in order to keep the world safe for democracy. You know, things like, "Could you get me a copy of that report?" or "Can you find a way to deal with that knucklehead Lex Luthor?"

Messages such as these can be made into a Task quite easily. To do so, follow these steps:

1. In Inbox, select the appropriate message, then drag and drop it onto the Task icon (or Task folder in the Folder list).

2. When the New Task tool appears, fill in the appropriate information (priority, due date, and so on).

3. Click Save and Close. Go out and save the world.

The Calendar offers another clever way to autocreate a Task. For instance, if you have an appointment or meeting that you need to have something ready for, making an associated Task with the Calendar item is a great idea. Jamie, for example, needs to have all her hospital pre-registration forms filled out by her next doctor's appointment, so the doctor's office can get them processed. To help her remember this, she makes a Task from the appointment on the Calendar:

1. Highlight the appointment item in the Calendar.

2. Drag and drop it onto the Task icon or into the Task folder.

13

3. A New Task tool appears with the appointment information in the note box (see Figure 13.9).

4. Add the needed information in the appropriate fields, then click Save and Close.

Figure 13.9.

Making sure you're prepared for an appointment.

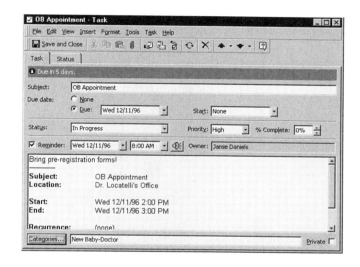

Finishing a Task

There's no greater satisfaction than a job well done, but how do you tell Tasks that you're done? There are four ways:

☐ When the Complete column is in view, as it is in Tasks' Simple List view, clicking the check box next to the finished Task will mark that Task as done.

☐ When the Status field is in view in the Information Viewer (that is, the Detailed List view), entering Completed in that field tells Tasks the job is done. You can also enter this value within a Task's Open Task tool.

☐ In the Task tool for the finished work, enter 100% in the % Complete field. Or, enter the same value in the % Complete field in Tasks' Detailed List view (see Figure 13.10).

☐ In the Task tool, click the Mark Complete button in the toolbar.

After you have marked a Task complete, it does not disappear from the Simple List view. Rather, it changes to a lighter, strikethrough text. This helps you keep track of the recent things you've accomplished, so you don't go through a "Did I do that?" anxiety crisis.

In the Active view, however, Tasks disappear as soon as they are marked complete. They are still around; you can see them if you switch back to the Simple List view. You must make a

13

small effort to make a Task disappear forever. See the "Deleting a Task" section in this chapter if you're one of those neat people who likes his screens tidy.

Figure 13.10.

Finishing off a Task.

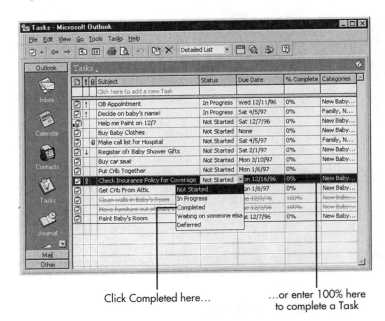

Click Completed here...   ...or enter 100% here
                                           to complete a Task

Editing a Task

Editing a Task is not difficult at all. If the item you wish to edit is visible in the Information Viewer, you can edit it directly without opening the Task tool.

After looking at her Tasks list, Jamie notices a typo in one of the Task subjects. Knowing her editor husband will tease her about it (editors do that), she decides to change it:

1. In any of the Information Viewer views, click on the Task that needs editing.

2. Place the cursor near the values that need changing. (Date fields give you the option of using a Date Navigator to change the information.)

3. Make the change. Click on any other part of the screen to exit this item, and the change is automatically saved (see Figure 13.11).

If you want to do more detailed editing, double-click on any Task in the Information Viewer. This opens up that Task's Task tool. Editing any of the fields on the Task tab is the same as creating the Task. But, there are other fields that can be edited—fields on the Status tab that deal with many things that come up during a particular job.

13

Figure 13.11.

*Editing a Task in the
Information Viewer.*

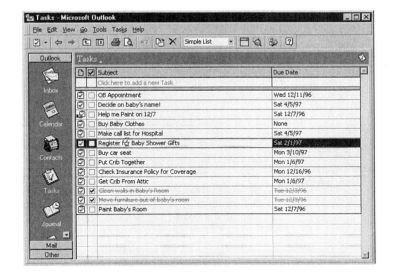

Take a look at the Status tab, visible in Figure 13.12. There's lots of stuff back there! Let's look at what each field can record for you.

Figure 13.12.

*The Status tab in the
Task tool.*

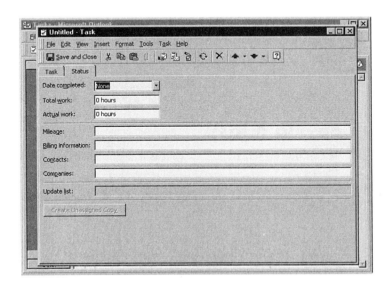

The Date completed field is automatically filled when a Task is marked complete. This is helpful when the Task is part of an overall project and you need to know who finished what when.

The Total work and Actual work fields are sort of misnomers. At least, the Total work field is. It should be called the Estimated work field, because you enter the estimated number of hours you think a Task will take to finish here. In the Actual work field, enter the number of hours the Task really took. (If this Task had been assigned, this would be a great way of monitoring someone's performance level.) Notice that the values of the field automatically change to day or week values.

TIME SAVER

> When hours are converted to days and weeks, the formula used is based on values you can set. The default values are eight hours equal one work day, and 40 hours equal one work week. If your office has a different schedule, change these conversion values by clicking the Tools|Options menu command in Tasks. In the Hours per day and Hours per week fields, change the values to what's right for you, and click OK.

The next four fields are self-explanatory: Mileage, Billing Information, Contacts, and Companies. If you need to keep track of this type of information, here's where to do it. Jamie could use the Mileage field to record her mileage to and from the doctor's office, which is tax-deductible.

TIME SAVER

> Instead of just typing names into the Contacts field, highlight the contact in Contacts, then drag and drop the information over to the Task tool's Contacts field.

Copying a Task

If you need to create a Task that is nearly identical to another, try this procedure to copy the Task:

1. In any of the Task Lists shown in the Information Viewer, click on the Task (or Tasks) you need to copy.
2. Type Ctrl+C, or click the Edit|Copy menu command.
3. Type Ctrl+V, or click the Edit|Paste menu command.

Now you can open the newly copied Task and make minor changes to make it unique.

An even faster way of doing this is to highlight the Task, and while holding the Ctrl key, drag the Task somewhere else in the Information Viewer. As soon as you release the key or mouse, voila! A copy is born!

13

Deleting a Task

As I've mentioned, when they are completed, Tasks do not just vanish into the air. They stick around, reminding you of all of the good (or not-so-good) work you've accomplished.

You can keep Tasks around until they are autoarchived, but you may want to clean house and sweep out these old Tasks sooner than that. You may even need to delete a current Task. In any case, to delete a Task, highlight the Task in question, then hit the Delete button on the Standard Toolbar in Tasks or on the toolbar within the Task tool.

Creating a Recurring Task

Modern society is based on repetition. We sleep every day, we bathe every day (I hope), and we do the same things every day, especially at work.

Most repeated jobs are easy to remember because of their repetition. It's not hard to remember to brush your teeth, but what if your doctor gives you new daily medication? If it's not "in the groove," it's hard to remember for a while. Jamie needs to take prenatal vitamins at a certain time every day and initially kept forgetting, so she made a recurring Task.

CAUTION

This is just a fictitious example, but if you do want to use Outlook to remind you of any kind of medical task (taking medication, taking blood samples, and so on), go ahead, *but make sure you have an alternate method to remind you of these things.* Computers crash, or the power can go out; never trust just one form of media to track these kinds of important details.

Unlike creating a recurring appointment in Calendar, Tasks does not allow you to create a recurring Task from scratch. Instead, you need to create a Task first, *then* make it recurring. After she has created the initial Task to take her vitamins, Jamie follows these steps to make the Task recur.

In the Task tool's toolbar, click the Recurrence button. This opens the Task Recurrence dialog, shown in Figure 13.13. In this figure, the Daily view is shown, although the default view is Weekly.

At the top of the dialog is the Recurrence pattern section. Here, depending on the type of pattern you chose, you will choose to recur your Task at a fixed time or a certain length of time after the last occurrence of the Task.

13

Figure 13.13.

The Daily Task Recurrence pattern.

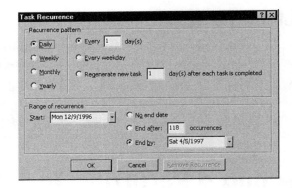

At the bottom of the dialog is the Range of recurrence section. This sets the length of time at which a Task will recur. The Start date defaults to the date you first created this Task and can easily be changed through the Date Navigator method or through direct data entry. The end date is variable. If the Task recurs indefinitely, the No end date radio button should be active. If a specific number of recurrences is known, this value can be entered in the End after: *x* occurrences field. If a specific end date is known, enter this value in the End by: field. Jamie's end date for this Task would be the arrival date of the baby.

Daily Pattern

If you refer to Figure 13.13, you will note the Daily pattern has only three options. The first, Every *x* day(s), lets you indicate what repetition pattern the Task should take. If it's every day, the value is 1. If it's every fourth day, the value should be 4.

The second option, Every weekday, is set when you need an appointment to occur every day within the Monday–Friday period.

The third option, Regenerate new task *x* day(s) after each task is completed, makes Tasks create a new Task only after the last occurrence of the Task has been completed for a certain number of days. One example of this type of recurring Task would be mowing the lawn in high summer. Once the lawn is cut, it should be mowed again a certain number of days later, not necessarily every week at the same time.

Weekly Pattern

At the top of the Weekly section (shown in Figure 13.14) is the Recur every *x* week(s) on field. The number in the middle of the sentence refers to the frequency you want the Task to recur. If you wanted to set a Task every second week, you would set the number to 2.

13

Figure 13.14.

The Weekly Task
Recurrence pattern.

The next part of the section contains check boxes for every day of the week. Check the appropriate days. If you have a Task that happens every business day but Wednesday, you would check off Monday, Tuesday, Thursday, and Friday.

The second option, Regenerate new task *x* week(s) after each task is completed, makes Tasks create a new Task only after the last occurrence of the Task has been completed for a certain number of weeks.

Monthly Pattern

The Monthly pattern (shown in Figure 13.15) has three options. The first option, Day *x* of every *x* month(s), is used to indicate that your Task happens on a specific date in the month and how often it occurs. If it's every month on the 15th, the values would be Day 15 of every 1 month(s). If it's every other month on the 21st, the values would appear as Day 21 of every 2 month(s).

The second option is used when the Task recurs on a specific day of the week. The *x x* of every *x* month(s) has two drop-down lists and a data value field. The first drop-down list has the values first, second, third, fourth, and last. The second list has the values of the days of the week, as well as day, weekday, and weekend day. The data value indicates the frequency of months, just as in the first option. For example, say you wanted to have the Task recur on every second Wednesday of every third month. Then the option should appear as The second Wednesday of every 3 month(s).

The third option, Regenerate new task *x* month(s) after each task is completed, makes Tasks create a new Task only after the last occurrence of the Task has been completed for a certain number of months.

13

Figure 13.15.
*The Monthly Task
Recurrence pattern.*

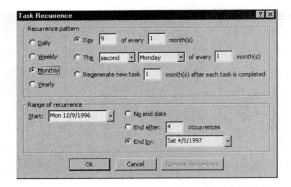

Yearly Pattern

The first option in the Yearly pattern view (see Figure 13.16) is Every *x x*. The first value, a drop-down list, specifies the months of the year. The second value is the specific date.

The second option allows the user to set a certain day of the week within a certain month once a year.

The third option, Regenerate new task *x* year(s) after each task is completed, makes Tasks create a new Task only after the last occurrence of the Task has been completed for a certain number of years. This may not happen very often, but hey, who knows?

Figure 13.16.
*The Yearly Task
Recurrence pattern.*

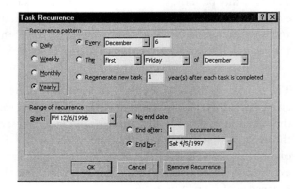

Figure 13.17 shows what the Task tool looks like after Jamie fills in information in the Daily view and clicks OK in the Task Recurrence dialog. Note the information displayed near the top, reminding her of the recurrence pattern she has set. Figure 13.18 shows the Task in the Simple List. The icon denoting it is the nifty Recurring Task icon.

13

Figure 13.17.
The recurring Task.

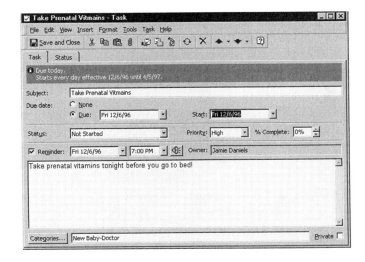

Figure 13.18.
The recurring Task in the Simple List view.

Recurring Task icon ————

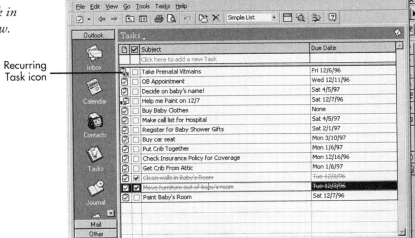

13

Summary

If you are a busy person, the frustration of dealing with so many different projects and jobs can be maddening. Tasks, as we've seen in this hour, can make life easier for you by creating neatly organized Tasks with as little fuss as possible.

But what if you are not alone in your little universe? What if you're a—gasp!—manager? The things to do for work suddenly don't have to be done just by you. Tasks can help you there, too, as you'll see in the next hour.

Q&A

Q Can I add attachments to Tasks?

A Yes, you can. You can add any kind of file or Office document in the Task tool's note box, as well as any Outlook item. Just select what you want to attach and drag-and-drop it in. You can also click the Attach button and add the file that way.

Q Can I skip the next occurrence of a recurring task?

A Such easy questions. If you open the recurring task, click the Task|Skip Occurrence menu command.

Q What if I need to stop a Task from recurring before its end date? Do I delete the Task?

A You can, if that Task will never be done. If it suddenly needs to be done just once, there's no need to delete it. Open the Task, click the Recurrence button, and in the Task Recurrence dialog, click Remove Recurrence.

13

Hour 14

Project Management with Tasks

The pharaohs of ancient Egypt had it easy. When they assigned a task, such as "Build me a big pyramid," their people said, "How high?" Today, we have unions that say, "How much will you pay us?"

In truth, things haven't changed much since those heady days on the Nile. Jobs that are too big, we get help for, whether it be from a co-worker or an assistant. Assigning a new job usually starts out with a meeting to explain the job at hand, followed by endless meetings and status reports to monitor the job. Wouldn't it be nice if, after that first big meeting, the need for all those status reports and status meetings simply vanished?

Think of Tasks, then, as Houdini. With it, you can assign Tasks to others, who can then accept, decline, or assign the Task to someone else. Once you have assigned a Task, it becomes the responsibility of the assignee, who now "owns" the Task, but you will still get status reports that will automatically be addressed to you.

Sounds good? Sit back a spell, and let's do some learning.

Assigning a Task

Outlook has a two-fold procedure when is comes to assigning Tasks to others—either create a fresh Task request or assign one of your current Tasks.

Once you've assigned a Task, it can be reassigned either by you or the new Task owner. This could happen after a Task has been declined or perhaps if you've changed your mind. There are various scenarios to do this, and we'll try to step through them all.

First, let's start at the beginning and create a new Task request.

Creating a New Task Request

There are three ways to create a new Task request. All of them need to be used with Outlook running, because you cannot make a Task request from scratch using the Microsoft Office Shortcut Bar. (You can, of course, create a new Task using the Shortcut Bar, and then assign it, as the section "Assigning a Current Task," explains later in this hour.) The following are the three methods:

- ☐ Click the Tasks|New Task Request menu command, as shown in Figure 14.1.
- ☐ Click the New Task Request command in the New Item button in the Standard Toolbar.
- ☐ Use the Ctrl+Shift+U shortcut keys.

Figure 14.1.

Starting a new Task request.

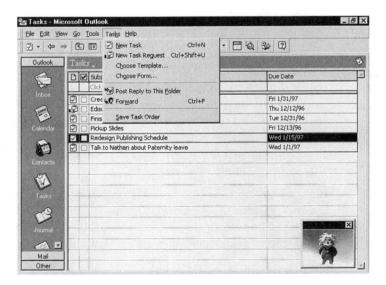

14

By using any one of these methods, you will quickly see the Task Request tool appear (see Figure 14.2). Looks kinda familiar, doesn't it?

Figure 14.2.

The Task Request tool.

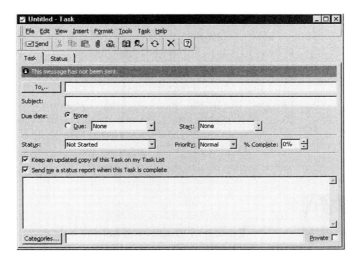

Indeed, the Task Request tool is almost exactly like the Task tool you reviewed in Hour 13, "Things to Do with Tasks." Only the addition of a few fields makes it different. These differing fields are

☐ To field—This field functions exactly like the field of the same name in the Inbox. If you click the To button, you get the Select Task Recipient dialog, which is identical to the Select Names dialog seen when clicking the To button in a new message. Look at Figure 14.3 if you don't believe me.

Figure 14.3.

The Select Task Recipient dialog.

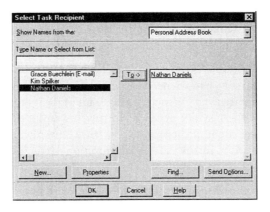

14

☐ Keep an updated copy of this Task on my Task List check box—This box, when
enabled, keeps a current version of the Task with you even after you have assigned
it. This does not mean you still own the Task. However, if you decide to assign the
Task to somebody else, you'll need to re-create an unassigned Task. If you have
kept this updated copy now, you won't have to re-create an entirely new Task later.
(I know, I know, it was confusing to me, too. An example or two should clear it up
for you.)

☐ Send me a status report when this Task is complete check box—This check box is a
bit easier to explain. When enabled, it attaches this same request to the Task
Request. When the recipient gets it, and if they accept the Task, every time they
want to give the Task's original owner an update on how things are going, all they
need to do is click the Status Report button to begin creating a status report already
addressed to the original Task owner.

JUST A MINUTE

Owners? Updates? Reports? What does it all mean?

This is how Outlook has defined ownership of Tasks, assigned or unassigned. Every time you create a Task, you are that Task's owner. You are
the owner of that Task for as long it remains assigned to you. Once you
assign the Task to someone else and he accepts it, he becomes the new
owner, while the most you will be is the recipient of a status report.

So, in the Outlook paradigm, a Task owner is not the one who initially
creates the Task, but the one who is *responsible* for the Task.

The difference between a status report and an updated copy is that a
status report only sends a message back to the proper individuals, while a
copy that can be updated actually updates all fields of the Task as if you
had opened it up and edited the Task yourself.

All the remaining fields in the Task Request tool, on both tabs, are exactly the same as the
Task tool. With this in mind, let's go through an example.

Lynn Stevens is the managing editor for Quantum Ink. It's her job to keep control of the
organized chaos generated on a daily basis between Editorial, Sales, Production, and
Manufacturing. As such, she has a lot of things to do. Some of these things she can get help
with. For instance, recently she gave her senior editors a bit more control in the day-to-day
management of their teams. So far, it's been working, but her bosses want some concrete
numbers to justify the new organizational structure. So, here is a Task to assign to Andy and
the other senior editors.

As you can see in Figure 14.4, after Lynn has entered the appropriate names in the To,
Subject, and Dates fields, she now needs to decide if she needs an updated copy left on her

14

Task List. Because she needs reports from all the senior editors, she shouldn't have any to reassign the Task too, right? Well, maybe. After all, what if one of them gets sick? So, she should keep an updated copy in case she has to reassign to one of the senior editors. But here's the rub: If a Task is assigned to more than one person, you can't keep an updated copy.

Figure 14.4.

Deciding on updates and reports.

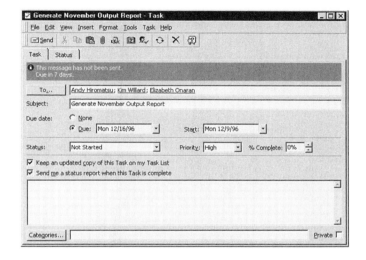

The reason for this is because once a Task is assigned to more than one person, only one of them becomes the owner (see top half of Figure 14.5). In fact, Outlook always gives Task ownership to the first person listed in the To field—something you should keep in mind. But now Outlook must use the ability to update Task copies within the new group, and cannot update "up" to another level at the same time (see the bottom half of Figure 14.5). In fact, if Lynn had left this box checked and clicked the Send button, she would have seen the warning dialog, shown in Figure 14.6.

Lynn will definitely need that status report to be sure the reports will be done on time. By a prior agreement, everyone at Quantum Ink spends the last part of their day making sure all their Task statuses are current, and that all assigned Tasks are sent status reports back to their owners. Figure 14.7 shows how the Task Request tool looks after Lynn is finished.

JUST A MINUTE

Your own organization may not be so detail-oriented. In general, however, it's a good idea to set up some guidelines on when status reports should be sent. If it's done on a case-by-case basis, be sure everyone involved knows this particular Task's needs.

The rule of thumb should be: The higher the priority, the higher the frequency of status reports.

14

Figure 14.5.
*How Task ownership
and updates work.*

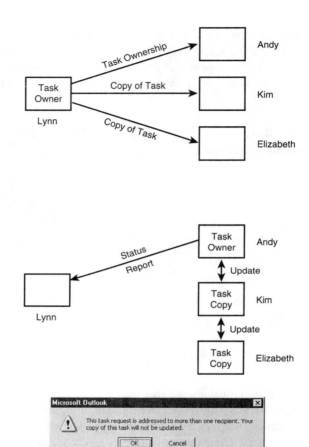

Figure 14.6.
*A warning about updates
and multiple Task
recipients.*

Now that the pertinent fields are complete, Lynn clicks Send and the Task is sent away. Her Task List, however, remains free of any mention of this Task. Now, Andy is the complete owner of the Task and has been entrusted with managing it. Lynn will still get status reports, but as far as Outlook is concerned, she no longer has the ability to reassign this Task.

If a Task is assigned to just one person, things are more straightforward. As shown in Figure 14.8, Lynn has assigned Nathan Daniels a Task and has kept an updated copy for herself. Notice that Nathan is now the owner of this Task.

14

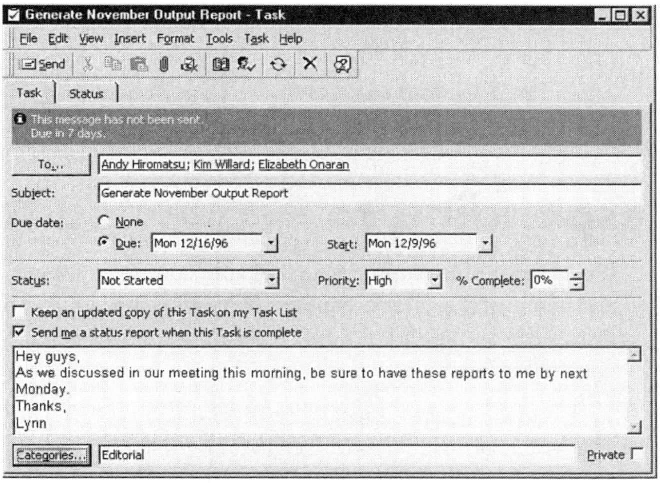

Figure 14.7.

The completed Task request.

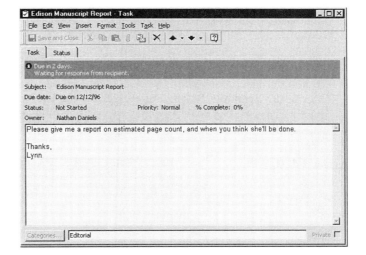

Figure 14.8.

Keeping a copy of a Task request.

Assigning a Current Task

If you have a Task that was assigned to you, or you have made for yourself, sometimes you may need to have someone else do it for you. Here are the steps to get this done:

1. After you have created or received a Task, open the Task by double-clicking on it in the Task List.

2. After the Task tool opens, click the Assign Task button in the toolbar, or click the Task|Assign Task menu command.

3. The Task tool changes to the Task Request tool. Fill in the correct information, and click Send.

Responding to Requested Tasks

Unless you are the supreme ruler of your company, sooner or later you will be on the receiving end of one of these Task requests. The important thing is to remain calm and make no sudden moves. By acting in a rational fashion, you should be able to deal with this beast without personal injury.

Task requests always appear first in your Inbox. If you are using Microsoft Exchange Server or a Microsoft Mail Postoffice, Task requests will appear as a request message, with a Task Request icon next to it. If you are using some other messaging systems, the requests will appear as ordinary mail messages. The difference here is that you will not be able to respond, update, or send status reports through Tasks. You will have to use e-mail and other forms of communication to pass this information around.

But, if you do have a Microsoft messaging system running, you are in luck. Task requests have their own special tool to help you quickly respond to them.

When Andy opens the Task request from Lynn, the Task request box appears, looking almost exactly like an Inbox message. The only difference is an information header saying who assigned the Task and when it is due, and a new toolbar, shown in Figure 14.9.

Figure 14.9.

The toolbar shown when a Task request is received.

As you can see, there are basically three options Andy can now take:

☐ He can accept the Task by clicking the Accept button.

☐ He can decline the Task by clicking the Decline button.

☐ He can reassign the Task to someone else by clicking the Assign Task button.

After looking at his own Task List and his Calendar, Andy decides to take on the Task. When he clicks Accept, a warning dialog will appear (see Figure 14.10).

14

Figure 14.10.

*Are you going to be terse
or eloquent today?*

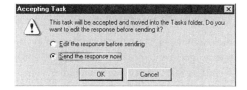

If he does not want to add any comments or stipulations, Andy can just click the Send the response now radio button. If he has something to say, he can click Edit the response before sending. A Task request tool will appear, only now with an information bar similar to the one in Figure 14.11. In the note box at the bottom of the tool, Andy can insert any reply he wishes. When finished, he clicks the Send button.

Figure 14.11.

*Formally accepting a
Task request.*

If the Task had been declined, the same options would have been presented. If the Task had been reassigned, Andy would have followed all the steps shown in the "Assigning a Current Task" section earlier in this hour.

Dealing with Changes

Sometimes, things don't always work out as planned. People get too busy to accept your Task request, or you may decide to assign a Task to someone else. The next few sections show you how to roll with these punches.

They Just Said No

This one happens sometimes. Maybe you just aren't the maniacal tyrant you used to be. Perhaps the seeds of rebellion are floating in your office. Perhaps—well, maybe they were just too busy.

When a Task is declined, it is sent back to your Inbox. If you need to reassign it or just do it yourself, you first need to get it back onto your own Task List. Double-click the message to open it. Then click the Task|Return to Task List menu command.

Now that the Task is back on your Task List, you just need to open the Task, click the Assign Task button, and try again to find a less busy (more loyal) person to help you.

14

I Changed My Mind

If you have decided that someone else may be better able to do the Task for whatever reason, you can reassign this Task to them. This will only work, however, if you have kept an updated copy of the Task in your own Task List:

1. Open the Task to be reassigned.
2. Click on the Status tab.
3. Click the Create Unassigned Copy button. When you do, a warning dialog (see Figure 14.12) will appear. Click OK.

Figure 14.12.

Creating an unassigned copy has its share of dangers.

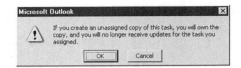

4. The field in the Task Request tool will open up, and a copy of the original Task request can now be edited as needed and sent to the new Task recipients.

So, what happens to the poor guy who was originally assigned the Task? Well, he will need to be notified of the change, so he can either delete the Task or keep working in tandem with the other assignees. What he will not be able to do is send Task updates to you anymore. Only the owner of the new Task can do this now. However, anyone who was on the status report list for the first Task will receive a status report indicating that this first Task has been completed, when the time comes.

Summary

You have just seen how easy it is to assign Tasks to someone else, so you can work harder at more of your own duties. Just remember these simple rules:

☐ When assigning Tasks, keep them simple. Try to break larger projects into smaller stages.

☐ Make sure everyone who might need to know about this project gets status reports.

☐ Even if you are the supreme ruler of your company, always be sure to say please, and be prepared to work out any scheduling conflicts. Bosses with iron wills give everyone else more stress than they need. Be especially polite if you are asking co-workers for help. Don't beg, but be ready to help them out when the time comes.

Having done all of this Task creating and assigning, are you getting a bit bored with this Task List view? Fear not, because in the next hour, we'll take a look at the Tasks in Outlook.

Q&A

Q Doesn't the use of Tasks seem a bit impersonal?

A To some extent. You'll recall that I said large jobs should be prefaced with meetings to explain in person what is going on. Tasks should not replace face-to-face meetings, but it should cut down the number of meetings, while still keeping everyone up-to-date.

Q Won't it be too difficult to assign Tasks without some kind of Microsoft messaging system?

A No, because at the very least, it saves you the step of separately e-mailing all parties, and you will still be able to update the original Task in your Task List as your assignees give their reports.

14

Hour 15

Configuring Tasks

Most of the fun of making something in the kitchen is not only getting it to taste good, but also to make it look good. Really, who wants mashed potatoes that look like moon rocks? Or chicken cordon bleu that looks flattened? Part of the appeal of food is how it looks. People are actually paid to photograph food professionally, of all things. That would be a photo shoot to see…"Come on, yes, you're steaming, broccoli! Yes, let me see more steam!"

The only exception to this is those peanut butter and cheese crackers in vending machines. I love them, but that orange is not a color found anywhere in nature.

It does take a lot of work to make a cake or pie look really good. But when all is said and done, it is usually worth it.

In the past two hours, you have been learning how to make Tasks, either for yourself or others. In this hour, we're going to learn how to make Outlook's Tasks look better.

Organizing the Really Big Jobs

If you look at Figure 15.1, you will see that the Daniels' list has grown a bit since Hour 13, "Things to Do with Tasks." It's also rather disorganized. Like many beginning Task Lists for really big projects, it is in the order of which things were thought of first.

Figure 15.1.

The Amtrak Task List: organized by train of thought.

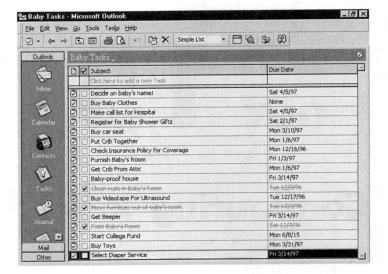

Now, at this point, you may be thinking that this is the part where the author guides you through an endless stream of different views in order to organize Tasks. Well, you're right, but there's a faster way to organize Tasks.

One of the nice things about Tasks (or any other table-based view in Outlook) is the ability to instantly sort an information field instantly just by single-clicking on the top of any column in the table.

You read that right. Let's give it a try. Nathan and Jamie Daniels, the authors of this fine Task List, would like to see this list sorted by due date, to give them a more chronological feel to the jobs ahead. Easily done. By single-clicking on the gray Due Date column head, they make the Task List sort chronologically, as shown in Figure 15.2.

But, there's a slight problem. The sort is in descending order, meaning that the date farthest in the future—June 8, 2015 (hey, they're Type A people, what can I say?)—is listed first. This is symbolized by the little arrow pointing down in the column head. To fix this, just click the column head again. Now, the arrow head points up, and the Tasks are listed in a more useful fashion (see Figure 15.3).

15

Figure 15.2.

Sorted by Due Date...sort of.

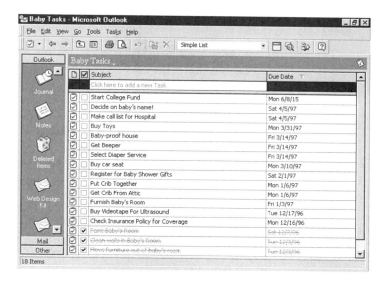

Figure 15.3.

Sorted by Due Date from now to then.

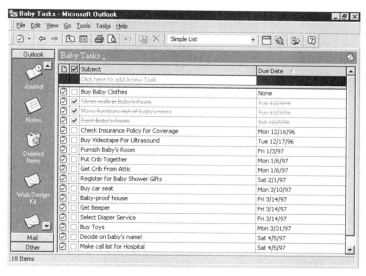

If the Daniels were librarians, perhaps they would want the Tasks listed alphabetically by subject. Clicking on Subject once will give them an ascending list of Tasks. Clicking on it again will make the Tasks' subjects descending. This technique works on any column field in any table view in Outlook.

Now it's time to see all the other views in Tasks.

Detailed List

The Detailed List view is my personal favorite. It contains all the information I think is relevant. Specifically, it shows the Icon, Priority, Attachment, Subject, Status, Due Date, % Complete, and Categories.

JUST A MINUTE

> All the table views in Tasks show the same first four fields, in this order: Icon, Priority, Attachment, and Subject. For the sake of avoiding a lot of redundancy, these will be referred to as the *default fields* from now on.

All Tasks, complete or not, are listed in this view (see Figure 15.4).

Figure 15.4.

The Detailed List view.

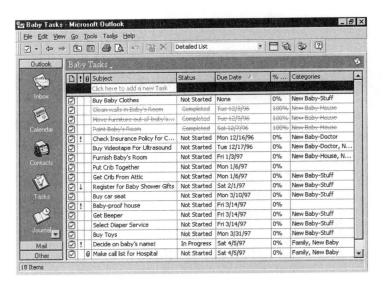

Active Tasks

In the Active Tasks view, the same fields as the Detailed List are shown, only now a filter has been applied. Remember, a filter lets only a certain type of data be shown at all. A view definition establishes how that data is displayed.

In this case, the filter basically says, "Show only the Tasks currently due (not completed) in the Detailed List view, and call it the Active Tasks view."

The results of this eloquent filter are shown in Figure 15.5.

15

Figure 15.5.

The Active Tasks view.

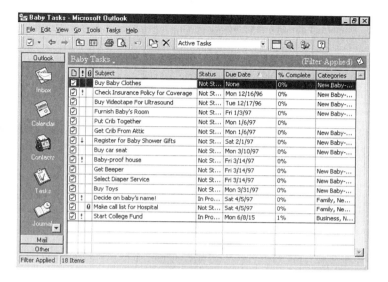

Next Seven Days

Again, the Next Seven Days view is a variant of the Detailed List view. This time, the filter lists only those Tasks with due dates that fall sometime within the next seven days (including today). This is a nice thing to have for those who like the short view (see Figure 15.6).

Figure 15.6.

The Next Seven Days view.

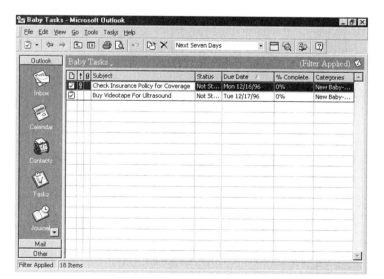

Overdue Tasks

Even with Tasks, nobody's perfect, and sometimes things will be forgotten or there just isn't enough time. That's where this next view comes in. By filtering out all but the overdue Tasks, the Overdue Tasks view allows you to see what you needed to get done yesterday. Although you can't tell in Figure 15.7, all items in this view are displayed in red for emphasis.

Figure 15.7.

The Overdue Tasks view.

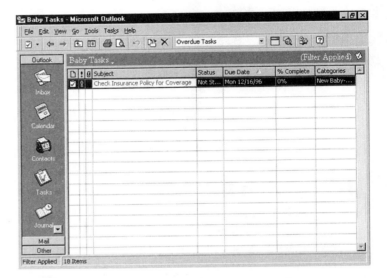

By Category

The By Category view gets away from the Detailed List variants a bit. The same information fields are still listed, and there is no filter, but now the Tasks are grouped into Group Boxes. In this view, the groups are the Tasks' categories (see Figure 15.8). As you will learn later this hour in the "Creating Your Own Views" section, groups can be of any information field you wish: Status, Subject, Due Date, and so on.

After looking at Figure 15.8, you may be wondering where the heck did all the Tasks go? They're there, only in a nice collapsed Group Box. To open (or expand, in Outlook lingo) a Group Box, just single-click on the tiny plus sign on the left end of the Group Box. Immediately, the plus sign changes to a minus sign, and the Tasks in this Group become visible, as seen in Figure 15.9.

15

Figure 15.8.

*The By Category view
(collapsed).*

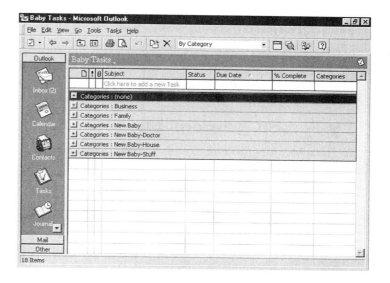

Figure 15.9.

*The By Category view
(expanded).*

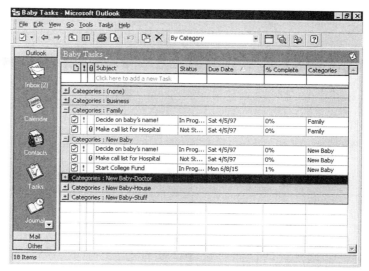

To reverse this procedure, just click on the minus signs.

Take a look at Figure 15.9 again. Notice that some of the Tasks are repeated across groups.
This happens with Tasks that are marked by more than one category. This view makes it easy
to cross-reference activities in Tasks.

Assignment

This next view is used to show all Tasks you have assigned to others and kept an update copy. Besides the default fields, Owner, Due Date, and Status are listed. The Owner field indicates who is the new owner of the Task (essentially, who is responsible for this duty).

By Person Responsible

If you have assigned a lot of Tasks to a bunch of different people, the By Person Responsible view will be of use to you. It shows the same fields as the Assignment view, only with Group Boxes sorted by the owner of the Task.

Completed Tasks

Always look ahead, that's my motto. But there are times when looking behind to see what you've done is important, too (such as at job evaluation time). The Completed Tasks view shows the default fields, Due Date, Date Completed, and Categories. A filter is used to show only those Tasks that have been finished. When you look at Figure 15.10, note that the completed Tasks in this view are no longer in a strikethrough font.

Figure 15.10.

The Completed Tasks view.

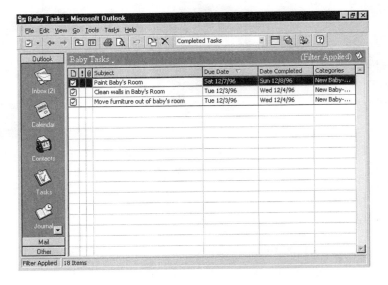

15

Task Timeline

The final view available in Tasks is surely the most unique. It is a timeline view of all the Tasks you have. You will learn a lot more about navigating through a timeline in Hour 17, "The Journal—My So-Called Diary," but let's walk through some of the basics now.

To open any Task you see, you would still double-click it to get the Task tool, so that's nothing new. Now, take a peek at Figure 15.11. You can see there are only two Tasks visible, but there's something important to note about them.

Figure 15.11.

Looking at the Task Timeline.

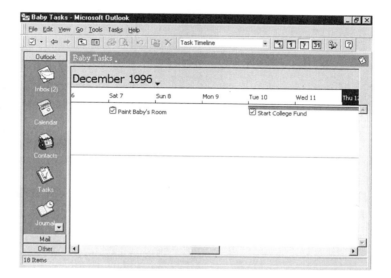

On the left is the Paint Baby's Room Task. On every other view (except Completed Tasks), this Task was finished and marked, complete with a strikethrough font. No longer. This view does not show you what's complete until you open a Task.

The next Task, Start College Fund, shows what a Task with a defined start and end date looks like. That gray bar extends all the way to the end date of the Task (in this case, June 2015).

If you look at the standard toolbar, you'll see that it has changed, too. It now sports Daily, Weekly, and Monthly view buttons, just as in Calendar. The view in Figure 15.11 is the Weekly Task Timeline, the default. Figure 15.12 shows the Daily view. Notice that the times for all the Tasks are at midnight of the Task's due date.

Figure 15.12.

The Daily Task Timeline.

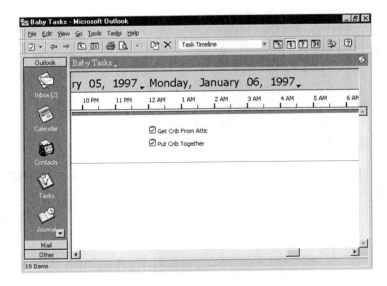

Figure 15.13 shows the Monthly view. Subjects of Tasks in this view are not visible until you move the mouse cursor over them, causing a label of the subject to appear.

Figure 15.13.

The Monthly Task Timeline.

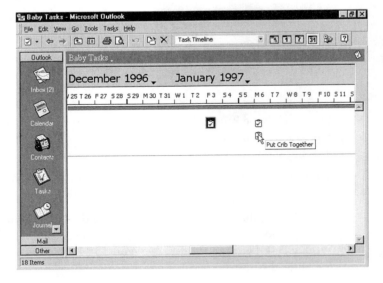

15

Moving around in the Task Timeline can be done in two ways, by using either the scrollbars at the bottom of the timeline (slow) or the Date Navigators. The Navigators have been cleverly hidden within each Day or Month heading in the upper section of the timeline. To make them visible, click on the little arrow next to a Date heading, as shown in Figure 15.14.

Figure 15.14.

The timelines' Date Navigator.

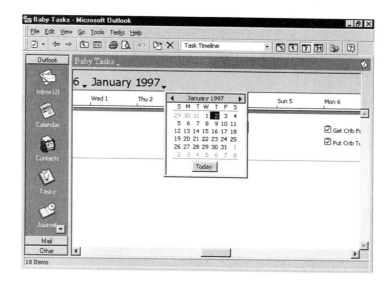

Remember, you can always get back to today by clicking the Today button in the Date Navigator or Standard Toolbar.

Creating Your Own Views

Like any other Outlook tool, Tasks lets you redefine or create any view of your Tasks you wish. (Remember, Tasks is part of Outlook, and Outlook is really one big database.) If you recall from Hour 12, "Configuring Calendar," there are three main ways to do this:

☐ Group Items

☐ Redefine Current Views

☐ Create a New View

Because we covered all these topics back in Hour 12, let's just concentrate a little bit on redefining Tasks' views and creating a new view.

Redefining Views

All of Tasks' views are in table form, which makes it easy to change things if you do not like what's being shown. When you click the View | Define Views menu command, the Define Views for "*Folder Name*" dialog appears. *Folder Name* is a placeholder for the name of the folder you are viewing. In this case, it's "Baby Tasks" (see Figure 15.15). From here, you can change the look of every Tasks view.

Figure 15.15.

The Define Views dialog.

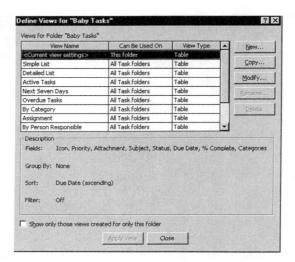

To change a current view, click the Modify button on the right side of the dialog. This brings up the View Summary dialog, as shown in Figure 15.16. This shows all the current settings for your current view and has five buttons that serve as jump points to other dialogs that can modify these settings. The functionality of these different dialogs is shown in Hour 12, so we won't repeat ourselves here.

Creating a New View

Creating a new view is much the same as modifying a current view. If you click the New button in the Define Views for "*Folder Name*" dialog, you will see the Create a New View dialog (see Figure 15.17). It enables you to give the new view a name and set what view type you want to base your view on. The radio buttons at the bottom allow you to choose who gets to see this new view and to which folder the view will apply. After clicking OK, a blank View Summary dialog appears, which you can modify just as you've learned in the last section and in Hour 12.

15

Figure 15.16.

The View Summary dialog.

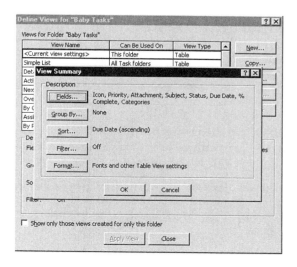

Figure 15.17.

The Create a New View dialog.

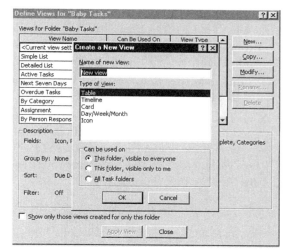

Summary

In this hour, you learned the ins and outs of organizing and viewing your Tasks. A lot of the functionality of defining these views is similar across all of Outlook's tools, so there should not have been anything to toss you for a loop.

What is important to remember from the last three hours is that when you first start to use Tasks, you need to stick with it. Despite how simple it is to enter a new Task, it may seem really tedious at first, and the short-term benefits do not seem all that special.

JUST A MINUTE

> Confessions of a convert: When I first started using Outlook, I hated Tasks. However, after using it faithfully, I really find it's a good tool to keep your head (and act) together.
>
> Be healed, brothers and sisters!

However, the long-term benefits are great because right now, it may not be hard to keep track of the things you need to do today, and even tomorrow, but what about next Tuesday? or next month? A little harder, isn't it?

So, if you stick to it, you will find Tasks to be a strong Outlook tool that you'll use every day.

Q&A

Q **How can I keep really detailed Tasks? I can't see these details in any of the standard views.**

A What I like to do is keep all the heavy details in the Task's note box or an attached file. Then I mark the Subject of the Task with an asterisk (*) to let me know there's more information I need to look at.

Q **I like to keep a simple text list on my computer to remind me of things to do. Will I have to retype all this in to Tasks?**

A Sort of. Try this: Create a Task with a dummy Subject line and dates. Then copy and paste this dummy Task until you match your number of things to do. After you open the document and arrange the windows so both Tasks and the To Do list are visible, you can select and drag your item to go right into the Task List, thanks to Office's OLE capabilities.

PART
VI

Notes and Journal: Small, Yet Savvy

Hour

Hour **16**

Not-So-Sticky Notes

The next time someone tells you that we will one day live in a paper-free society, feel free to laugh in his or her face. We will never be totally free of paper or its influence—at least, not for a very long time. Say, five or six centuries, give or take a decade.

This is not just an author trying to justify his medium. The art of the written word will long survive the passing of paper. This isn't the ranting of some tree-phobic, either. I like trees, and I recycle paper as much as possible.

This argument is based on the physical concept of inertia. Paper, archeologists estimate, has been around since papyrus was first used in ancient Egypt over 4,700 years ago. That's a lot of momentum built up.

Once an idea gets into humankind's collective head, it becomes a difficult thing to change society's mind. Money is a good example. Computers are just about sophisticated enough to handle almost any financial transaction we need, but there is still that need to have cash on hand. ATM cards are great, but it's also nice to see the moolah once in a while.

And computers can handle any kind of document you can think of. Indeed, the invention of the computer also brought about the invention of quite a few new kinds of documents. However, people who use computers every day still think in terms of paper. For instance, "How many pages is that Word document?" or "Where is the network printer located?" These topics are always there, lurking in the background.

Once in a while, a form of paper is so good, it gets translated directly into electronic form. The spreadsheet is a good example. The whole row/column/cell metaphor didn't just appear in some programmer's head. Spreadsheets were huge sheets of paper with sometimes hundreds of rows and columns of financial data, which accountants had to spread out over big tables and check by hand.

In this hour, we will look at another kind of paper that has made the leap directly to electrons: the sticky note. Outlook has taken the entire sticky note phenomenon and made a whole new computer version of it—right down to the ubiquitous pastel color schemes.

Passing Notes

Okay, electronic sticky notes are a novel idea, you say, but what good are they?

I say a lot. Notes in Outlook are sort of a cross between a Task, an Appointment, and a Contact. Notes let you jot down any kind of information you want—activities, reminders, phone numbers—and let you keep them indefinitely. If you use Outlook as much as I think you will, Notes should be one of your primary tools. As we will see later this hour, once you save something in Notes, it's there to stay and can easily be transferred to a more functional part of Outlook: Tasks, Calendar, even the Inbox.

Because of all this flexibility, Notes has some limitations. Notes cannot be set to remind you of something with a beep and a dialog message. Nor can a Note be directly sent to someone else via e-mail. A Note doesn't have a lot of fancy controls and display settings, and it cannot recur.

By creating a new Note, you'll be able to see just what a Note can and cannot do for you.

Creating a Note

There are five ways to start a new Note, shown in the following list:

☐ If you are not in Outlook, you can click the New Note button on the Microsoft Office Shortcut Bar, shown in Figure 16.1.

☐ If you are in Notes, you can click the Note | New Note menu command or the New Note button on the Standard Toolbar.

16

☐ If you are in a Note item, click on the Note icon in the upper-left corner, and then click the New Note menu command.

☐ If you are in some other part of Outlook, you can click on the New Note command on the New Item drop-down list in the Standard Toolbar (see Figure 16.1).

☐ Finally, if you like shortcut keys, hit Ctrl+N if you are in Notes and Ctrl+Shift+N if you are anywhere else in Outlook.

Figure 16.1.
Starting a new Note.

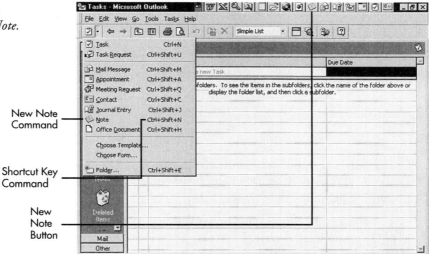

New Note Command

Shortcut Key Command

New Note Button

Once you do any of these procedures, a little yellow box is going to pop up onto your screen, as seen in Figure 16.2.

JUST A MINUTE

Just a quick word about colors. Because all of the money in this book was spent on the exorbitant author wages (ha, ha), this book was printed in black and white. Notes uses blue, green, pink, yellow, and white for background colors. Yellow is the default, and that is what will be used unless otherwise noted.

So, you'll just have to believe me.

Let's look at this intricate Note closely. You can see a document icon in the upper-left corner and a close window button in the upper-right corner. In the bottom of the Note is a section containing the time and date the Note was created and a resizing tool in the lower-right corner.

Figure 16.2.

*A brand-new, empty,
yellow Note.*

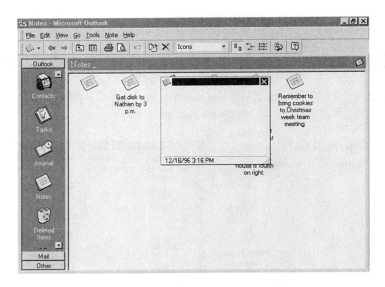

That's it. No menus, no save buttons…not even the omnipresent Windows OK button. So, it's safe to move onto the next hour, right? Not exactly. After all, a simple lever can move the world, if put in the right place.

To write a Note, simply type the message you want into the Note, such as the one Barney of Quantum Ink has created in Figure 16.3. Once you have done this, you can save it as is or set some of the Note's parameters, so you can organize it. Because we will want the full functionality of Notes, let's not save the Note yet.

Figure 16.3.

A little Note of Horrors.

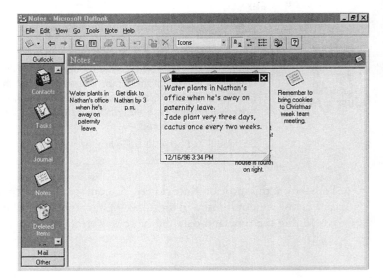

16

Notes have two main parameters with which they can be organized: color and categories. You may use one or both, or none, if you prefer. Barney likes to use both. To access these parameters, Barney clicks on the Notes icon in the Note and sees the menu shown in Figure 16.4.

Figure 16.4.

Setting more Note detail.

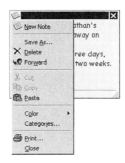

To change the color of a Note, click on the Colors command, then on any of the five color choices presented to you (see Figure 16.5). This is a personal reminder for Barney, and he codes them as blue.

Figure 16.5.

Chasing those naughty blues.

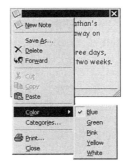

To assign a category to the Note, click the Categories command. The Categories dialog appears, as shown in Figure 16.6, where any number of categories can be assigned to the Note. As you learned in Hour 10, "Keeping Track of Your Life," additional categories can be added by clicking the Master Category List button. Once you choose the categories you want, click OK, and you'll see that the Note has not changed in the slightest. Categories are only shown in selected views of Notes' Information Viewer screen, as you will see later in this hour.

After you have done all that you need to do to the Note, click the close window button to instantly save it to Outlook's database. You could save it into another format by using the Save As command you saw on the Note document menu, but I do not recommend it for time-saving reasons.

Figure 16.6.

*Establishing a Note's
categories.*

JUST A MINUTE

Notes are continuously saved, even after their initial creation. If you open
a Note (new or otherwise), make a change, and click anything outside the
Note, that change is instantly reflected in all the views of Notes' information viewer.

After closing the Note, it will appear in the information viewer (see Figure 16.7). In the Icon
view (Notes' default view), the first paragraph of every note is displayed, no matter how long
or short.

Figure 16.7.

*Viewing Notes in the
Icon view.*

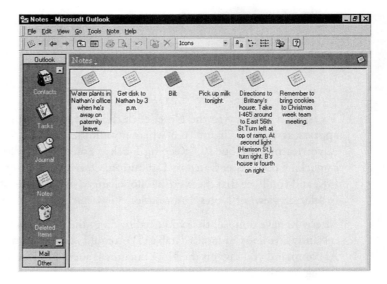

16

JUST A MINUTE

When you create a Note, it is recommended that you keep the first paragraph of the Note short, yet descriptive. If it is too long, way too much screen real estate will be hogged by the Note, but beware of letting it be too short (see Figure 16.7). The Note to Bill in Figure 16.7 tells us nothing in Icon view.

16

Editing a Note

If you see something in a Note that needs to be changed, click on the Note item in any Notes view. The Note will open, and you can make your changes in the Note's text, color, or categories.

You can also resize an open Note. To do this, move the mouse until the cursor is on the lower-right corner of the Note. When the cursor changes to the diagonal resizing cursor (see Figure 16.8), click the left mouse button and size the Note to your heart's content. When you are done, let go of the mouse button. This is a handy way of seeing all of the Note's text at once.

Figure 16.8.

Resizing a Note.

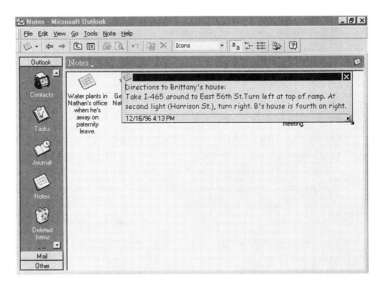

TIME SAVER

Like any other window in Windows 95, you can also use the pop-up menu for the Note in the Taskbar to Maximize the Note to full screen.

If you do this, be forewarned: The window can no longer be resized, and (more annoying) every subsequent Note will appear like this. To get smaller Notes, use that same pop-up menu and click Restore.

If the need for your Note has passed, highlight the Note and click the Delete button in the Standard Toolbar. If the soon-to-be-vaporized Note is open, click the Note document menu, followed by the Delete command.

Organizing and Configuring Your Notes

When I was in school, I had my notes all very organized. Notes to Lisa were in one side of the desk's drawer, notes to Gretchen on the other, and notes to Aubrey in the middle. This may not seem all that important, but I still remember the trouble I got into the one time I goofed up this system. Fifth-grade girls can really *punch*.

While your motivations may not be so life-threatening, it's still nice to be able to get all your Notes into some kind of pattern, so they can more easily help you.

To aid you in this endeavor, Notes has five different views to see your Notes. We have already seen the first: the Icon view.

The remaining four views of Notes are all table views, which you should be familiar with by now. A quick look at them will allow you to make a decision on which view you prefer.

The Notes List view shows the Icon, Subject, Created, and Categories information fields. The icons are colored with the same color the Note has been created or edited with. The Subject shows the first paragraph of the Note. If it is too long, ellipses indicate that the Subject continues. Created shows the date the Note was first made. It is the default sorting column for the Notes List view, meaning that all the Notes are sorted from newest to oldest created. The Categories field shows the categories the Note falls under.

Another default setting for the Notes List view, as you can see in Figure 16.9, is the AutoPreview, allowing you to read the first few lines of the Note's contents. This feature can be deactivated by clicking the AutoPreview button in the Standard Toolbar.

The next view, Last Seven Days, also has a default AutoPreview setting. In fact, it is identical to the Notes List view in every way, except that now a filter has been applied to the data. This filter only allows Notes modified in the last seven days to be displayed. On Barney's Notes list, only one old Note drops out (see Figure 16.10), but this view is nice if you use Notes a lot.

16

Figure 16.9.

The Notes List view.

The AutoPreview button

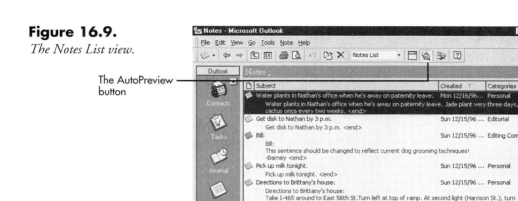

Figure 16.10.

The Last Seven Days view.

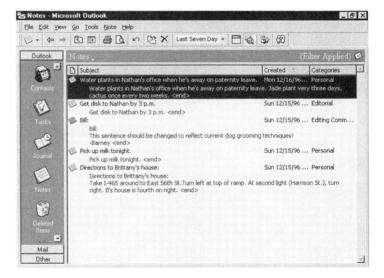

The By Category view only displays three information fields: Icon, Subject, and Created. This time, the Notes are grouped into their respective categories.

The default view of the By Category view has all the groups closed, but this can be changed by clicking on the little box with the plus sign in it on the left side of the group box. This expands the category, as seen in Figure 16.11. To collapse the category again, simply click on the minus sign in the group box.

Figure 16.11.

The By Category view.

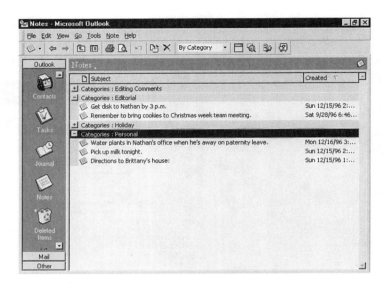

The last view provided by Notes is the By Color view. This view is identical to the By Category view, although now the Notes are grouped by their color (see Figure 16.12).

Figure 16.12.

The By Color view.

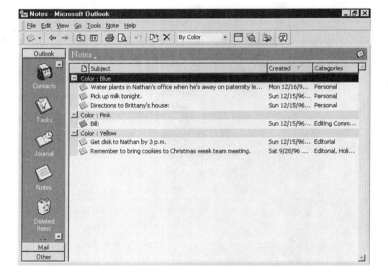

16

TIME SAVER

For the sake of example, we showed Notes that were organized by color and category. In real life, this kind of detail would probably be really silly and counter-productive as well. This is especially true, given the presence of these last two views.

I recommend using the following organizational techniques, based on your needs:

Organized with	If...
Color	...you have five or less loose groups you want to organize your Notes in
Category	...you have a lot of more organized groups for your Notes
Both color and category	...you have a group that can be subdivided into smaller groups

Like any other tool in Outlook, all these views can be customized to suit your needs. Because this has been shown in some detail in Hour 12, "Configuring Calendar," see that hour for more information.

There is one other set of configuration parameters you can set in Notes, the Note item itself. To do this, click on the Tools | Options menu command in Notes. This activates the Options dialog, shown in Figure 16.13.

Figure 16.13.

The Tasks/Notes tab of the Options dialog.

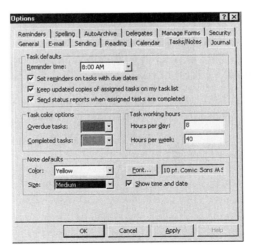

Most of the Tasks/Notes tab is dedicated to the Tasks tool, but down at the bottom of the dialog there's a little Notes default section that is of interest to us.

The Color drop-down list sets the default color of the Note when it is first created. It can be set to any of the five available colors of Notes.

The Size drop-down list sets the default size of the Note. The differences of the three sizes (small, medium, or large) can be seen in Figure 16.14.

Figure 16.14.

Would you like small, medium, or large fries with your order?

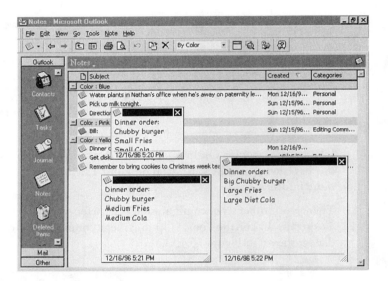

The Font button, when clicked, activates the standard Windows Font dialog (see Figure 16.15). With it, you can set the size, appearance, and color of the Notes font. When you are finished, a sample of the font appears in the field just to the right of the Font button.

Finally, the Show time and date check box causes a new Note to display this information when a new Note is created in the Note itself.

After changing any of these controls, click Apply or OK to apply the changes to the next new Note created.

Figure 16.15.

So many fonts, so little time.

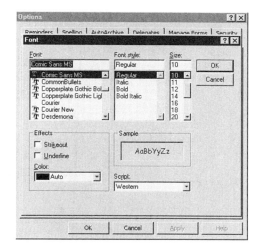

Putting Notes in Their Place

One nice feature of Notes is that they can be directed to other parts of Outlook, even other files on your computer. To be truthful, this feature is available with any Outlook item: a Task, a Contact, or whatever. However, with Notes, it's a lot faster (and therefore easier) to use because of the very small file size a Note has.

The very nature of a Note—sort of a sticky note slapped on a bigger document—also lends itself to this kind of use.

To send a Note to another part of Outlook, click once on the Note item in any view, and drag the Note until it superimposes any of the icons in the Outlook bar or any of the folders in the Folder list.

When you send a Note to another part of Outlook, you essentially begin the AutoCreate function. For example, sending a Note to Contacts will AutoCreate a new Contact with the body of the Note appearing within a New Contact dialog (see Figure 16.16). Notice that the Category for the Note has been moved into the Contact's category field.

Figure 16.16.

The Note is now in the note box of the new Contact.

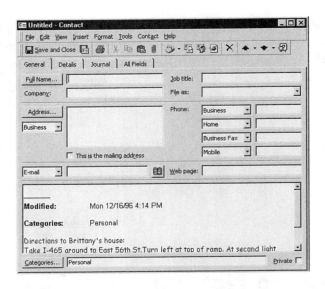

This action is repeated whenever you send a Note to any part of Outlook. If you want to have a Note appear as an attached object inside of an Outlook item, the procedure is slightly different:

1. To attach a Note to an Outlook item (for this example, let's say a Contact), open that item first.

2. Click on the Insert | Item menu command.

3. In the Insert Item dialog (see Figure 16.17), navigate until the Notes folder is highlighted above and you can see the contents of the Notes folder below.

Figure 16.17.

Finding a Note to attach.

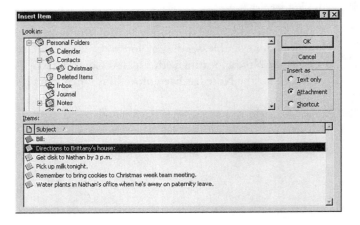

16

4. Be sure the Insert as setting is set for Attachment. Click OK.

Now, a Note item will be embedded within your Contact item, as seen in Figure 16.18. To open this Note, simply double-click it whenever the item it's attached to is open.

JUST A MINUTE

Whenever you attach a Note to any Outlook item, its icon always appears as yellow, despite any other color it has within Notes.

Figure 16.18.

The Note is now attached to the Contact.

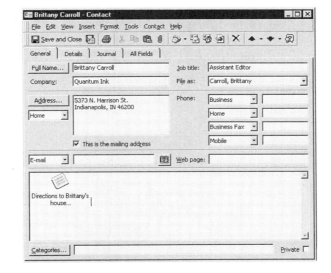

Summary

By now, you should have a good idea of how to quickly create and organize Notes in Outlook. Use them for those in-between things that don't quite fit into a Task or Calendar item.

If used in this manner, Notes will soon become the glue that holds Outlook together.

Q&A

Q I really don't like any of the pastel colors of Notes. Can I change them?

A No. Unfortunately, there is no way (short of programming) to add more color choices to Notes.

Q Can I attach a Note to my desktop?

A With ease. Select the note, and drop it anywhere on the desktop. It will turn yellow, but that will be the only change to the Note from seeing it in Icon view.

Q I have tried to drag and drop a Note into my Word document, and all I get is text information. I can't find the Note to attach it from Word, either. Can I do this?

A Yes, but first you have to get the Note out into the open as a separate file. Notes are generally just data items in Outlook's big database. However, if you drag the Note out to the desktop first, the Note becomes a separate *.msg (Microsoft Mail Message) file, which you then can drag into your Word document as an embedded file, complete with a little yellow Note icon. (By the way, you can do this with any Outlook item.)

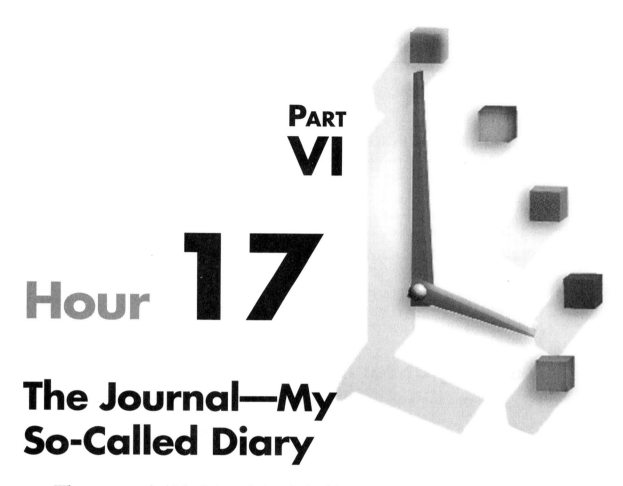

PART VI

17

Hour

The Journal—My So-Called Diary

When many people think of a journal, they think of their sacred diaries of their youth. These tiny books, kept under lock and key, contained thoughts and feelings that could never be shared with anyone else.

And then there were the rest of us, trying to sneak a peek at them.

Journals have been kept by people both famous and infamous ever since writing started. At first, they were probably just used to help someone with a faulty memory keep track of just what they did that day. Then, along came publishers and lucrative book contracts, and suddenly "Spent day shopping at the mall for a blender," became "For the entire day, I began the search for the one perfect item that would brighten my kitchen."

Outlook's Journal is not quite as flowery as that. It is a very utilitarian tool that gets back to the real roots of journal-keeping. In other words, it helps you and your faulty memory keep your work straight.

To do this, Journal automatically records any activity you do with Outlook or Office 97. It also lets you manually record accomplishments or activities. This may not sound like a big deal. Think about it this way: Try to recall the actual filenames of *all* of the files you worked on the day before yesterday. Can you? If you can, you're good. Now think of the files you worked on a week ago Tuesday.

If any of these questions stumped you, don't let it bother you too much. Some days, I can't remember what I worked on that morning. But sooner or later, you will need to get a hold of that file you sent to your boss last week, and darned if you can remember the filename.

Or, a more likely scenario would be this: What if you need to get a hold of the next-to-last version of the document because the last version's changes were unsatisfactory?

Tracking these kinds of things down by filename and version would take a lot of time. But Journal allows you to look at your workday not by which files you worked on, but by which files you worked on *when*. For a lot of us, this is a much easier way to perceive our workday.

Looking at Journal

When you first look at Journal, it seems quite a bit different from the other tools in Outlook. Figure 17.1 shows Journal in its default view, By Type. There are other views of Journal, of course, but in this hour let's stick with this one. A closer examination of all the Journal views is in Hour 18, "Configuring Journal."

Figure 17.1.

The Journal in Outlook.

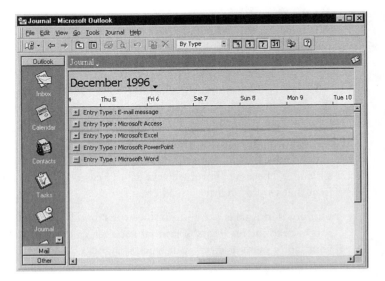

17

This view of Journal is called a timeline view. All of the Journal items appear on a specific date and time of the timeline. This date reflects when the item was created or when the last version of the item was saved. Of course, we can't see these items because the group boxes in this view are all collapsed.

Group boxes allow you to group Outlook items by any criteria you want. Here, the document type is the grouping criterion. Type, in this case, is the kind of Office 97 document.

CAUTION

If you have just upgraded from an older version of Office, you are going to find that Journal will be rather empty for a while, because Journal will not autorecord anything other than Office 97 and Outlook events.

If Outlook is your only installed Office 97 product, you will find the functionality of Journal extremely limited. All Office-based events will have to be manually recorded.

Like group boxes in other areas of Outlook, the items within them expand or collapse using the small plus/minus sign box on the left side of the group box. Clicking on a plus sign expands the group, while clicking on a minus sign collapses it (see Figure 17.2).

Figure 17.2.

Open and shut groups.

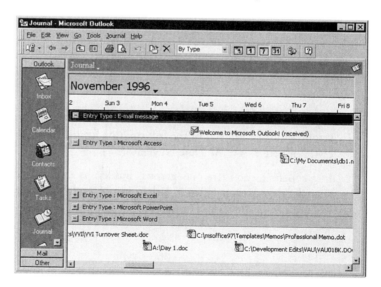

In the expanded groups, you will see tiny icons with one-line tags next to them. These tags will either be a filename and its full directory path, or perhaps the subject of a mail message or meeting request. Also, notice the icons. They all bear striking resemblances to the icons of their parent programs—little Word icons for Word documents and little Mail icons for Outlook's Inbox items—except for one difference. In the lower-left corner of each icon (squint now) is a tiny clock. This additional symbol is Journal's clever way to indicate that this item is *not* a Word or Excel document. Instead, it is a Journal entry for that document.

The distinction here is important to get a handle on now. Otherwise, if you double-click one of these items expecting to get the actual document, you will get a surprise. A Journal entry for a document (or Outlook item) contains information on when the document was created, who created it, and how long it was opened last, among other things. Figure 17.3 shows an open Journal entry and the kind of information it contains.

Figure 17.3.

A Journal entry for a Word template.

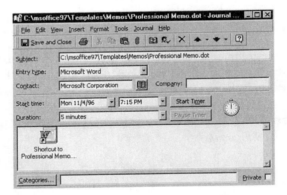

Navigating around the timeline views in Outlook is fairly simple. You can either use the scrollbars at the bottom of the information viewer to move forward and backward in time or (even better) use the Date Navigator.

In a timeline, the Date Navigator is hidden in a rather sneaky way. See those little black triangles next to each day or month heading? If you click on one of them, the Date Navigator will appear, as shown in Figure 17.4.

Figure 17.4.

The timeline Date Navigator.

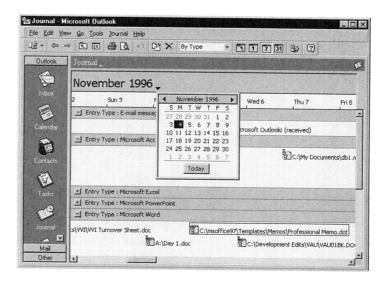

If you want to see what's in today's Journal, simply click the Today button in the Date Navigator or the same button in the Standard Toolbar.

Is This Thing On?

At this point in the hour, I usually start telling you about how to create a new item in whatever part of Outlook that's being discussed. Life is full of surprises, because now it's time to show you how Journal can create new entries for you.

Journal will automatically record three types of activities:

- ☐ Any Office 97 document created from an Office 97 program. This includes any future members of the Office 97-compatibility club.
- ☐ Any e-mail, message request and response, or task request and response to and from any Contact you wish.
- ☐ Any phone call that you make from Outlook.

When you install Outlook, there are a number of default settings for what gets automatically recorded and what doesn't. To get at these options, click on the Tools | Options menu command in Journal. The Options dialog, shown in Figure 17.5, will appear.

Figure 17.5.

The Journal Options dialog.

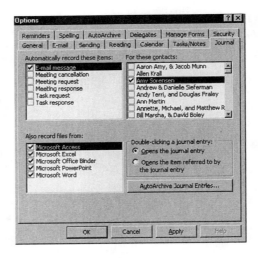

Three of the four sections in this dialog are used to set recording configurations. The two at the top are directly related to each other. The section on the left, Automatically record these items, gives you a choice of what kind of Outlook transaction you want Journal to monitor. The For these contacts section lets you pick whose transactions you will monitor. For example, I might want to record all e-mail messages between myself and my friend Amy, which is the setting shown in Figure 17.5.

One thing to keep in mind: You can't monitor one kind of Outlook transaction for one set of people and another transmission type for another group. If you choose e-mail, tasks, and so on, those transactions *all* will be recorded for *all* the Contacts you choose.

TIME SAVER

There is another way to begin recording interactions with a certain Contact. Try this:

1. Open the Contact item.
2. Click on the Journal tab.
3. Click the Automatically record journal entries for this contact check box.
4. Click Save and Close.

From now on, everything Outlook can automatically record will be done for that person.

17

The Also record files from option lets you set which Office 97 document types you want to record. This is pretty straightforward. You can record any combination of Office documents.

The remaining section in this dialog box is dicussed on later in this hour.

I did say that you could also automatically record phone calls made from Outlook, and the Options dialog appears to have made a liar out of me. After all, there was no phone call setting, was there? This is one of those hidden tricks of Outlook. To exploit this trick, follow these steps:

1. From any part of Outlook, click on the Tools | Dial | New Call menu command, or press the Ctrl+Shift+D shortcut key combination.

2. In the New Call dialog (see Figure 17.6), enter the name of the person or organization you want to call.

Figure 17.6.

The New Call dialog.

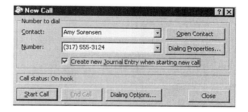

3. If the person is in your Contact list, click on the correct phone number choice in the Number field. Otherwise, type in the phone number in the Number field.

4. If you want Journal to record this call, click the Create new Journal Entry when starting new call check box.

5. Click the Start Call button. The call will go through, and an Entry will be added to the Journal.

Activate Manual Override

Journal is not limited to just recording these few things. In actuality, Journal can record pretty much anything you do on and off your computer. This function is called manually recording something, and it's simple to use. Before I show you how to accomplish these feats of daring do, it would be better to first show you around the Journal Entry tool, the place where you will always end up.

Figure 17.7 shows a Journal Entry tool for a Word document Andy Hiromatsu was working on for Quantum Ink's Web site.

Figure 17.7.

The Journal Entry tool.

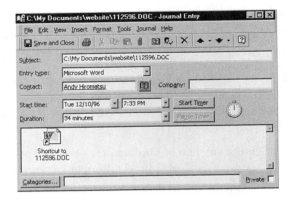

The Subject field contains a full DOS path to the file. It can contain anything, as long as it's related to the document. You wouldn't want to call a Web site document Journal Entry, "Recipe for Barbecue Ribs," after all.

The Entry Type field is comprised of a large drop-down list that contains all the choices you should need to define this Entry (see Figure 17.8). If what you want is not there, you are going to have to improvise, as direct entry to this field is not allowed. The only way more choices can be provided is when a new Office-compatible program is installed.

Figure 17.8.

Some of the Journal Entry types available.

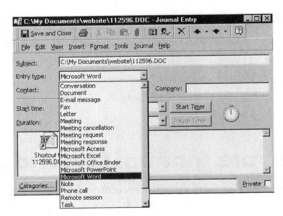

The Contact field contains the name of anyone associated with the document, whether it be creator, collaborator, or editor. If the name is underlined, this means the person or company is in your Contact list. Just to the right of the Contact field is an Address Book button. If you click this, the Select Names dialog, shown in Figure 17.9, appears. By highlighting the names on the left, then clicking Add, you can quickly move people to the right column. When you are done, click OK, and all the names on the right will appear in the Contact field.

17

Figure 17.9.

The Select Names dialog.

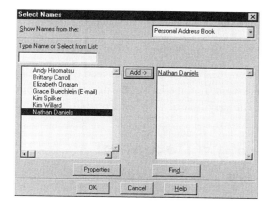

The Company field is a text-only field where you can enter a company associated with the Entry.

TIME SAVER

> To keep the number of Categories in the Master Category List down, I sometimes use the Company field to record the name of a larger project the Entry may be a part of. When I view the Entries in one of Journal's table views, I can easily see the items associated with this project.

The next section gives the time and date details for the Entry. The Start time fields show the date and time the document was last edited.

JUST A MINUTE

> Always remember that the Start time does not necessarily reflect the creation date of a document. If the Journal Entry is not for the original version of the document, the Start time shows the time the last editing session was begun.

You can change these times, but it will only have the effect of moving the Entry on the Journal timeline. It will not change the document's actual times. So, Andy could change the Journal to show this document was edited on Dec. 9, but anyone looking at the document's own information will know otherwise.

The Duration field shows the total time the document was last opened. It too can be changed manually, but it only affects the Journal Entry, not the document itself.

The neatest use for the Duration field is as a stopwatch. Want to time a meeting or a phone call? Click the Start Timer button. When you are finished, click the Pause Timer button. Now your event is accurately timed.

The next three fields—the Notebox, Categories, and Private fields—are old acquaintances to you by now, so let's not spend time on them. Two more things to note before we end this little tour are the Previous and Next Item buttons in the toolbar.

These buttons enable you to proceed through all the Journal Entries one at a time, forward or backward. If you click on the drop-down menus, you can also move to the adjacent item, or to the very first or very last Entry in the Journal.

Entering a Document

At this point, you may be getting a bit nervous about all of this. This seems like a lot of information you have to enter, so why would you even bother?

Well, you will soon see that manually recording something is not as manual as you might think.

Take recording a document. Think you have to enter all of the DOS path in the Subject field? Think again. To enter a document into the Journal, follow these steps:

1. Open Outlook and your preferred file navigator (Windows Explorer will do nicely).
2. Arrange it so both applications' windows are visible on the screen.
3. Click and drag the file over to the Journal icon on the Outlook bar or the Journal folder in the Folder List.
4. A new Journal Entry tool will appear. You can enter any pertinent information into it now.
5. Click Save and Close.

Now an Entry for this document will appear in Journal. Easy, eh?

Entering an Outlook Item

The procedure for entering an Outlook item is even more simple because you don't have to fuss with window positioning. To manually record an Outlook item, follow these steps:

1. Find the item you want to record in Outlook.
2. Click and drag the file over to the Journal icon on the Outlook bar or the Journal folder in the Folder List.
3. A new Journal Entry tool will appear (see Figure 17.10). You can enter any additional information into it now.
4. Click Save and Close.

17

Figure 17.10.

Recording an Outlook Task.

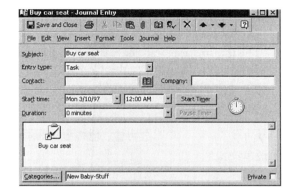

Again, not too hard. Journal Entries are designed to be automated. In fact, they even show up in other parts of Outlook.

Entering a Contact Activity

Many activities that can be recorded in Journal often have a Contact or two associated with them. After all, it takes two to tango, right? If you are the kind of person who remembers things by people association, you are in luck. Outlook lets you assign Journal Entries related to a Contact from the Contact item itself.

When you want to do this, use the following procedure:

1. Open the Contact item you need to work with.
2. In the Contact tool, click the Journal tab. If you have already set Journal to automatically record for this Contact, the tab should look similar to Figure 17.11.

Figure 17.11.

A Contact's Journal tab.

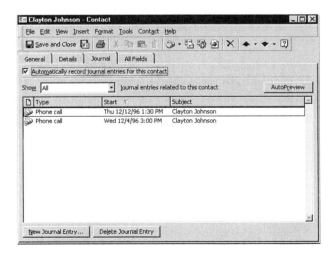

3. If you click the New Journal Entry button toward the bottom of the tab, a new Journal Entry tool will appear.

4. The information fields have default information already entered, showing a phone call about to be made to this Contact (see Figure 17.12). You can quickly change this to another type of activity.

5. After making your changes, including timing the activity, click Save and Close.

Figure 17.12.

Recording a phone call to a Contact.

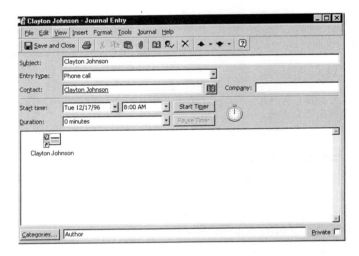

Entering Everything Else

This happens to me all the time: you're walking down the hall to your office, pondering perplexing issues. Invariably, you run into someone who immediately starts discussing an entirely different topic. You only half-listen—the perplexing issue is rapidly consuming all your brain's processing power. You nod in the right places, mumble a departing comment, then rush back to your office.

Now, if what that person in the hall was talking about was important, if you don't write it down quickly, you may forget all about it. This is where Journal can help you. You can record the gist of the conversation, who it was with, and when it happened.

When you want to do this, you need to open a new Journal Entry tool. Use one of the following methods to activate the tool:

☐ From anywhere in Windows, click the New Journal Entry button in the Office Shortcut Bar.

☐ Anywhere in Outlook, click the File | New | Journal Entry menu command.

17

☐   In another part of Outlook, click the Journal Entry command in the New Item drop-down list on the Standard Toolbar.

☐   In Journal, click the New Journal Entry button on the Standard Toolbar.

☐   Also in Journal, click on the Journal | New Journal Entry menu command.

☐   Use the shortcut keys: Ctrl+N in Journal and Ctrl+Shift+J anywhere else in Outlook.

Fill in the pertinent information in the Journal Entry tool, then click Save and Close.

Using Journal

Journal can do more for you than just act as a memory jogger. It can also serve as a time-based file manager of sorts, letting you open files and items based on *when* the document was used. If you need to talk to the people who have been using a document, Journal lets you automatically link to them.

Opening Files and Outlook Items

As stated earlier this hour, when you double-click a Journal item, you don't get that document opened automatically. Instead, you get the Journal Entry for that item, with an attached shortcut to the document inside. Wouldn't it be nice if you could skip this middle step and go straight to the document?

Fear not, citizens, there is a way! Actually, two: a fast way and a faster way.

To use the fast way, follow these steps:

1.   Right-click the Journal item.

2.   On the pop-up menu (see Figure 17.13), click the Open Item Referred To command.

To use the faster way, follow these steps:

1.   In Journal, click the Tools | Options menu command.

2.   In the Options dialog, click the Opens the item referred to by the journal entry radio button in the Double-clicking a journal entry section.

3.   Click Apply and OK or just OK.

Now Journal becomes just like a little historical file manager, because every item will open with just a double-click. Pretty nifty, eh? But, there's a trade-off. You no longer can open the Journal Entry of the item by double-clicking it. However, if you use the pop-up menu method previously described and click on the Open Journal Entry command, you will be able to access the Entry.

Figure 17.13.

Go directly to the document with this pop-up menu.

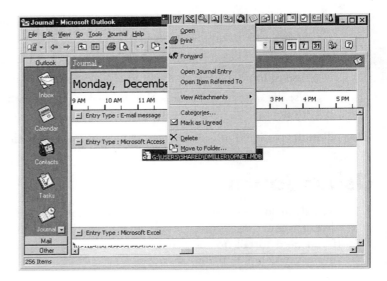

Opening Contacts from Journal Entries

If you need to open any Contacts associated with a document or recorded Outlook item, try this simple two-step method:

1. Open the Journal Entry.
2. Double-click any underlined names in the Contact field.

This calls up the Contact tool for that person. If the name is not underlined, that means this person is not on your Contact list. If you want to be able to automatically track Journal activities for him or her, or just get in touch, you should add the name into Contacts as soon as possible.

TIME SAVER

Sometimes names are not underlined, yet you know they are in the Contact list. (Perhaps they were added to Contacts after the Journal entry was created.) To resolve names in the Contact field, click the Check Names button in the toolbar. If the name still does not become underlined, check the spelling of the name.

17

Summary

Journals have come a long way since those little lock-and-key books.

In Journal, you have a really powerful tool that will not only track your work and activities, but will also call up old work in a chronological fashion.

The only drawback to Journal is that you can't write how you felt when you got kissed by the monkey bars at recess and hide your diary under your pillow.

Q&A

Q I have a Contact to autorecord who I know is in the Contact list, but I can't see the name in the Options dialog. What gives?

A Either (a) the person is in the Twilight Zone, or (b) the Contact item is not in the main Contact list. If the Contact is in a subfolder, it won't be read by Journal. Move or copy the Contact into the main Contact folder, and all will be well. If it's (a), you're on your own.

Q Can I delete Entries?

A Yes. Simply highlight the Entry and click the Delete button on the Standard Toolbar.

Hour 18

Configuring Journal

Hey, kids, try this nifty philosophy experiment with your friends: Take an object, any object, and hold it up to someone. Then ask, "What is this?"

Because of the vagaries of human nature, I can almost guarantee that you will not get the same answer very often. If it's a blue racquetball, for instance, the answers might be something like "a ball," "a blue ball," "a racquetball," or "something that's in my face."

People, in general, tend to apply subjective labels to everything, even when we are being objective. The scientific method, often called "an objective way of looking at the world," is itself just another way of looking at things.

Together, we never see the same things, and what's more, we like it that way. So much so that we shape the world around us to match our preferences. We decorate our homes, we buy groovy clothes, and (here it comes) we customize Outlook.

So, in celebration of human nature, this hour covers customizing the look of Outlook's Journal.

Look at Me; I'm Not Half the View I Used to Be...

Before diving into the techniques of customizing Journal, a look at what Journal has to offer is in order. In the last hour, we used the timeline view By Type to look around Journal. This view is shown in Figure 18.1.

Figure 18.1.

Another look at the By Type view.

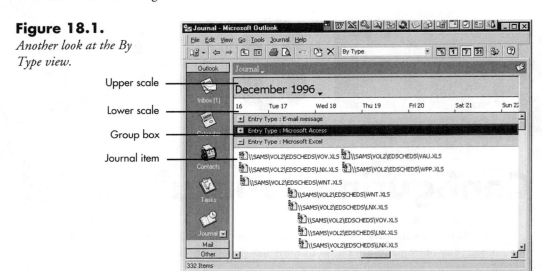

Upper scale
Lower scale
Group box
Journal item

Remember, this is the default view of Journal, and it shows the Week view, one of the three types of timeline views. You can tell this by looking at the increments in the two scale bars above the groups and items. The lower scale shows the dates with the days of the week, and the upper scale shows the month and year.

Note how the items are stacked on top of each other, but are not quite aligned. This is because the items fall on the time they were created on that particular day. So, by looking at Dec. 18, it can sort of be told that two Excel documents were edited at around midday. If a more detailed timeline is needed, clicking the Day view button in the Standard Toolbar will create a Day view much like the one in Figure 18.2.

As you can see, the two Excel documents are there (close to 1:50 and 2:30 p.m., actually), but now there are items for three other Excel documents between 8:30 and 10 a.m. Why were they not in the Week view?

18

Figure 18.2.

The Day timeline view.

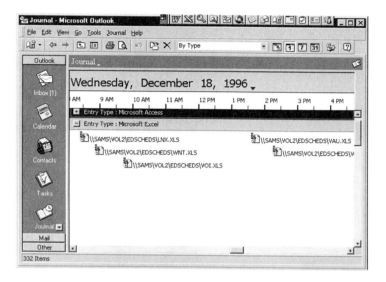

Well, they were, but they were located farther down on the timeline. You see, the timeline views have this criteria for display: The entire label of an item must be visible and cannot be overlapped. So, to fit all of the items in, items in the timeline are displayed farther and farther down on the screen. This makes things difficult to read sometimes. If, back in Figure 18.1, we would have used the scrollbar to move down the screen, we would have come upon the three Wednesday morning spreadsheets. The afternoon documents have room, so they appear on the top of the group.

TIME SAVER

There is a way to clean up this mess a bit. Click on the View | Format View menu command. In the Format Timeline View dialog, down in the Labels section, adjust the number of characters that are displayed in the label to a smaller number. (Try 20.)

You may think this is silly, especially if your labels show file pathnames. After all, now they will be cut off, and you won't be able to tell what they signify. Ah, there's another trick here. Whenever labels are truncated (really shortened, in English) in Journal, you can move the cursor over them, and a little pop-up label showing the full label content will appear.

The third view of a timeline is the Month view. Take a look at Figure 18.3. Because the increments in the lower scale are so narrow, Journal doesn't even try to show the items' labels by default. The items look more aligned along the timeline, but they are not. It's subtle at this scale, but the items still fall on the approximate time of day they were created or edited.

Figure 18.3.

The Month timeline view.

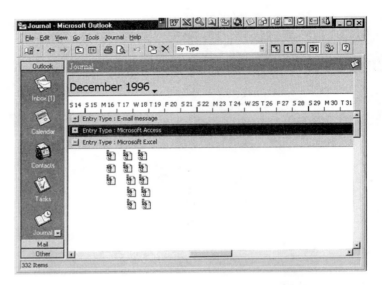

TIME SAVER

Just can't live without those labels? Don't like the little yellow pop-up labels? Rest easy, and click on the View|Format View menu command. In the Format Timeline View dialog, down in the Labels section, click the Show label when viewing by month check box.

If you do this, your timeline is going to vertically expand by leaps and bounds because items will have to be stacked to avoid label overlap.

You should be pretty familiar with the By Type view by now. Let's take a look at the other six views of Journal before learning how to customize a timeline.

By Contact View

If you communicate with a lot of people or share a lot of files, be prepared to see a lot of group boxes in this view. By Contact is identical to By Type, except the Journal Entries are grouped by contact (see Figure 18.4).

It is important to know just what is meant by contact in this context. It is not just who you talk to or send e-mail to.

18

Figure 18.4.

The By Contact view.

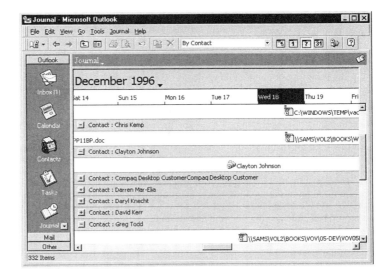

Inside every Office document is summary information that contains the time of original creation, the original author, time of last edit, and so on (this is true in Office 97 *and* 95). If you want to change this information manually, click on the File | Properties menu command in any Office program (except Access and Outlook) when the document is open. It is the name in the Author field that Journal uses as the Contact name.

This is all very nice, but it can lead to problems. Some files carry a lot of summary baggage with them, and that can clog up your timelines with a lot of weird group boxes. If you really hate this kind of thing, you can select any group box, then click the Delete button in the Standard Toolbar.

By Category View

In contrast to the last view, the By Category view groups (take a wild guess) by category. But I suspect the first time you open it, you are going to find very few category group boxes (see Figure 18.5).

This is because for all its cool AutoRecording, Journal does not automatically assign a category to anything it records for you. So, a great majority of Journal's Entries do not have categories. If you have not manually recorded an Entry, none of them will.

Figure 18.5.
The By Category view.

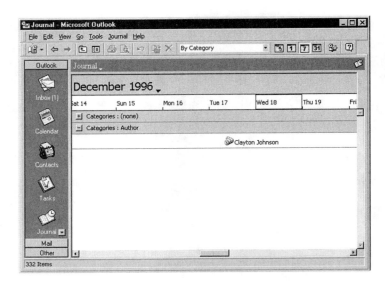

This sort of limits the usefulness of this view, unless you are diligent in going back and assigning categories to Entries.

TIME SAVER

There is a fast way to bulk assign categories to Journal Entries. While holding down the Ctrl key, click on all the items you want to assign to the same category.

When you have selected all of the items, right-click on one of the selected items. In the pop-up menu that appears, click the Categories command. In the categories dialog that appears, select all the appropriate categories, and click OK.

If you don't want to keep on top of this kind of organization, I recommend that you do not use this view very often. There is one positive use for this view, however. In the Categories: (none) group, you can easily see the order in which you worked on any file, regardless of type or contact.

Entry List View

The Entry List view is the first of the three table views in Journal. The information fields are displayed in a more familiar form, as seen in Figure 18.6.

Figure 18.6.

The Entry List view.

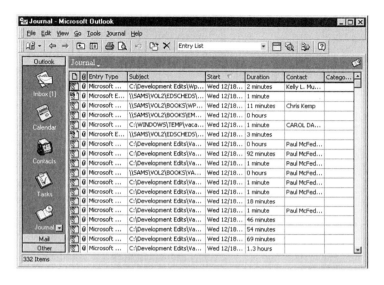

The fields displayed in this view are the Icon, Attachment, Entry Type, Subject, Start, Duration, Contact, and Categories.

The Icon and Entry Type columns show exactly the same information—what type the Journal item is. One just uses icons rather than English, that's all. Such redundancy is usually not needed and also eats up screen real estate. I recommend that one of these columns be deleted.

TIME SAVER

Hour 12, "Configuring Calendar," presented the process of defining a view in Outlook. There is a faster way to delete a particular column from a table view, though. Follow these steps:

1. Click and drag a column header box up or down on the screen.

2. As soon as the column box leaves the heading area of the table, a large black "×" will appear over it.

3. Unclick the box. It will disappear, as will the entire column of data.

You can also use this technique to shift the order of columns.

When you switch views, a dialog box appears asking if you want to save this new column arrangement as a new view, update the current view with these settings, or discard the changes you made.

The Attachment column tells the user, with the presence of a paper clip icon, that a document or Outlook item is linked to this item. This may seem superfluous because most things automatically recorded in Journal *are* documents. If you just use Journal to only record Office documents, you should delete this column from Journal's table views. It's only a little space savings, but like they say in the federal government: A million here, a million there, and pretty soon you're talking real savings.

The Subject field contains the same information as the icon labels in the timeline views. This shows the complete information, even if you resized the label information in the Format Views dialog, as shown earlier this hour.

The Start field shows the start date and time the Entry was recorded. The Duration field indicates the time the document was edited or created, or the length of time manually recorded for the Journal Entry.

The last two fields, Contact and Categories, are no different from any other part of Outlook.

This field has no groups or filters applied, so you can see all of your data at once.

Last Seven Days View

The next table view in Journal uses the same columns as the Entry List view. But, as you can see in Figure 18.7, a filter has been applied to the data. This filter only allows Entries from today to a week ago to be displayed, hence the name of the view.

Figure 18.7.

The Last Seven Days view.

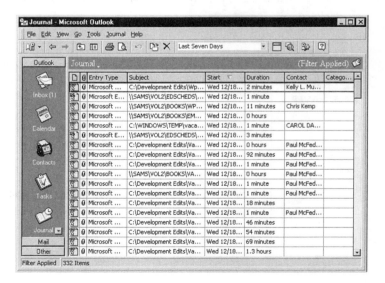

Phone Calls View

The last table view predefined for Journal is the most restrictive of the views. The filter applied to the Journal data lets just the phone call items get displayed.

In Figure 18.8, you can see the effect of this. Note the loss of one information field: the Entry Type column. Journal's designers recognized its redundancy with the Icon field and, at least in this view, chose not to display it.

Figure 18.8.

The Phone Calls view.

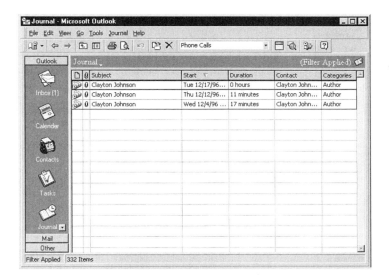

Creating Your Own Views

Did you ever get one of those model kits as a kid? Weren't they great? You'd crack off all of the pieces from the plastic molding, then one by one cement them together.

Then came time for the painting, and the decals. But, for me, it proved difficult to get the paints right. So, all the Starships *Enterprise* I had growing up were suspiciously white.

Outlook, as we all know by now, lets you do your own detailing of the views it has, giving the different tools such as Journal your own personal look and feel—no need for plain, generic Journal views.

In the now-infamous Hour 12, the methods of changing your viewpoints were fairly well outlined. However, changing the look of a timeline view is a bit different than the day/week/month or table views. So for the rest of this hour, let's review the configuration techniques as they apply to timelines in Journal.

Defining Views

If you want to create a new timeline view in Journal, I would recommend you take a current view and modify it to meet your needs.

Click the View | Define Views menu command and the Define Views for "Journal" dialog appears (see Figure 18.9). With this one dialog, you can modify the look of every Journal view at one time.

TIME SAVER

If you ever want to modify just one aspect of a view in Outlook, you can save a step and go straight to the needed tool without using the Define Views dialog. The following table illustrates the menu commands needed to go straight to the right tool.

To define...	...Use this command...	...And this dialog will appear
The displayed fields	View	Show Fields...	Show Fields
How data is grouped	View	Group By...	Group By
How data is sorted	View	Sort...	Sort
What data is shown	View	Filter...	Filter
The "cosmetic" look	View	Format View...	Format *View Type* View

If you want to format more than one of these view aspects, it still would be a good idea to use the Define Views dialog, so its Description section can help you keep track of all the changes you have made.

Figure 18.9.

The Define Views dialog.

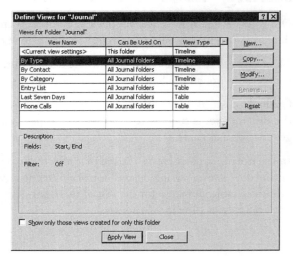

To change a current view, click the Modify button on the right side of the dialog. This brings up the View Settings for *View* dialog, as shown in Figure 18.10. Like the Description section of the Define Views dialog, this dialog shows all the current settings for the view you are in right now and has those five nifty buttons that activate the dialogs for modifying these settings.

However, one of those five buttons, Sort, is all gray, which is the universal Windows symbol for a disabled function. This makes sense if you think about it. A timeline should only be able to sort by chronology, so Journal does not let the user have the option to change this.

JUST A MINUTE

When you are creating or modifying any view type where all view aspects are allowed to be modified, this dialog is called a View Summary dialog.

For any view type where access to a certain view aspect has been disabled, this dialog is called View Settings for *View*.

This seems kind of silly, especially when you consider that of the five Outlook view types, only Table enables modification to all view aspects.

Figure 18.10.

The View Settings dialog.

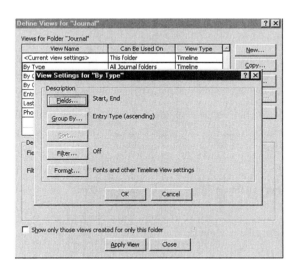

Displaying Timeline Fields

If you click the Fields button in the View Settings dialog, you see the Date/Time Fields dialog (see Figure 18.11). Here you can choose what information will be visible in the timeline view. This does not seem to be a very powerful function. After all, there are only three available fields to choose from: End, Modified, and Start. By default, the Start field in a timeline is assigned the Start data, and the End field is assigned the End data. If you decide to use the Modified data in one of these two fields, the time of modification will be shown on the timeline.

Figure 18.11.

The Date/Time Fields dialog.

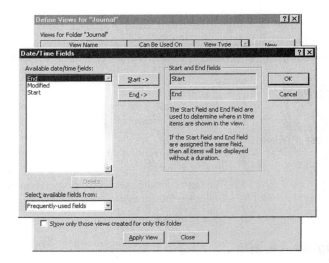

There are more data fields available for use as a timeline's Start or End field than just these three. To access them, click on the Select available fields from list box in the Date/Time Fields dialog.

If you click on any of other options, the list in the Available data/time fields box will reveal item-specific fields to use. This is handy if you are creating views to look at specific Outlook items.

Grouping Timeline Data

To change the grouping structure of a timeline, click the Group By button. This opens the Group By dialog, shown in Figure 18.12. You see that there are four nearly identical sections, each containing a drop-down list box and ascending and descending radio buttons.

In the first section, Group items by, you see the current grouping criteria for the view you are in. Because this is the By Category view, items are being grouped by, well, categories in ascending order. For timelines, the Show field in view check box is disabled because this applies to columns in table views.

The second section's list box, which is expanded in Figure 18.13, allows you to establish a second level of timeline grouping criteria.

18

Figure 18.12.
The Group By dialog.

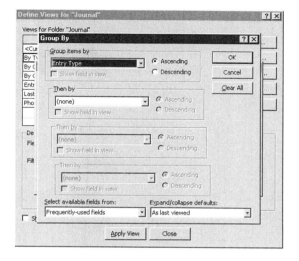

Figure 18.13.
Some of the available fields in which to group timeline data.

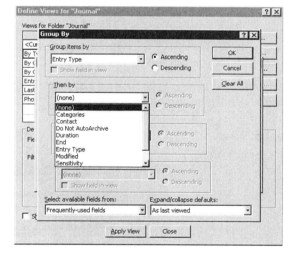

18

The rest of the sections let you group down to a fourth grouping level, if you wish. At the bottom of the dialog is the Select available fields from list box, which lets you choose which field set you can pick your grouping fields from. Next to this is the Expand/collapse defaults list box, which sets the default view for any expandable group heading.

Filtering Timeline Data

If you want to restrict what data gets displayed, click the Filter button to get the Filter dialog, shown in Figure 18.14.

Figure 18.14.

The Filter dialog.

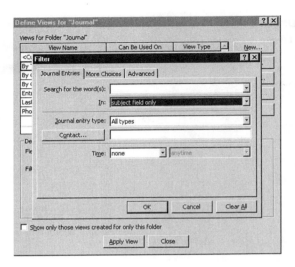

To use the Filter dialog, enter the information value you want Journal to show. The functionality is the same as any other Outlook view. Figures 18.15 and 18.16 show the More Choices and Advanced tabs, respectively, of the Filter dialog, to give you an idea of the different tools you can use to hone your data.

Remember, to view *all* your data again, re-enter the Filter dialog and click the Clear All button. All data in Journal will be visible again.

Figure 18.15.

The Filter dialog's More Choices tab.

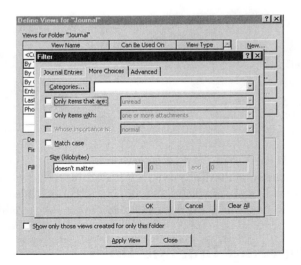

18

Figure 18.16.

The Filter dialog's Advanced tab.

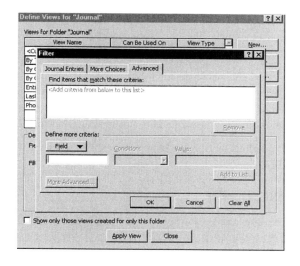

Changing a Timeline's Look

The last button to click in the View Settings dialog, Format, brings up the Format Timeline View (shown in Figure 18.17).

Figure 18.17.

The Format Timeline View dialog.

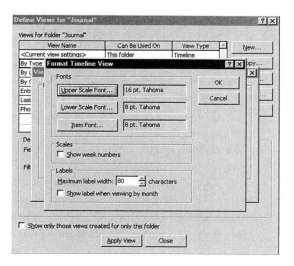

18

There are three areas of a timeline that can be modified: the upper scale, the lower scale, and the item label. The corresponding Font buttons each activate a standard Windows Font dialog. After you change the font settings, samples of the new font appear next to the Font buttons.

The Scales section has just one check box: Show week numbers. If this is checked, Week N, where N is 1 through 52, will appear next to the date in the upper scale for the Day and Week views of a timeline and as the only unit label in the Month view.

The Labels section has already been reviewed earlier this hour.

Summary

The clues are in, and there is only one conclusion: Journal is much more than a simple record of the work you have done. Part file manager, part version tracker, and, yes, part diary, Journal enables you to manage all your work in a focused, organized manner.

This hour marks the end of Part VI, "Notes and Journal: Small, Yet Savvy," and the end of in-depth looks at the individual parts of Outlook. Beginning with the next hour, the remainder of the day will be spent learning how to fine-tune Outlook and use all the pieces as a single cohesive tool.

Q&A

Q I thought only document attachments would show the Attachment icon. But it's showing up in some of my phone call and remote messaging Journal entries. What's with this?

A The Attachment icons apply to attached documents and Outlook items. If you have made a phone call, sent an e-mail, or faxed someone your Contact list, the paper clip will appear. You can use this to your advantage to update your Contacts. Modify or create a new table view in Journal that will sort by Attachment, then Entry Type. Look at the items you have frequently sent to someone *not* in Contacts. These would be good candidates for addition, no?

Q Is there any way to shorten the vertical size of some of the timeline groups? They get so tall sometimes that they're hard to manage.

A Other than decreasing the font size of your items, no. This is a valid concern because it makes the timelines one of the more awkward parts of Outlook.

18

PART VII

Getting a Better Outlook

Hour

Hour **19**

Maintaining Outlook

Like any database, your Personal Folders File in Outlook can become quite large as you fill it with more and more e-mail, Contacts, Journal entries, appointments, and Notes. I have been using Outlook for about four months, and already my Personal Folders File (mailbox.pst) is over 35MB.

You can do a few things to maintain your Outlook database and keep it as small as possible. This chapter covers the techniques of archiving, exporting, and compacting, and gives you a few tips to reduce the size of your Outlook file.

Checking Out Your Personal Folders File

The first thing you should know is where your Personal Folders File is stored on your computer. To find its location, choose Tools | Services. In the Services dialog box, select the Personal Folders File and click the Properties button. The Properties screen will appear, as displayed in Figure 19.1.

Figure 19.1.

When you view the properties of Personal Folders, you can find out the location of your .PST *file, set a password to prevent other people from accessing your personal folders, and compact an offline folder to make it smaller.*

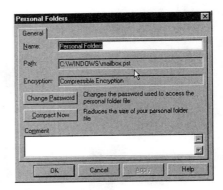

Archiving

Archiving is a way of removing old data from your Outlook file, but removing it in a way that you can get it back anytime you need it. It's an operation that could be compared to filing old bills and receipts. You probably don't refer to them very often (if at all), but you have to keep them somewhere in case the IRS ever wants to audit you. Hopefully, you have filed and stored your old paperwork in a place where you can access it easily and be able to use it again.

The same principles apply when you are archiving items from your Outlook file. Archiving removes the old data from your Outlook database and stores it in an archive file, usually called Archive.PST, which can be read by Outlook whenever you want to refer to the data again. In fact, an archived file will look exactly like it did when it was part of your main Outlook Folders File. The same folders and structures will remain.

Setting Up AutoArchive

You can choose to allow Outlook to automatically archive information, based on a schedule that you designate. You can schedule an archiving session to take place as often as every day or as infrequently as every 60 days. It really depends on how you work and how much hard drive space you have available.

To configure the AutoArchive feature, choose Tools | Options and click on the AutoArchive tab, as shown in Figure 19.2.

19

Figure 19.2.

The AutoArchive tab allows you to specify how frequently, if at all, you want Outlook to perform automatic archiving sessions.

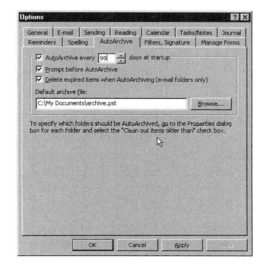

Notice that there is a note at the bottom of the dialog box that instructs you to go to each folder and set the properties for autoarchiving. This is an important procedure for the AutoArchive feature to work properly. If you do not perform this task for each folder, nothing will happen when Outlook tries to archive your files.

The Journal module in Outlook is the only one that can be set up for AutoArchive in the Options dialog box. Click on the Journal tab and then click the AutoArchive Journal Entries button. A dialog box will appear in which you can specify how often, if at all, you want Journal entries to be cleaned out. The limit to the frequency at which the Journal entries can be archived is much bigger than the 60-day limit that is placed on the other modules. In this dialog box, you can choose to archive the entries or simply delete them once they reach a certain age.

Whenever it's time for Outlook to perform archive operations, a notice appears on your screen that looks like Figure 19.3. The notice alerts you that Outlook is ready to begin archiving. You can choose to accept or decline. If you decline, the notice will appear each time you open Outlook until you accept the operation or until you reset the AutoArchive schedule in the Option|AutoArchive dialog box.

19

Figure 19.3.

Before archiving auto-matically, Outlook will alert you with a message.

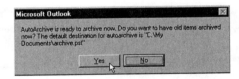

Archiving Manually

If you prefer to archive your Outlook database manually, you can do so by choosing File|Archive. The Archive dialog box allows you to archive according to the AutoArchive settings, which can differ from folder to folder, depending on how you set the properties. Otherwise, you can choose to archive entire folders by the same standard, such as archiving all items older than August 1, 1996.

This is a good way to archive items and folders if you want to clean off a specific project that has been completed. In Figure 19.4, Mark wants to archive all the messages within the folder labeled "Sanjaya's Book," because the project has been completed. To set the properties, he does the following:

1. He selects only the Sanjaya's Book folder in the list.
2. He chooses to archive all items older than July 1, 1996, which is when the project began.
3. He names the archive file in a way that identifies the project, which is `Sanjaya_Jan97.pst`.
4. He clicks OK to begin the archiving operation.
5. If the file is small enough, which it should be, he can move it to a floppy disk and store it with the contract for the book.

Figure 19.4.

The Archive dialog box appears when you want to manually perform archive operations.

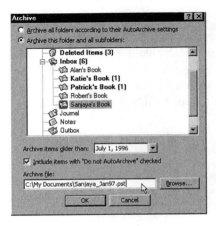

19

Removing a Folder after Archiving

If you archive all the items in a folder, the folder still will remain in the Personal Folders File until you remove it. To remove it, right-click on the folder and choose Delete. Another way to delete it is to select it, go to File|Folder, and choose Delete *name of folder*.

Restoring from an Archive

You can restore from an archive in two ways. You can open the archive as a separate Personal Folders File or you can import the archived items into your current Personal Folders File. Which one should you choose when you want to restore from an archive? It depends on how you want to use the data. If you want to use the data temporarily, you should probably use the Open Special Folder command. If you want the data back in your current Personal Folders File permanently (or for a more extended period of time), you should use the Import and Export command, located under the File menu.

Opening an Archive as a Separate Personal Folders File

If you want to restore an archived file, a quick way to do it is to open it as a Personal Folder. It will show up within Outlook as an additional Personal Folder to your main Personal Folder. Once it's open, you can copy items, open messages, and do all the things with the items that you need to do. You can open multiple Personal Folders within Outlook at the same time. Perform the following steps for opening a Personal Folder:

1. Click on File|Open Special Folder|Personal Folder, and choose the .PST file to which you want to connect.
2. Click OK.

You will notice that there are two Personal Folders files showing in the Folder List. By clicking on the plus (+) sign, you can expand the list of folders to find the archived items that you need. When you have finished using the archived items, you can disconnect the Personal Folders File by right-clicking on it and choosing Disconnect from the drop-down menu.

Importing an Archive into Your Personal Folder File

To import an archive into the Personal Folders File, you must complete the following steps:

1. Click on File|Import and Export.
2. Choose Import from a Personal Folders File (.PST), and click Next.
3. Choose the .PST file to import and decide how you want duplicates to be handled. Click Next.

4. Select the folder that you want to import and whether you want subfolders to be imported as well. You can import items in the current folder or in the same folder in the Personal Folders File you select.

5. Click Finish and the items will appear in their respective places in your Personal Folders File.

Exporting Items

The difference between exporting and archiving items is that archiving removes them from your Personal Folders File and exporting makes a copy of them. Exporting also gives you the option of exporting the data as a Personal Folders File, which can be read by Outlook or Windows Messaging, or as a file, such as a text file, an Excel spreadsheet file, or a database file.

Exporting is a good way to share Outlook items with other Outlook users. Maybe you want to give your Contacts database to someone else, whether that person uses Outlook or not. It's also an easy way to copy Outlook folders and place them into other Outlook files that you maintain. For instance, if you work with Outlook at work and home, you can export items from work and import them into your Outlook file at home. Because the entire Personal Folders File can become so large that it's impossible to copy onto a floppy diskette, you can easily export individual folders and items to transport them.

Exporting to a Personal Folders File

To export to a Personal Folders File, complete the following steps:

1. Choose File | Import and Export.

2. Choose Export to a Personal Folder File (.PST) and click Next.

3. Choose the folder to export and indicate if you want to export the subfolders with it.

4. If you want to filter the information, click the button and set up the criteria for the filter. Click OK and then click Next.

5. Give the exported file a name and designate a location for it.

6. If you are exporting to a file that is already created, decide if you will allow duplicates or if you want the duplicates to replace the items already in the file.

7. Click Finish.

Exporting to Other File Formats

To export a file to another file format, complete the following steps:

1. Choose File|Import and Export.
2. Choose Export to File and click Next.
3. Choose the folder to export and click Next.
4. Pick a file type from the list and click Next.
5. Name the file, designate the location, and click Next.

Once you have saved the file, find it in the Explorer and double-click on it to open it. If you chose to export to a tab- or comma-delimited file, the file will be an unformatted file in which the fields are separated by either commas or tabs and the records are separated by paragraph marks.

Tips on Making Your Outlook File as Small as Possible

There are a few things you can do periodically to save space on your computer while you use Outlook. Here are some suggestions:

☐ Empty the Deleted Items folder frequently by selecting it and choosing Tools|Empty Deleted Items Folder. You can also right-click on the Deleted Items Folder and choose Empty Deleted Items.

☐ If you want items to automatically be deleted permanently each time you exit Outlook, choose Tools|Options|General tab, and check the box marked Empty Deleted Items Folder upon exiting.

☐ If you request receipts when you send e-mail messages, check the box marked Delete receipts and blank responses after processing in the Tools|Options|E-mail tab.

☐ Turn off the option to save messages that you send. In the Tools|Options|Sending tab, uncheck the option to save messages in the Sent Items Folder. You can always specify on an individual basis if you want to save a message that you are sending.

☐ Even if you don't turn off the option to save items in the Sent Items folder, at least turn off the option to save copies of forwarded messages. This option can be found in the same tab in the Options dialog box.

☐ Be conservative in choosing options to be tracked as automatic Journal entries. Go to Tools|Options|Journal tab, as shown in Figure 19.5.

19

Figure 19.5.

Being conservative when you choose automatic recording of Journal entries will help to keep your Outlook file smaller.

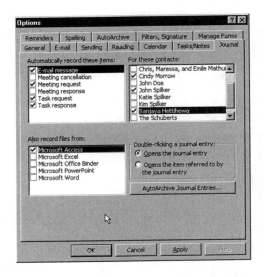

☐ Archive frequently by choosing AutoArchive or archive manually, as described at the beginning of this chapter.

☐ Compact your Personal Folders by choosing Tools | Services. Select Personal Folders and click the Properties button. Choose Compact Now.

Summary

This chapter guides you through the different ways to maintain your Outlook database. You learned how to archive folders by scheduling automatic archiving sessions and manually archiving. You also learned some tips and tricks for keeping your Outlook database as small as possible. Finally, you learned how to restore information that you have archived.

Q&A

Q If you try to archive and nothing happens, what could be wrong?

A There are two different steps required before archiving will work properly. Check the properties of each folder, such as Calendar, Journal, and Inbox, and click on the AutoArchive tab to complete the options for archiving. If you have set the options for each folder, check the Options dialog box under the Tools menu to complete the main instructions for archiving in Outlook.

Q **Where should you look to find out what is being recorded by the Journal?**

A Go to the Tools menu option and choose the Options command. Click on the Journal tab to see which items are being recorded (such as Word, Excel, individual Contacts, Tasks, and other events).

Q **What is the difference between exporting and archiving?**

A Exporting allows you to export information from Outlook to a separate Personal Folders File or to another file format, such as ASCII. The information is simply copied, not removed from your Outlook database as it is when you archive.

19

Hour 20

Integrating Outlook with Office 97

If you think Microsoft has the patent on office tool integration, think again. It has been done before. The most widely used integrated tool appeared in offices, schools, and homes as early as the mid-nineteenth century.

The first part of the device had been in existence in one form or another since the Aztec civilization. Its most modern form was invented by the Germans in the sixteenth century, and until 1812, their device dominated the world market.

It was then that William Monroe opened an American business to create this device, and soon broke the German hold on the market, and gave America more independence from yet another European nation.

The second part of the device was added in 1858, by Philadelphia inventor Hyman Lipman, thus creating a truly integrated tool. Surely the whole is greater than the sum of its parts, as any of us who uses a wooden pencil with rubber eraser knows.

Office 97, like its predecessors, integrates its components as much as possible, in order to get that greater sum of tools. Some of the integrative methods are fairly obvious, thanks to document Object Linking and Embedding. Other aspects of the integration are more subtle, and don't always leap out at you.

Such is the integration between Outlook and the other Office 97 programs. Some of it screams out at you, such as WordMail, and some of it is kind of quiet, such as scheduling a meeting from the middle of a PowerPoint slideshow.

You have already learned in Hour 17, "The Journal—My So-Called Diary," about the biggest way Outlook deals with documents created by its Office compatriot: Journal. With Journal, you can access a document, workbook, presentation, or (ahem!) database created in Office, as well as track revisions to these Office documents.

This hour covers different ways Outlook interacts with its Office buddies and how it can make your work go quite a bit smoother.

Outlook and Word

If you think of Office as a family, Outlook is sort of like John-boy, and Word is like Grandpa Walton. Both are valued members of the family, but it is quite clear who has the experience and power in the family.

This is not so strange, if you think about it. Since its inception, a document-centric ideal has been promoted by Office. All Office files were documents of one form or another, the argument went, and what better place to put most of the document controls but Word? That argument still holds true today in Office 97, even though Outlook items are not really documents, but rather database entries.

JUST A MINUTE

Actually, Outlook items, when saved as separate files, are Mail Message files. You can see this every time you drag and drop a Task or other Outlook item out onto the desktop, which is essentially saving the item to a separate file.

Appropriately, Word and Outlook have the most levels of interaction. Using both programs, you can send e-mail messages, create mail merge documents, and create tasks.

20

WordMail

When you send e-mail messages from Outlook's Inbox, there are some pretty good tools to format your message. You can apply bold, underline, or italic fonts, change the base font and its size, and create bulleted lists—not a bad list.

But sometimes you want to make it better. No offense, but Outlook's message tool is not a word processor. So, Outlook gives you the option of using Word as its e-mail editor.

TIME SAVER

Admittedly, using a full-blown word processor as your e-mail editor is going to make creating a message a bit slower. In fact, Microsoft recommends that your computer has at least 16MB of RAM before even using WordMail.

The biggest advantage of using WordMail is sending really nice formatted documents to other people. But if the recipient does not use WordMail, most of your formatting is for naught. The message will only be read as plain text.

If either of these two criteria apply to you, I recommend you continue to use Outlook's Inbox editor.

If you decide to use WordMail, you will need to tell Outlook about it. The way to do this is to click on the Tools | Options menu command. In the Options dialog that appears, click on the E-mail tab, as shown in Figure 20.1.

Figure 20.1.

The Outlook Options dialog.

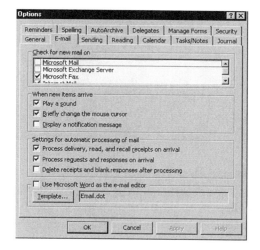

20

All that needs to be done is click on the Use Microsoft Word as the e-mail editor check box, then OK. Poof! That's it. The next time you start to create a new mail message, you will see a little message box that says `Starting Word as your e-mail editor`, followed by the appearance of a brand-new message tool that looks like the Outlook message tool (see Figure 20.2). Gee, how exciting.

Figure 20.2.

The super-duper deluxe WordMail Message tool. Really!

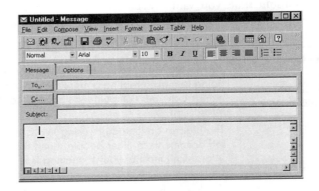

Hold on! It's really different. Look at those toolbars again! There's a lot more tools in them! To help see the difference, compare Figure 20.2 with Figure 20.3, which shows a standard Outlook message tool.

Figure 20.3.

The mild-mannered Outlook Message tool.

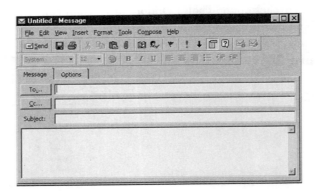

Tools of the Trade

You can see that the toolbars and menus of the WordMail Message tool have more in common with Word 97 than Outlook. The Formatting toolbar has expanded to match Word's, and the Standard Toolbar has been replaced with the Send Mail toolbar (see Figure 20.4).

20

Figure 20.4.

The WordMail Message tool's toolbars.

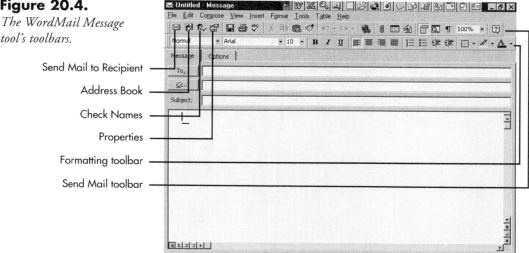

Send Mail to Recipient

Address Book

Check Names

Properties

Formatting toolbar

Send Mail toolbar

TIME SAVER

In case you are wondering, the WordMail function does not go both ways. You can't send a Word-formatted e-mail message directly from Word, even if the WordMail option is on.

What you can do is send an e-mail with the most recent version of the open Word document attached. Just click on the Send to Mail Recipient in the Reviewing toolbar of Word 97.

A majority of the tools in the aforementioned toolbars are familiar to Word 97 users. On the far-left end of the Send Mail toolbar are four buttons that have the most use for a WordMail message.

The Send Mail to Recipient button, when clicked, sends the completed message to whomever it is addressed to. It is the counterpart of the Send button in the Outlook Message tool.

The next two buttons are direct émigrés from Outlook: the Address Book and Check Name buttons. Clicking the former brings up the Outlook Address Book dialog. Clicking the latter helps you resolve any names in the To and Cc boxes.

The Properties button is more functional than you might think. Usually, properties of a document are something only a real stickler for detail messes around with, right? In WordMail, properties are more important. Take a look at the Send Mail toolbar again. See any message priority buttons? Interested in the Properties button now? If you click it, the Properties dialog, shown in Figure 20.5, appears.

20

Figure 20.5.

*The WordMail Proper-
ties dialog.*

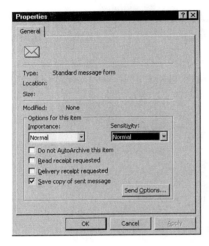

With this dialog, you can set the Importance and Sensitivity of the message, as well as whether you want to get delivery and read receipts, and how you want to save and archive the message.

CAUTION

> If you click the Send Options button, the Send Options for this Message dialog appears. But, the options are all for a fax message, not an e-mail!
>
> My presumption is that this dialog was originally coded for Microsoft Fax, and this button is a holdover from that. It doesn't hurt anything, but I would leave it be, so Outlook can't get the message types confused.

Once you are finished with the Properties dialog, click OK, and you'll return to the Message tool. As for the rest of the buttons and fields, you will find that they function like Word 97's Standard and Formatting toolbars. The To, Cc, and Subject fields work exactly like Outlook's Message tool.

It's Got the Look

There is, though, one more thing WordMail can do to make your messages sparkle. Using templates, you can create an entirely new look for an e-mail message. Follow these steps to attach a new template to a message:

1. Enter the Inbox in Outlook.

2. Click on the Compose | Choose Template menu command (see Figure 20.6).

3. In the Choose Template dialog, click on the template you want, then click OK.

Figure 20.6.

The Choose Template dialog.

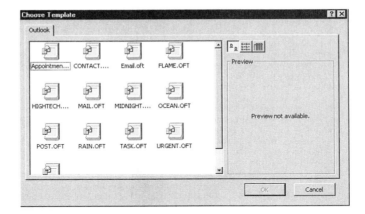

The next time a new message is created in that Outlook session, that template will be used. Figures 20.7 and 20.8 show examples of the same message, using the Hightech and Ocean templates.

Figure 20.7.

The Hightech template.

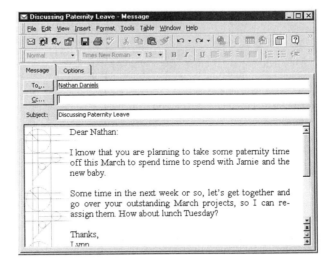

If you are really entranced by one of these templates, you can make it your default template for every e-mail message you create with WordMail. Follow these steps to set up this:

1. In Outlook, click on the Tools | Options menu command.

2. In the Options dialog, click the E-mail tab.

3. Click the Template button.

4. In the WordMail Template dialog (see Figure 20.9), click the template you like.

Figure 20.8.
The Ocean template.

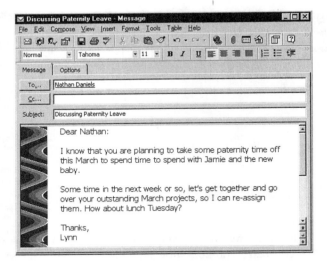

Figure 20.9.
The WordMail Template dialog.

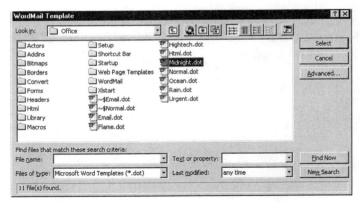

5. Click the Select button.

6. Make sure the correct template name appears in the Options dialog. If it does, click the OK button.

If you ever have enough of WordMail, simply open the Options dialog in Outlook again and uncheck the Use Microsoft Word as the e-mail editor check box. Outlook then will use its own Message tool again.

Mail Merge

I have a confession to make: Mail merges give me the willies. I know I'm not alone. However, Word 95, and now Word 97, have made them a lot easier.

20

Now that I've made you nervous, let me first explain what a mail merge is, for those not in the know. Simply put, mail merging is the process used by Word to create a form letter, envelope labels, or any other document that needs multiple copies generated for many people. Instead of creating a separate copy for each person, you create one master document, with a list of the different names and addresses. Word then places the data in the master document in the right order, and voila! You too can be a junk mail king!

The data can come from a lot of different sources: an Excel spreadsheet, an Access database, and now Outlook's Address Book.

Before we rush into the procedure to create a mail merge document, some questions must be asked. Table 20.1 shows the Outlook fields that can be directly merged into Word 97. After looking at this table, ask yourself these questions:

- ☐ Will my master document need fields in this table?
- ☐ Will my master document need an Outlook field that's not in this table?
- ☐ Will my master document need a completely new custom field?

Table 20.1. Merge-capable fields.

Contact field name	Word field name
Assistant's Name	Assistant_Name
Assistant's Phone	Assistant_Phone
Business Fax	Business_Fax
Business Phone 2	Business_Phone_2
Business Phone	Business_Phone
City	City
Company	Company
Country	Country
Department	Department
E-Mail	Email_Name
First Name	First_Name
Home Address City	Home_City
Home Address Country	Home_Country
Home Address Postal Code	Home_Zipcode
Home Address State	Home_State
Home Address Street	Home_Address
Home Fax	Home_Fax

20

continues

Table 20.1. continued

Contact field name	Word field name
Home Phone 2	Home_Phone_2
Home Phone	Home_Phone
Job Title	Title
Last Name	Last_Name
Mailing Address	Mailing_Address
Mobile Phone	Mobile_Phone
Office Location	Office
Other Address City	Other_City
Other Address Country	Other_Country
Other Address Postal Code	Other_Zip
Other Address State	Other_State
Other Address Street	Other_Address
Other Fax	Primary_Fax
Other Phone	Other_Phone
Pager	Pager_Phone
Spouse	Spouse
State	State
Street Address	Street_Address
Suffix	Generation
Title	Courtesy_Title
ZIP/Postal Code	Zipcode

Your answers to these questions will determine the method you need to get the merge data into Word. Not to worry, you'll learn how to answer each one.

TIME SAVER

Before you begin any of these methods, it would be a great idea to create a new Contacts folder, and copy the appropriate people into it. That way, you can be sure you will get only the correct people for your mail merge document.

My Document Uses Only the Standard Merge Fields

You are the conformist that makes books like this easy to write. Take pride in your conformity. Now, let's merge:

1. Start Word 97.

2. Open an existing document to mail merge, if you have one.

3. Click the Tools|Mail Merge menu command. The Mail Merge Helper dialog appears.

4. In Section 1, click the Create button. Click the appropriate document type you want to create (see Figure 20.10).

Figure 20.10.

The Mail Merge Helper dialog.

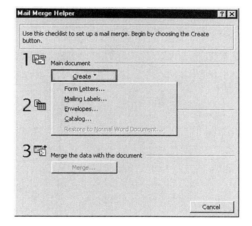

5. Once you click on the right document type, a query will pop up (see Figure 20.11), asking if you want to use the currently open document or create a new document for the master document.

6. In Section 2, click the Get Data button (see Figure 20.12).

TIME SAVER

Should you happen to perform a mail merge without this trusty book by your side (shame on you), keep an eye on the very top section of the Mail Merge Helper dialog. It will tell you what needs to be in the right sequence.

20

Figure 20.11.

Use what you have, or make a new master document.

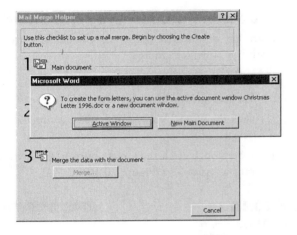

Figure 20.12.

The data source choices.

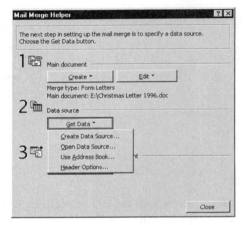

7. Click the Use Address Book command. The Use Address Book dialog appears (see Figure 20.13).

8. Select the Outlook Address Book option, then click OK.

9. In the Mail Merge from Contacts Folder dialog (see Figure 20.14), select the folder you want to use, then click OK.

10. Unless you are using an old master document that already has merge fields, you will get a message box asking you to insert merge fields. Click Edit Main Document to begin this process.

11. Click the Insert Merge Field button, and select the appropriate fields to place in your document (see Figure 20.15).

20

Figure 20.13.

The Use Address Book dialog.

Figure 20.14.

Choosing the correct folder.

Figure 20.15.

Inserting the merge fields.

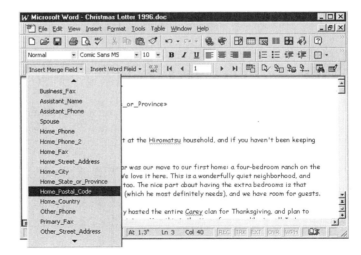

20

TIME SAVER

> To make your documents look their best, treat each merge field as an actual single word, using the correct punctuation and spacing you normally would.

12. When finished, click the Mail Merge Helper button.

13. In Section 3, click the Merge button.

14. In the Merge dialog (see Figure 20.16), select the options you need. Click the Merge button when ready.

After some processing from the computer, your document will soon be merged with the Outlook data.

Figure 20.16.

Finalizing your merge options.

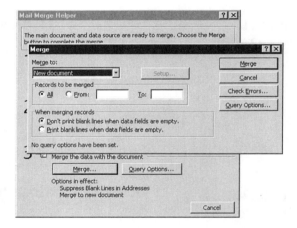

My Document Uses Outlook Fields, but Not All Are Standard

If you want to use fields that are not on the standard merge list, you will need to prepare the data in Outlook first before Word can use it. Before you start the merge process in Word, follow these steps:

1. In Outlook, click the File | Import and Export menu command.

2. In the first screen of the Import and Export Wizard (see Figure 20.17), select the Export to a file option and click the next arrow.

20

Figure 20.17.

Selecting the Export to a file option in the Import and Export Wizard (1 of 5).

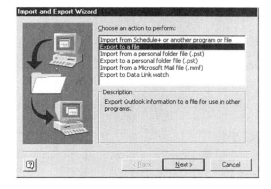

3. In the second screen, select the folder from which you want to export (see Figure 20.18).

Figure 20.18.

Selecting the folder from which you want to export (2 of 5).

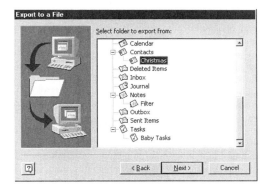

4. In the third screen, select the export file's type (see Figure 20.19).

Figure 20.19.

Using the Import and Export Wizard to select the export file's type (3 of 5).

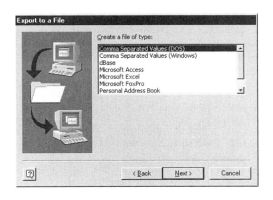

20

TIME SAVER

When you are exporting files to use in Word 97 or PowerPoint 97, choose the Windows version of the Tab or Comma Separated file types.

5. In the fourth screen, enter the name for the soon-to-be exported data file (see Figure 20.20). Use the Browse button for more ease.

Figure 20.20.

Enter the name for the exported file in the Import and Export Wizard (4 of 5).

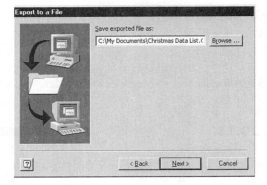

6. The fifth and final screen of the Wizard (see Figure 20.21) shows just what actions will be taken once the Finish button is pushed. Because you are using non-standard merge fields, click the Map Custom Fields button.

Figure 20.21.

The final actions in the Import and Export Wizard (5 of 5).

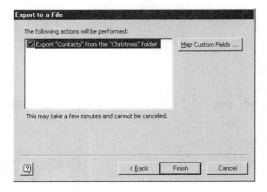

7. In the Map Custom Fields dialog that appears (see Figure 20.22), you can assign the "stick out like a sore thumb" fields from Contact to corresponding Word merge fields.

20

Figure 20.22.

The Map Custom Fields dialog.

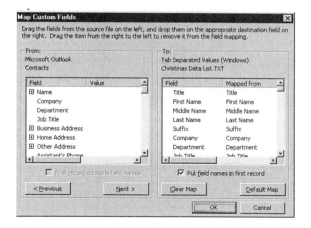

TIME SAVER

If you can't find a field among the Word fields that's close to your oddball Contact field, go ahead and choose an oddball Word field—one that you would not normally need. The field's name won't matter when you create your master document.

8. Once the non-standard fields are mapped (assigned) to Word fields, click OK, and then click Finish in the Wizard. Outlook will then export the assigned data to the file named earlier in the Wizard.

Now, start Word 97 and follow steps 1 through 6 of the mail merge setup process, shown in the section, "My Document Uses Only the Standard Merge Fields." These steps are the same in any of the mail merge processes. However, things change when you get to step 7:

9. After clicking the Get Data button, click the Open Data Source command. The Open Data Source dialog appears (see Figure 20.23).

Figure 20.23.

Choosing the data source file.

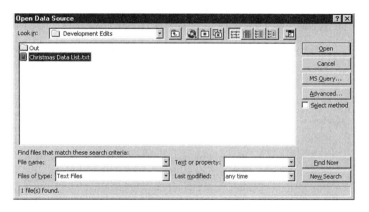

20

10. Select the correct data source file, then click Open.

Skip step 9 in the mail merge process outlined in the section "My Document Uses Only the Standard Merge Fields," and proceed with the remainder of the steps (10-14) in that section.

My Document Uses Custom Fields

If your Outlook file is using a completely customized field, the mail merge procedure is exactly the same as that outlined in the last section: Prepare the Contact data, then open a data source file, as opposed to using the Outlook Address Book directly. However, instead of exporting the Contacts, you will manually create the data source file, using the following steps:

1. In Contacts, create a new table view containing the fields you need.
2. In that new view, select all the Contacts you need for the merge.
3. With the Contacts still selected, create a Clipboard copy of them by using the Ctrl+C shortcut keys, or the Edit|Copy menu command.
4. Open a new document in Word 97.
5. Using the Edit|Paste menu command or the Ctrl+V shortcut keys, paste the selected contacts from the Clipboard.
6. Save the document. Remember the name, because this will be your data source file.
7. Open the Word document you want to use as the master mail merge document and begin the mail merge process.

Now let's look at the third big thing you can do with Word and Outlook: create a Task from Word.

Creating Tasks

Back when you were learning about Tasks and their creation in Hour 13, "Things to Do with Tasks," you may have been saying that sure, Tasks were cool, but to stop what I'm working on, switch to Outlook, make the Task—this isn't very productive.

And, I would agree with you. No one likes it when their train of thought is disrupted. So why do it? In Word 97, you can create a Task from the document you are working in. This Task will have the open document linked to it, for more convenience.

TIME SAVER

If you ever want to just create a Task from wherever you are working, you can always click the New task button in the Microsoft Office Shortcut bar. It won't have a link to what you are working on, but this is not always needed anyway.

20

To create the Task from the open document, you should be in Word 97 with the document open. Complete the following steps:

1. Right-click on any toolbar in Word.
2. Select the Reviewing toolbar from the pop-up menu.
3. On the Reviewing toolbar (see Figure 20.24), click the Create Microsoft Outlook Task button.
4. A Task tool will appear, like the one in Figure 20.25, with the filename in the Subject field, and a shortcut to the document and the first line of the document in the note box. Finish filling in the rest of the Task information and click Save and Close.

Figure 20.24.
The Word 97 Reviewing toolbar.

Create Microsoft
Outlook Task button

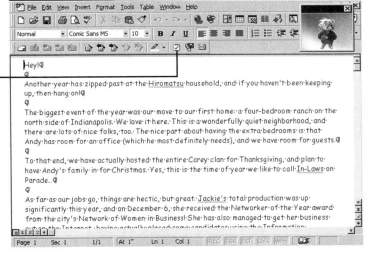

Figure 20.25.
The document-related Task.

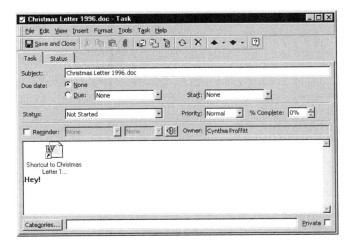

TIME SAVER

If you make a lot of these document-related Tasks, you can move the Task button in the Reviewing toolbar into the Standard or Formatting toolbars. Then you'll have the tool present all of the time. To move the button, have the Reviewing toolbar open, as well as the destination toolbar:

1. Right-click on any of the toolbars.
2. Click on the Customize command in the pop-up menu that appears.
3. When the Customize dialog appears, ignore it. Click and drag the dialog down until all of the toolbars are uncovered.
4. Click and drag the Task button from the Reviewing toolbar to the place you want it on the destination toolbar.

When you close Word 97 you will be asked to save changes to the current template. If you say yes, this toolbar change will remain in place until you move another button.

Outlook and Access

As you have probably deduced, because Outlook is a database and Access is a database creation tool, they ought to be able to share everything, right?

Pretty much, but the transition is not one-to-one. Outlook, a descendant of Exchange, uses a database format slightly different from that of Access. Fortunately, it is not too hard to share information between the programs.

Exporting Data to Access

If you need to let Access use the data contained within Outlook, you must first export the data to an Access 97 database file.

Follow these steps to export your Outlook data to Access:

1. In Outlook, click the File | Import and Export menu command.
2. In the first screen of the Import and Export Wizard, select the Export to a File option and click the next arrow.
3. In the second screen, select the folder from which you want to export.
4. In the third screen, select the export file's type—in this case, Microsoft Access.
5. In the fourth screen, enter a name for the exported Access file. Be sure to give it an .mdb extension. Use the Browse button for more ease.

20

6. The fifth and final screen of the Wizard shows what actions will be taken once the Finish button is pushed.

7. Click Finish in the Wizard. Outlook then exports the assigned data to the Access file named earlier in the Wizard.

Importing Data from Access

So far, all the interactions with Office programs have been one way; the other programs use Outlook's data for their own maniacal purpose.

Now Outlook can get even, by importing data from an Access database. This function is helpful when you want to get a lot of data quickly into Outlook.

Importing data is exactly the same as exporting data. The Import Wizard screens all have the same functionality as the Export Wizard. In fact, only the last screen has a difference, and it's minor: a Change Destination button that gives you one more chance to choose the destination folder of the new data.

Outlook and Excel

After all of the great interactive stuff you learned about Word and Outlook, you're in for a letdown. Excel 97 and Outlook can do only two things together: create a workbook-related Task and share data.

To create a Task, follow these steps in the open Excel workbook:

1. Right-click on any toolbar in Excel.

2. Select the Reviewing toolbar from the pop-up menu.

3. On the Reviewing toolbar (see Figure 20.26), click the Create Microsoft Outlook Task button.

4. A Task tool will appear with a shortcut to the workbook in the note box. Finish filling in the rest of the Task information, and click Save and Close.

If you anticipate creating a lot of workbook-related Tasks, use the Tip procedure suggested in the previous section and move the Task button to another toolbar.

If you need to share data between the two programs, use Outlook's Import and Export Wizard, as described in the "Outlook and Access" section earlier this hour.

20

Figure 20.26.

The floating Excel 97 Reviewing toolbar.

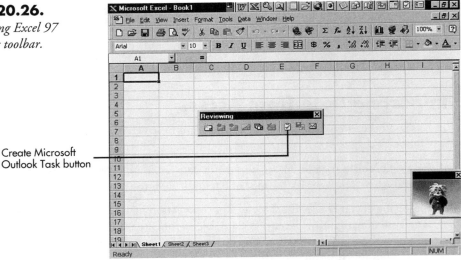

Create Microsoft
Outlook Task button

Outlook and PowerPoint

If you look at these two programs, no two could seem more different. One's a personal information manager, and one's a slide show maker, so how can there be any commonality between them?

The key is to remember that PowerPoint is not just a "slide show maker." It's a business presentation tool, and that one word—"business"—is the common connection with Outlook. However, as you were warned earlier in the hour, the interactivity is not easy to see.

After you have created a presentation in PowerPoint, one of your options is to use a computer terminal to project the presentation. While the presentation is made, PowerPoint's Meeting Minder can take notes, schedule a meeting, or create a Task. It's those last two capabilities that relate directly to Outlook.

Scheduling a Meeting

Scheduling a meeting with PowerPoint's Meeting Minder is simple. If you right-click anywhere in a slide show presentation, a pop-up menu will appear (see Figure 20.27).

When you click on the Meeting Minder command, the Meeting Minder dialog appears, as seen in Figure 20.28.

If you click the Schedule button, a Meeting tool appears. Using this, you can quickly schedule a meeting without entering Outlook.

20

Figure 20.27.

The Slide Show pop-up menu.

Figure 20.28.

The Meeting Minder dialog.

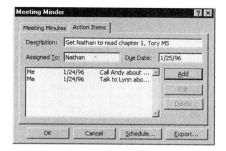

Creating Tasks

You can also use the Meeting Minder to create some Tasks. If you click the Action Items tab, you can enter the task's subject into the Description field and the due date and assignee into their respective fields. When this information is entered, click the Add button.

You can add as many action items as you want. When you are finished, don't click the OK button. Click the Export button instead. This will activate the Meeting Minder Export dialog (see Figure 20.29).

This dialog gives you two choices. You can export any meeting minutes and action items you have into a Word 97 document or export just the action items into Outlook. If you check this latter option and click Export Now, the action items will be placed directly into Tasks, as seen in Figure 20.30.

Summary

In this hour, you learned about all the different ways that Outlook can interact with the other Office 97 programs. With the capability to share data, e-mail tools, and create Tasks from most of the Office programs, Outlook is truly part of the Office 97 "puzzle," and demonstrates that the whole is indeed greater than the sum of its parts.

20

Figure 20.29.

The Meeting Minder Export dialog.

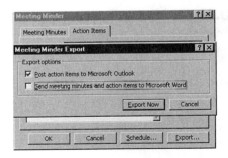

Figure 20.30.

The exported action items now in Tasks.

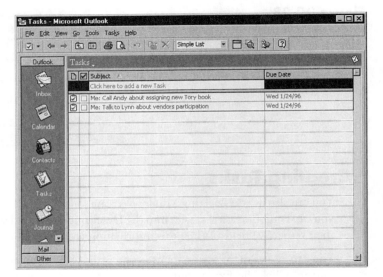

In Hour 21, "Remote Control: Delegating with Outlook," you will learn how Outlook can be used by others to manage mail, tasks, and schedules. Doesn't sound very exciting? Well, this will be other people using *your* Outlook files to manage *your* mail, *your* tasks, and *your* schedule.

20

Q&A

Q Can Outlook share data with other non-Office programs?

A Yes, it can. It can import and export data between Outlook and FoxPro, dBASE, and Schedule+.

Q Can I use another word processor as my e-mail editor?

A Nope.

Q I am having problems with exporting mail merge data. Do you have any hints?

A It depends on the problem. If you are not getting all your data, remember that you can only specify one Outlook folder at a time when mail merging from Word, and subfolders do not count. You should perform separate mail merges with each contact folder, or (better) copy all of the right contacts into a new special folder and mail merge from that.

If the problem is too much data, it may be because you had a filter on your contacts. When Word mail merges, it ignores filters and picks up all data in a folder. Again, copy the data into a new folder and mail merge from that.

20

Hour 21

Remote Control: Delegating with Outlook

CAUTION

Reading this hour without Exchange Server has been known to cause severe frustration and anger. You are recommended to move to the next hour until you or your company acquires access to an Exchange Server.

Feel free to make a copy of this hour to show to your boss or MIS so you can wave it in their face and say, "See? *This* is what we could do with Exchange Server!"

Do you have an assistant? Do you treat them well all the time, or do you just take them for granted until Secretaries' Day, when you might send them a bouquet? I ask merely because I don't have one and I'd like to know the proper way to treat them.

After watching bigwigs and their assistants, I have seen that assistants schedule meetings and appointments, answer mail, answer the phone—mostly things that Outlook can do. So, now that Outlook is here, the bosses will be able to take care of themselves, right?

Now that you've stopped laughing, let's get real. Managers will always need someone to take care of things for them, big or small. Even if they don't have an actual assistant, there are those rare times when they leave the office (vacations, appendectomies, conventions, the usual) and someone else needs to be in charge.

So for all those Napoleons among us, Outlook has something really great. By assigning delegates, Outlook users can let someone else answer their e-mail, assign tasks, and schedule appointments.

Back to Sharing Time in Romper Room

All right, before you begin to learn how to use Delegate Access, it's important to understand just what it is. Whenever you deal with Exchange Server, sooner or later you will hear talk about shared folders, public folders, and Delegate Access. It will probably scramble your head a bit. (This is your head. This is your head on Exchange…)

Table 21.1 attempts to clear up the confusion by indicating the differences between these terms.

Table 21.1. Share and share alike.

Term	Definition
Shared (private) folder	Allows someone to enter your Exchange folder and look at its data and that's it
Delegate Access	Lets someone enter your Exchange folder and send things such as meeting and task requests on your behalf
Public folder	Lets everyone look inside your Exchange folder

This hour is going to focus on Delegate Access, but because it is a more open form of a shared private folder, a lot will be picked up about that along the way, too.

Begin at the Beginning

Just because you have Exchange Server installed does not mean you will automatically be able to use the Delegate features. The first time you want to use it, you will likely have to install them in Outlook.

21

To see if you need to install the Delegate add-in, click the Tool|Options menu command in Outlook. Do you see a Delegate tab? No? Then it's time to install the add-in:

1. Click the General tab in the Options dialog box.
2. Click the Add-In Manager button.
3. If the Delegate Access add-in appears in the list of loaded add-ins (see Figure 21.1), make sure it is checked. Once it is, click OK. The Delegate tab will appear in the Options dialog.

Figure 21.1.

The Add-Ins dialog.

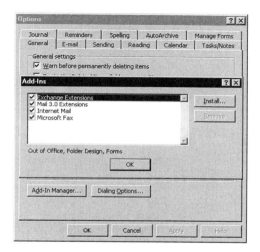

If the add-in is not listed in the Add-In dialog, it needs to be installed.

4. Click the Install button. The Install Extension dialog (see Figure 21.2) opens.
5. There are a number of Outlook add-ins presented. Select `Dlgsetp.ecf` and click Open.
6. The Delegate Access option is now in the Add-in dialog. Make sure it is checked, then click OK.

The Delegate tab is now in the Options dialog. Now, let's use it.

21

Figure 21.2.

The Install Extension dialog.

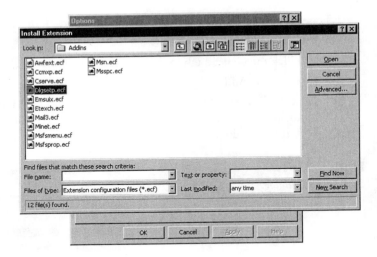

Delegating Outlook Folders

When it comes time for you to give someone Delegate Access to your Exchange folder, you are going to have to set it up in the Options dialog:

1. In Outlook, click the Tools|Options menu command.

2. In the Options dialog, click the Delegates tab.

3. If the delegate is already in the Delegates box, skip to step 6; otherwise click the Add button.

4. In the Add Users dialog, type the name of the delegate-to-be you want to set permissions for in the Type name field.

5. Click Add, then OK.

6. In the Delegates box, select the delegate you want.

TIME SAVER

Want to assign access to more than one delegate? Select multiple names in the Delegates field.

7. Click the Permissions button, and then choose the permissions for the folders you want the delegate(s) to access. These permissions are explained in Table 21.2.

21

Table 21.2. Delegate permissions.

Permission	What the delegate can do
Author	Read and create items, as well as change and delete only the items they have created.
Editor	Read, create, change, and delete any item in the folder.
Reviewer	Read-only. (This level is moot if the Send meeting requests and responses only to my delegates, not to me check box is checked on the Delegates tab. Read-only permission would be useless in this situation because all the information is going straight to the delegate's Inbox anyway.)
Custom	Some variant of the above three levels, defined by the delegator.
None	No permissions given.

8. Outlook will send a message to the new delegates of their new status and their permissions. To do this, click the Automatically send a message to delegate summarizing these permissions check box.

Repeat these steps whenever you want to change a present delegate's access permissions—just skip steps 3–5.

Once you no longer need delegates, you can remove them very quickly. To do so, complete these steps:

1. Open the Delegates tab of the Options dialog.
2. Select the names of the delegates you want to remove.
3. Click Remove.

TIME SAVER

> If you use the same delegates a lot, instead of completely removing them, change their assigned permissions to None. Then they will still be in your Delegates list later.

The remainder of this hour shows you what to do when you get tapped on the electronic shoulder as a delegate.

21

Handling the Inbox as a Delegate

One thing that never stops, even when someone is gone, is mail. The slogan "through rain, snow, or dark of night" certainly applies to electronic messages—even more so because e-mail does not stop on Sundays and national holidays.

On average, Americans with e-mail get about five messages a day. Corporate workers receive an average of 12 per day. Neither of these numbers sounds like a lot, except when you consider they all usually have to be answered. Messages have become like phone calls—the immediacy of their arrival promotes the speed of the reply.

It's for this reason Outlook has Delegate Access, so messages can get answered quickly, even when you are unavailable.

Replying to Messages

Answering a delegator's e-mail is not a complicated process, as seen in the following steps. Remember, to do this, the delegate must have author or editor permission assigned to him:

1. In Outlook, click the File | Open Special Folder | Exchange Server Folder menu command.
2. Type the name of the delegator into the Name field, or click the Name button and choose from the Select Names dialog.
3. In the Folder field, select the Inbox folder.

JUST A MINUTE

These first three steps are used to open any delegator's Outlook folder. For the rest of the hour, these three actions will be named the "Open the delegator's folder" step.

4. Select the message that you want to reply to.
5. Click the Reply button on the Standard Toolbar, click the Compose | Reply menu command, or type the Ctrl+R shortcut keys.
6. Compose the reply message as you normally would.
7. Click the Send button.

As you can see, replying to a message from someone else's Inbox is exactly like doing it from your own. What the recipient of the reply receives, however, is a little different than the usual message. They will see the delegator's name in the Sent On Behalf Of field, and the delegate's name in the From field.

Sending Messages

Delegates can do just more than reply to mail. They can create entirely new messages on behalf of the delegator. If you have received delegate permission, follow these steps to send a message on behalf of someone else:

1. In Inbox, click the New Mail Message button in the Standard Toolbar, or click the Ctrl+N shortcut keys.

2. In the Message tool, click the View | From Field menu command. The From field will appear in the Message tool (see Figure 21.3).

Figure 21.3.

The From field.

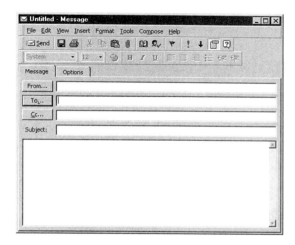

3. In the From field, type the name of the delegator.

4. Complete the rest of the message as you normally would. When finished, click the Send button.

Again, the recipient will see the delegator's name in the Sent On Behalf Of field, and the delegate's name in the From field.

Handling Tasks as a Delegate

Sometimes when a person is out of the office, he needs to have things done for him besides just monitoring his communications.

The steps to create a Task or a Task request on behalf of the delegator are exactly like those detailed in Hour 13, "Things to Do with Tasks," except that you must first open the delegator's Tasks folder. You can also change the order of the delegator's Task list. To respond to a Task request, a delegate must first enter the delegator's Inbox.

21

TIME SAVER

Do you often have to use someone else's Inbox, Tasks folder, or Calendar? If so, you can add a shortcut to the Outlook bar to that folder.

Right-click on the background of the Outlook bar, then click the Add to Outlook Bar command on the pop-up menu. Navigate down the Shared Private Folders branch in the Add to Outlook Bar dialog until the correct folder of the correct person is selected. Click OK.

Now the delegator's folder is just a click away.

The criterion to take any of these actions is that the user must have Delegate Access with Editor permission.

Handling Calendar as a Delegate

Again, handling someone else's Calendar is the same as handling your own. Appointments and meeting requests are created from the delegator's Calendar, and the acceptance or declination of a meeting request is done through the delegator's Inbox.

To have this kind of ability, the delegate must have (you guessed it) Delegate Access and Editor permission.

Summary

As if you don't have enough work to do already, Outlook and Exchange Server enable you to handle the work of someone else. While I am sure this has you jumping for joy, it does allow the office to continue to hum along in someone's absence.

And, if you are a delegate for a manager, this not only gives you a chance to show your stuff, but also a way to get your feet wet in a job you might want someday.

In the next hour, you will learn one of the high-end ways you can customize Outlook, using Office 97's underlying programming technology: Visual Basic for Applications.

Q&A

Q **Getting into a delegator's folders seems easy enough, but how do I get back to my own?**

A This is easy, too. When you are done with the delegator's folders, click any of the icons in the Outlook bar. You will automatically be brought back to your folder.

Q **Throughout this book you have mentioned Exchange Server. Where can I get more information?**

A On the Web, navigate your browser to `http://www.microsoft.com/exchange`.

21

Part
VIII

Cutting-Edge Outlook

Hour

Hour **22**

Automating Outlook with VBA

by Paul McFedries

It is interaction with others which teaches man all he knows.

—Euripides

Users of Office 95 had to rely on three separate tools to manage their electronic lives: the Windows Messaging System, the Windows 95 e-mail client, and Schedule+, the Office address book and time-management program. Although these applications were a large step up from sticky notes and postage stamps, the combination was never a satisfying one. Why? Well, let me count the ways:

☐ Although Windows 95's Exchange client was to be admired for its capability to combine multiple e-mail systems and faxing in a single Inbox, it was woefully lacking in features. Items such as message filtering and automatic signatures, although available for years in other clients, were nowhere to be found in Exchange. (However, the client that shipped with Exchange Server was a noticeable improvement.)

☐ Schedule+ had some interesting and useful features, but it suffered from a clunky interface. And its piggish use of system resources made you reluctant to leave it open all the time (usually considered a prerequisite for a scheduling tool!).

☐ Exchange and Schedule+ didn't know how to work with each other. For example, the programs couldn't share a common address book, or even exchange addresses via some common file format.

☐ Neither program was set up to properly handle the groupware services offered by Microsoft Exchange Server.

To solve these problems, Microsoft came up with a new program to replace both the Exchange Client and Schedule+. It's called Outlook and not only does it combine the functionality of Exchange and Schedule+ in a single package, but it also includes a boatload of new features that turn it into a truly useful information management tool. This hour takes you through a number of methods for taking advantage of Outlook's e-mail and groupware capabilities, both on a forms level and a programming level. If you don't care about programming, take this hour off and head on over to Hour 23 "It Takes a Licking..."

A Summary of Outlook's Programmable Features

When designing Outlook, one of Microsoft's goals was to give as many people as possible the ability both to customize the program and to take advantage of its dynamic properties. To accomplish this, the designers added many features that enable users to "program" Outlook without doing any programming. The following changes have been examined for each Outlook tool in previous hours:

☐ Changing the folder view

☐ Sorting messages

☐ Grouping messages

☐ Filtering messages

☐ Defining a custom view

☐ Using rules to process messages automatically

☐ Creating public folders

On a slightly higher level, you can gain even more control over the operation and appearance of Outlook by getting your hands a little more dirty:

☐ Create custom forms by modifying any of Outlook's built-in forms (such as Message and Contact), which you have already learned in previous hours.

22

☐ Add VBScript code to a form in order to control the form programmatically.

☐ Incorporate Office 97 documents into Outlook's forms, and then use VBA macros embedded in these documents to control the operation of the form.

☐ Use Automation to control Outlook's objects from any VBA application.

Accessing Outlook Via Automation

Referencing Automation objects in VBA takes a little more work than regular objects (although, as you'll see, it's really just a few extra keystrokes). Specifically, you need to use the `Dim` and `Set` statements to let VBA know that you want to work with an Automation object. In theory, there are three ways to go about this: the `New` keyword, the `CreateObject` function, and the `GetObject` function. In practice, however, you can only reference Outlook's Automation interface by using `CreateObject`. Here's the syntax used with this function:

```
CreateObject(Class)
```

> Class   The *programmatic identifier* that specifies the Automation server application and the type of object to create.

The `Class` argument is a string that always takes the following form:

```
Application.ObjectType
```

Here, `Application.ObjectType` specifies the Automation object class, where `Application` is the name of the application as it appears in the Object Browser's Project/Library drop-down list, and `ObjectType` is the object class type.

Note that you normally use `CreateObject` within a `Set` statement and the function serves to create a new instance of the specified Automation object. For example, if `ol` is an object variable, you'd use the following statements to create a new instance of Outlook's Application object:

```
Dim ol As Outlook.Application
Set ol = CreateObject("Outlook.Application")
```

Note that there's nothing else you need to do to use the Automation object. With your variable declared and an instance of the object created, you can use that object's properties and methods directly. I'll show you some examples when I discuss Outlook's object model in the next section. (Note as well that your code should clear the object variable—that is, it should set the variable to `Nothing`—to save resources.)

T

The CreateObject function loads Outlook, but you never see Outlook onscreen. This is the desired behavior in most Automation situations. However, if you *do* want to see what Outlook is up to, set the Application object's Visible property to True, like so:

```
ol.Visible = True
```

Automation and the Outlook Object Model

As you've seen when designing forms, Outlook has an amazing number of options for customizing objects without forging any code. These options were designed for end-users who lack programming skills and for developers who need to get low-level applications up to speed quickly. However, this is a programming chapter, so I can assume not only that you have programming skills, but also that you'll eventually need to create higher-level Outlook applications. So I'll spend the rest of this hour showing you how to build programmability into Outlook, both indirectly (by using VBA to control Outlook's Automation interface) and directly (by using VBScript in a form).

Before we get down to the brass tacks of Outlook programming, however, we need to examine Outlook's object model. This will give you an idea of what kinds of objects you can manipulate and how you can manipulate them. Throughout the rest of this section, I'll introduce you to the object model and show you how to use this model to work with Outlook via Automation in your VBA applications.

JUST A MINUTE

As always when dealing with Automation, your first chore is to set up a reference to the required object library in your VBA project. In this case, highlight your project and select Tools | References in the Visual Basic Editor, activate the check box beside Microsoft Outlook 8.0 Object Library in the Available References list, and then click OK.

Also note that this hour assumes you're familiar with Automation concepts, as well as the Visual Basic Editor. For the best tutorial on general VBA programming, check out *VBA Programming Unleashed*, by Paul McFedries (Sams Publishing).

22

The Application Object

The top-level object in the Outlook hierarchy is the Application object. You use this object to return information about the current Outlook session and to gain access to the rest of the Outlook hierarchy. As I mentioned earlier, to establish an Automation connection with this object, use the CreateObject function.

The Application object has four second-level objects:

☐ Assistant—This is a property of the Application object, and it returns an Assistant object that represents the Microsoft Office Assistant. (This object is common to all the Microsoft Office application hierarchies.)

☐ Explorer—This object references the window in which Outlook is displaying a folder's contents. See "The Explorer Object" section later in this hour.

☐ Inspector—This object references the window in which Outlook is displaying an item's contents. See "The Inspector Object" section later in this hour.

☐ NameSpace—This object acts like a sort of "abstract root" object for the Outlook application.

The NameSpace Object

You use the NameSpace object to log on and off, return information about the current user, and more. To return a NameSpace object, you use the GetNameSpace method with the MAPI argument (which is the only argument currently supported by this method). Here's an example:

```
Dim ol As Outlook.Application
Dim ns As NameSpace
Set ol = CreateObject("Outlook.Application")
Set ns = ol.GetNameSpace("MAPI")
```

Logging On to a MAPI Session

Once you have the NameSpace object, you can then log on to establish a MAPI session by invoking the Logon method:

NameSpace.Logon(*Profile, Password, ShowDialog, NewSession*)

NameSpace	The NameSpace object.
Profile	The name of the Outlook profile to use in the MAPI session.
Password	The password used with the profile.
ShowDialog	A Boolean value that determines whether Outlook displays the Logon dialog box. Use True to display the dialog box.

NewSession	A Boolean value that determines whether Outlook creates a new MAPI session. Set this argument to True to start a new session; use False to log on to the current session.

For example, the following statement logs on to a MAPI session using the Windows Messaging Settings profile (assuming the current NameSpace is represented by a variable named ns):

```
ns.Logon "Windows Messaging Settings"
```

Logging Off a MAPI Session

When you've completed your labors in a MAPI session, you can log off by running the NameSpace object's Logoff method:

NameSpace.Logoff

NameSpace	The NameSpace object.

Working with MAPIFolder Objects

The NameSpace object also acts as a root folder for all the Outlook folders. This means you can use it to return a reference to a folder and then work with that folder. Note that in the Outlook object model, folders are MAPIFolder objects.

One way to return a MAPIFolder object is to use the GetDefaultFolder method. This method returns the default folder for a given type in the current profile. Here's the syntax:

NameSpace.GetDefaultFolder(*FolderTypeEnum*)

NameSpace	The NameSpace object.
FolderTypeEnum	A constant that specifies the type of folder. You can use any of the following defined constants: olFolderCalendar, olFolderContacts, olFolderDeletedItems, olFolderInbox, olFolderJournal, olFolderNotes, olFolderOutbox, olFolderSentMail, and olFolderTasks.

Alternatively, you can use the Folders property to return a Folders object that represents all the MAPIFolder objects in the namespace. To reference a specific folder, use Folders(*Index*), where *Index* is either an integer value—where the first folder is 1—or the name of a folder, such as Folders("Public Folders").

Listing 22.1 shows a procedure that enumerates the first- and second-level folders in the namespace.

TYPE

Listing 22.1. A procedure that enumerates the first- and second-level folders in the Outlook namespace.

22

```
 1: Sub EnumerateFolders()
 2:     Dim ol As Outlook.Application
 3:     Dim ns As NameSpace
 4:     Dim folder As MAPIFolder, subfolder As MAPIFolder
 5:     '
 6:     ' Establish a connection and log on
 7:     '
 8:     Set ol = CreateObject("Outlook.Application")
 9:     Set ns = ol.GetNamespace("MAPI")
10:     ns.Logon
11:     '
12:     ' Run through the first-level folders
13:     '
14:     For Each folder In ns.Folders
15:         Debug.Print folder.Name
16:         '
17:         ' Run through the second-level folders, if any
18:         '
19:         If folder.Folders.Count > 1 Then
20:             For Each subfolder In folder.Folders
21:                 Debug.Print "   " & subfolder.Name
22:             Next 'subfolder
23:         End If
24:     Next 'folder
25:     '
26:     ' Log off the session
27:     '
28:     ns.Logoff
29:     Set ol = Nothing
30: End Sub
```

The code begins by declaring several object variables (lines 2–4), and then it sets up the references to Outlook's Automation objects (lines 8 and 9) and logs on (line 10). Then a For Each...Next loop runs through each object in the Folders collection (lines 14–24). The second-level folders are derived by using the Folders property of the MAPIFolder object (lines 20–22). The name of each folder is displayed in the Visual Basic Editor's Immediate window (the Debug.Print statement in lines 15 and 21; activate the View|Immediate Window command to see the results).

The Explorer Object

As mentioned earlier, the Explorer object represents the window Outlook is using to display a folder's contents. There are two ways to return an Explorer object:

☐ *Application*.ActiveExplorer—This method returns an Explorer object that represents the currently displayed window for the specified Outlook *Application* object. If no window is currently displayed, this method returns `Nothing`.

☐ `MAPIFolder`.`GetExplorer`—This method returns an Explorer object that represents a new window for the specified `MAPIFolder`. Here's the syntax:

`MAPIFolder`.GetDefaultFolder(*`DisplayMode`*)

`MAPIFolder`   The MAPIFolder object.

`DisplayMode`   A constant that determines how the Explorer object will display the folder. You have the following choices:

DisplayMode	*Description*
`olFolderDisplayFolderOnly`	Displays only the folder contents and the folder banner.
`olFolderDisplayNoNavigation`	Displays the folder contents and the folder banner without access to the folder list.
`olFolderDisplayNormal`	Displays the folder contents, folder banner, and Outlook bar.

Here are some Explorer object properties and methods:

☐ `Explorer`.`CommandBars`—Returns the `CommandBars` collection, which represents the CommandBar objects associated with the specified `Explorer` object.

☐ `Explorer`.`CurrentFolder`—Returns or sets a MAPIFolder object that represents the folder associated with the specified `Explorer` object.

☐ `Explorer`.`Close`—Closes the window associated with the specified `Explorer` object.

☐ `Explorer`.`Display`—Displays the window associated with the specified `Explorer` object.

Listing 22.2 shows a procedure that checks for an existing Explorer object and creates a new Explorer object if one doesn't exist.

Listing 22.2. A procedure that logs on to a MAPI session and then displays an Explorer object.

TYPE

```
1: Sub DisplayDefaultInboxFolder()
2:     Dim ol As Outlook.Application
3:     Dim ns As NameSpace
4:     Dim folder As MAPIFolder
5:     Dim exp As Explorer
6:     '
7:     ' Establish a connection and log on
8:     '
```

22

```
 9:     Set ol = CreateObject("Outlook.Application")
10:     Set ns = ol.GetNamespace("MAPI")
11:     ns.Logon
12:     '
13:     ' Get the default Inbox folder and set the Explorer
14:     '
15:     Set folder = ns.GetDefaultFolder(olFolderInbox)
16:     Set exp = ol.ActiveExplorer
17:     '
18:     ' If no folder is displayed, create a new one and display it
19:     '
20:     If exp Is Nothing Then
21:         Set exp = folder.GetExplorer(olFolderDisplayNoNavigation)
22:         exp.Display
23:     End If
24:     Set ol = Nothing
25: End Sub
```

After the usual variable declarations and logon (lines 2–11), the default Inbox folder is set to the folder variable (line 15), and then the active Explorer is set to the exp variable (line 16). If there is no current Explorer (that is, if the ActiveExplorer method returns Nothing; see line 20), a new Explorer is created (line 21) and displayed (line 22).

The Inspector Object

When you open an Outlook item (such as an e-mail message or a Contact), the window in which the item appears is an Inspector object. As with the Explorer object, there are two ways to return an Inspector object:

☐ Application.ActiveInspector—This method returns an Inspector object that represents the currently displayed item window for the specified Outlook Application object. If no window is currently displayed, this method returns Nothing.

☐ Item.GetExplorer—This property returns an Explorer object that represents a new window for the specified Item. (See "Working with Item Objects," later in this hour.)

The properties and methods of the Inspector object are similar to those of the Explorer object. Here's a summary of a few of the most useful members of this class.

Inspector.CommandBars returns the CommandBars collection, which represents the CommandBar objects associated with the specified Inspector object.

Inspector.CurrentItem returns or sets an Item object that represents the item associated with the specified Inspector object.

Inspector.ModifiedFormPages returns a Pages object that represents the various tabs in the specified Inspector object.

Inspector.Close closes the window associated with the specified *Inspector* object.

Inspector.Display displays the window associated with the specified *Inspector* object.

Inspector.HideFormPage hides a form page in the specified *Inspector* object. Here's the syntax:

Inspector.HideFormPage(*PageName*)

Inspector	The Inspector object you want to work with.
PageName	The name of the page you want to hide.

Inspector.IsWordMail returns True if the specified *Inspector* object uses WordMail; it returns False, otherwise.

Inspector.SetCurrentFormPage displays a page in the specified *Inspector* object:

Inspector.SetCurrentFormPage(*PageName*)

Inspector	The Inspector object you want to work with.
PageName	The name of the page you want to display.

Inspector.ShowFormPage makes a previously hidden page visible in the specified *Inspector* object. Here's the syntax:

Inspector.ShowFormPage(*PageName*)

Inspector	The Inspector object you want to work with.
PageName	The name of the page you want to show.

Working with Item Objects

Once you've logged on to a MAPI session and referenced the MAPIFolder object you want to work with, you can then use the Items collection to deal with the various items in the folder. This section discusses the various types of items available and shows you how to create new items.

Types of Item Objects

Depending on the type of folder you're using, the Items collection will contain one or more of the objects listed in Table 22.1. In each case, you can return an item by using Items(*Index*), where *Index* is either an integer (where the first item in the folder is 1) or a value from the default property listed in Table 22.1.

22

Table 22.1. Outlook's item object types.

Item	Default property	Description
AppointmentItem	Subject	This object represents an appointment or meeting in a Calendar folder.
ContactItem	FullName	This object represents a contact in a Contacts folder.
JournalItem	Subject	This object represents a journal entry in a Journal folder.
MailItem	Subject	This object represents a mail message in an Inbox folder. (Note that the Inbox folder type represents any mail folder, not just the Inbox folder.)
NoteItem	Subject	This object represents a note in a Notes folder.
TaskItem	Subject	This object represents a task in a Tasks folder.

JUST A MINUTE

Table 22.1 lists the main item types, but there are also five other types you'll come across: MeetingRequestItem, PostItem, RemoteItem, ReportItem, and TaskRequestItem. Because these types often co-exist with other types in a single folder, you often need to know the type of item you're dealing with. To do this, use the TypeName(*Item*) function, where *Item* is the item object you're working with.

A Closer Look at MailItem Objects

Each of the item object types listed in Table 22.1 has dozens of properties and methods, which is a reflection of the tremendous attention to detail that characterizes the Outlook product. Rather than going through each property and method for each item object (which would probably double the size of the book), I'll use this section to examine the object you'll probably use most often in your VBA applications: the MailItem object.

MailItem Object Properties

The MailItem property boasts over 60 different properties that cover everything from the message recipients to the assigned sensitivity. Here's a listing of the most useful MailItem properties.

MailItem.AlternateRecipientAllowed returns `True` if the specified *MailItem* can be forwarded; it returns `False`, otherwise. You can also set this property.

MailItem.Attachments returns the `Attachments` object—the collection of all attached files it—for the specified *MailItem*. Use the `Attachments` object's `Add` method to add an attachment to a message:

```
mItem.Attachments.Add "C:\My Documents\Memo.doc"
```

MailItem.BCC returns the display names (separated by semicolons) of the addresses listed as blind courtesy copy recipients for the specified *MailItem*. See the `Recipients` property to learn how to add e-mail addresses to a message.

MailItem.Body returns or sets the body text for the specified *MailItem*.

MailItem.CC returns the display names (separated by semicolons) of the addresses listed as courtesy copy recipients for the specified *MailItem*. See the `Recipients` property to learn how to add e-mail addresses to a message.

MailItem.ConversationIndex returns the index of the conversation thread associated with the specified *MailItem*.

MailItem.ConversationTopic returns the topic of the conversation thread associated with the specified *MailItem*.

MailItem.CreationTime returns the date and time that the specified *MailItem* was created.

MailItem.DeferredDeliveryTime returns or sets the date and time that the specified *MailItem* is to be delivered.

MailItem.ExpiryTime returns or sets the date and time that the specified *MailItem* is to expire.

MailItem.Importance returns or sets the importance level for the specified *MailItem*. This property can be one of the following constants: `olImportanceHigh`, `olImportanceLow`, or `olImportanceNormal`.

MailItem.ReadReceiptRequested returns `True` if the sender has requested a read receipt for the specified *MailItem*; it returns `False`, otherwise.

MailItem.ReceivedTime returns or sets the date and time that the specified *MailItem* was received.

MailItem.Recipients returns a `Recipients` object—the collection of recipients—for the specified *MailItem*. You use the `Recipients` object's `Add` method to add new recipients to a message:

MailItem.Recipients.Add(**Name**)

    MailItem   The message to which you want to add the recipient.

22

Name   The e-mail address of the recipient. If the recipient is in the address book, you can just use the display name.

To determine the message line to which the recipient will be added (To, Cc, or Bcc), set the `Type` property of the new recipient. Use `olTo` for the To line; `olCC` for the Cc line; or `olBCC` for the Bcc line. For example, assuming `newMessage` is an object variable that represents a MailItem, the following statements add two recipients, one on the To line and one on the Cc line:

```
newMessage.Recipients.Add("Biff").Type = olTo
newMessage.Recipients.Add("bob@weave.com").Type = olCC
```

`MailItem.SaveSentMessageFolder` returns or sets the MAPIFolder object in which a copy of the specified `MailItem` will be saved once it has been sent.

`MailItem.SenderName` returns the display name of the sender of the specified `MailItem`.

`MailItem.Sensitivity` returns or sets the sensitivity level for the specified `MailItem`. This property can be one of the following constants: `olConfidential`, `olNormal`, `olPersonal`, or `olPrivate`.

`MailItem.SentOn` returns the date and time that the specified `MailItem` was sent.

`MailItem.Size` returns the size of the specified `MailItem`, in bytes.

`MailItem.Subject` returns or sets the subject line for the specified `MailItem`.

`MailItem.To` returns the display names (separated by semicolons) of the addresses listed in the To line of the specified `MailItem`. See the `Recipients` property to learn how to add e-mail addresses to a message.

`MailItem.UnRead` returns `True` if the specified `MailItem` has not been read; it returns `False`, otherwise. You can also set this property.

`MailItem.VotingOptions` returns or sets the voting options (separated by semicolons) for the specified `MailItem`.

`MailItem.VotingResponse` returns or sets the voting response for the specified `MailItem`.

Listing 22.3 shows a procedure that utilizes a few of these properties.

TYPE   **Listing 22.3. A procedure that reads Inbox data into a worksheet.**

```
1: Sub ReadInboxData()
2:     Dim ol As Outlook.Application
3:     Dim ns As NameSpace
4:     Dim folder As MAPIFolder
```

continues

Listing 22.3. continued

```
5:        Dim ws As Worksheet
6:        Dim i As Integer
7:        '
8:        ' Establish a connection and log on
9:        '
10:       Set ol = CreateObject("Outlook.Application")
11:       Set ns = ol.GetNamespace("MAPI")
12:       ns.Logon
13:       '
14:       ' Get the default Inbox folder and
15:       ' set the Receive Mail worksheet
16:       '
17:       Set folder = ns.GetDefaultFolder(olFolderInbox)
18:       Set ws = Worksheets("Receive Mail")
19:       '
20:       ' Run through each item in the Inbox
21:       '
22:       For i = 1 To folder.Items.Count
23:           '
24:           ' Make sure we only grab MailItems
25:           '
26:           If TypeName(folder.Items(i)) = "MailItem" Then
27:               With folder.Items(i)
28:                   '
29:                   ' Record the sender, subject, size,
30:                   ' received time, and some of the body
31:                   '
32:                   ws.[A1].Offset(i, 0) = .SenderName
33:                   ws.[A1].Offset(i, 1) = .Subject
34:                   ws.[A1].Offset(i, 2) = .Size
35:                   ws.[A1].Offset(i, 3) = .ReceivedTime
36:                   ws.[A1].Offset(i, 4) = Left(.Body, 100)
37:               End With
38:           End If
39:       Next 'i
40:       '
41:       ' Log off the session
42:       '
43:       ns.Logoff
44:       Set ol = Nothing
45: End Sub
```

The code declares a few variables and then logs on to a MAPI session (lines 2–12). The procedure then runs through the items in the default Inbox folder (the For...Next loop in lines 22–39), and then records the SenderName (line 32), Subject (line 33), Size (line 34), ReceivedTime (line 35), and the first 100 characters of the Body (line 36) onto a worksheet. (Note the use of VBA's TypeName function, described earlier, in line 26 to make sure we only work with MailItem objects.)

22

Creating a New MailItem Object

When you need to send an e-mail message, you first need to create a new MailItem object. You do this by invoking the Application object's CreateItem method:

Application.CreateItem(*ItemType*)

Application	An Outlook Application object.
ItemType	A constant that specifies the type of item you want to create. For a MailItem, use olMailItem. (The other constant values you can use are olAppointmentItem, olContactItem, olJournalItem, olNoteItem, olPostItem, or olTaskItem.

Listing 22.4 shows a sample procedure.

Listing 22.4. A procedure that uses worksheet data to send an e-mail message.

```
 1: Sub SendFromWorksheet()
 2:     Dim ol As Outlook.Application
 3:     Dim ns As NameSpace
 4:     Dim ws As Worksheet
 5:     Dim newMessage As MailItem
 6:     '
 7:     ' Establish a connection and log on
 8:     '
 9:     Set ol = CreateObject("Outlook.Application")
10:     Set ns = ol.GetNamespace("MAPI")
11:     ns.Logon
12:     '
13:     ' Data is in the Send mail worksheet
14:     '
15:     Set ws = Worksheets("Send Mail")
16:     '
17:     ' Create the new MailItem
18:     '
19:     Set newMessage = ol.CreateItem(olMailItem)
20:     '
21:     ' Specify the recipient, subject, and body
22:     ' and then send the message
23:     '
24:     With newMessage
25:         .Recipients.Add ws.[B2]
26:         .Subject = ws.[B3]
27:         .Body = ws.[B4]
28:         .Send
29:     End With
30:     '
31:     ' Log off the session
32:     '
33:     ns.Logoff
34:     Set ol = Nothing
35: End Sub
```

This procedure creates a new MailItem object (line 19) and uses data from an Excel worksheet (declared in line 15) to set the MailItem object's recipient (line 25), subject (line 26), and body (line 27). With that done, the Send method is invoked (line 28) to send the message.

MailItem Object Methods

With the methods available to the MailItem object, you can send messages, reply and forward messages, move messages to a different folder, and more. Here's a summary of some of the MailItem object methods:

MailItem.Close closes the Inspector object in which the specified *MailItem* object is displayed. This method uses the following syntax:

MailItem.Close(*SaveMode*)

MailItem	The MailItem object you want to work with.
SaveMode	A constant that determines how the Inspector is closed:

Save Mode	Description
olDiscard	Closes the Inspector without saving changes.
olPromptForSave	Prompts the user to save changes.
olSave	Saves changes automatically.

MailItem.Copy creates a copy of the specified *MailItem* object.

MailItem.Delete deletes the specified *MailItem* object.

MailItem.Display displays the specified *MailItem* object in a new Inspector using the following syntax:

MailItem.Display(*Modal*)

MailItem	The MailItem object you want to work with.
Modal	Use True to make the Inspector a modal window; use False for a non-modal window.

MailItem.Forward forwards the specified *MailItem* object. This method returns a new MailItem object that represents the message to be forwarded.

MailItem.Move moves the specified *MailItem* object to a different folder using the following syntax:

MailItem.Move(*DestFldr*)

MailItem	The MailItem object you want to work with.
DestFldr	The MAPIFolder object to which you want to move the message.

MailItem.PrintOut prints the specified *MailItem* object.

22

MailItem.Reply replies to the sender of the specified *MailItem* object. This method returns a new MailItem object that represents the reply to be sent.

MailItem.ReplyAll replies to all the recipients of the specified *MailItem* object. This method returns a new MailItem object that represents the reply to be sent.

MailItem.Save saves the specified *MailItem* object.

MailItem.SaveAs saves the specified *MailItem* object under a different name or path using the following syntax:

MailItem.SaveAs(**Path,** *Type*)

MailItem	The MailItem object you want to work with.
Path	The path to which you want to save the MailItem.
Type	A constant that specifies the file type you want to use:

olDoc	Word format (*.doc)
olMsg	Message format (*.msg)
olRTF	Rich Text Format (*.rtf)
olTemplate	Outlook Template format (*.oft)
olTxt	Text Only format (*.txt)

MailItem.Send sends the specified *MailItem* object.

Controlling Forms Via VBScript

HTML lets you create increasingly interactive and dynamic pages—from links to forms to database queries to ActiveX controls. If you know VBA, you can put that knowledge to good use by building some client-side intelligence into your pages. In other words, you can insert snippets of VBA-like code into your pages; this code will run automatically on users' machines when they download your page.

The secret of this is an offshoot of the VBA language called *VBScript*. In a browser that understands how to run VBScript programs (such as Internet Explorer), you can implement programs to validate form data, customize pages based on, say, the current time or the browser being used, get the various objects on the page to communicate with each other, and much more. These *scripts* (as they're called) can be as simple as displaying a message box when the user clicks a page object, or as complex as full-fledged games and applications.

However, VBScript is no one-trick pony. The same advantages that VBScript applies to Web forms can also be realized when working with Outlook forms. That's because Microsoft designed Outlook forms to handle VBScript procedures that can work directly with form objects and respond to form events. This enables you to add dynamic characteristics to your forms and to go well beyond the relatively simple validation features that are implemented as object properties. This section shows you how to implement VBScript in your custom Outlook forms.

The Differences Between VBA and VBScript

VBScript is designed as a strict subset of VBA. In other words, all elements of VBScript are present in VBA, but some VBA elements aren't implemented in VBScript. Table 22.2 summarizes the VBA language features that aren't present in VBScript.

Table 22.2. VBA language elements that aren't implemented in VBScript.

VBA Category	Not in VBScript
Arrays	Arrays declared with lower bound <> 0
	Array function
	Option Base
	Private, Public
Collection	Add, Count, Item, Remove
Conditional Compilation	#Const
	#If...Then...#Else
Control Flow	DoEvents
	For Each...Next
	With...End With
	GoSub...Return, GoTo
	On Error GoTo
	On...GoSub, On...GoTo
	Line numbers, line labels
Data Conversion	CCur, CVar, CVDate
	Format
	Str, Val
Data Types	All intrinsic data types except Variant
	Type...End Type
Date/Time	Date statement, Time statement
	Timer

22

22

VBA Category	Not in VBScript
DDE	`LinkExecute, LinkPoke, LinkRequest, LinkSend`
Debugging	`Debug.Print`
	`End, Stop`
Declaring Variables	`Declare`
	`Public, Private, Static`
	`New`
	`Const`
	Type-declaration characters
Error Handling	`Erl`
	`Error`
	`On Error...Resume`
	`Resume, Resume Next`
File I/O	All
Financial Functions	All
Object Manipulation	`CreateObject`
	`GetObject`
	`TypeOf`
Objects	Clipboard
	Collection
Operators	`Like`
Options	`Deftype`
	`Option Base`
	`Option Compare`
	`Option Private Module`
Strings	Fixed-length strings
	`LSet, RSet`
	`Mid statement`
	`StrConv`

Other than the restrictions outlined in Table 22.2, the rest of the VBA universe is at your disposal. You can use `If...Then...Else` statements, `Do...Loop` structures, functions such as `MsgBox` and `Format`, and whatever else your code requires.

Adding Scripts to a Form

To enable you to attach scripts to a form, the Forms Designer has a Script Editor feature. This is a simple text editor in which you write your VBScript event handlers, functions, and procedures. To open the Script Editor, make sure you're in the Forms Designer and then select the Form|View Code command. Figure 22.1 shows the Script Editor window with some VBScript code already added.

Figure 22.1.

Use the Form Designer's Script Editor to create your VBScript procedures.

```
Script Editor:
File  Edit  Script  Help

' This event handler runs whenever the user reads the item. The procedure updates the
' custom ReadCounter property, which monitors the number of times the item has been read.
'
Function Item_Read()
    '
    ' Increment the current value
    '
    Item.UserProperties.Item("ReadCounter").Value = _
        Item.UserProperties.Item("ReadCounter").Value + 1
    '
    ' Save now to avoid the user being prompted to save changes unnecessarily
    '
    Item.Save
End Function
' This event handler fires when the item is opened. The procedure displays the number
' of times the item has been read.
'
Function Item_Open()
    '
    ' Don't display the message if we've just created the item (i.e., the ReadCounter
    ' property is still 0).
    '
    If Item.UserProperties.Item("ReadCounter").Value <> 0 Then
        MsgBox "This item has been read " & _
            Item.UserProperties.Item("ReadCounter").Value & _
            " times."
    End If
End Function
```

Bear in mind that the Script Editor does not have the fancy IntelliSense features that you may have grown to depend upon in the Visual Basic Editor. There are no syntax colors, no pop-up hints, no case adjustments, and no automatic syntax checks. If you'd prefer to have these features around in order to keep your code on the straight and narrow, you might consider building your VBScripts in the Visual Basic Editor and then transferring them to the Script Editor when you're ready to try them out. If you go this route, however, make sure you use only the language elements that are part of the VBScript subset.

VBScript and the Form Object

Because your VBScripts exist at the form level, it makes sense that they'll spend much of their time manipulating either the form itself or one of the fields or controls defined on the form. This section examines how VBScript interacts with the form, and I'll discuss fields and controls a bit later.

In all your VBScript procedures, you use the Item keyword to reference the form object. This makes sense because a form is really a particular variation on the Outlook item theme, be it a MailItem, ContactItem, or whatever. Therefore, all of the properties and methods that are native to the type of item you're working with are fair game inside your VBScript routines. In a MailItem form, for example, Item.Save saves the form, Item.Send sends the form, and Item.Close closes the form.

Form Events

The Item keyword not only gives you access to a form's properties and methods, but also to any one of the many events that are associated with the item. Most item events are common to all the item types, and they cover actions such as reading the item, sending the item, and closing the item.

To add an event handler stub procedure to the Script Editor, select the Script|Event command to display the Events dialog box, shown in Figure 22.2. Highlight the event you want to work with and then click Add.

Figure 22.2.

Use the Events dialog box to select the event you want to handle.

The Script Editor inserts a stub procedure with the following general structure:

```
Function Item_Event(Arguments)

End Function
```

Here, *Event* is the name of the event you highlighted and *Arguments* is a set of one or more arguments that are passed to the procedure. (Note that many of the event handlers have no arguments at all.) As usual with these procedure stubs, you define the event handler by adding code between the Function and End Function statements.

Here's a rundown of the various events you can trap:

The Close event fires when the user closes the item or when your code invokes the Close method.

TIME SAVER

All of Outlook's event handlers are implemented as Function procedures. This means you can cancel any event by setting the function's return value to `False`. To cancel the `Close` event, for example, you'd add the following statement to the event handler:

```
Item_Close = False
```

The `CustomAction` event fires when the user or your code runs a custom action. This procedure uses the following syntax:

```
Item_CustomAction(ByVal Action, ByVal NewItem)
```

    Action   The custom action.

    NewItem   The new item that is created in response to the custom action.

The `CustomPropertyChange` event fires when the user or your code changes the value of a custom control. Here's the syntax:

```
Item_CustomPropertyChange(ByVal Name)
```

    Name   The name of the custom property.

I'll discuss custom properties in more detail when I discuss working with controls in your VBScript procedures, later in this hour. See "Working with Controls (Custom Properties)."

The `Forward` event fires when the user forwards the item or when your code invokes the `Forward` method. Here's the syntax:

```
Item_Forward(ByVal ForwardItem)
```

    ForwardItem   The new item that will be forwarded.

The `Open` event fires when the user opens the item. Note that this event fires after the `Read` event, discussed later.

The `PropertyChange` event fires when the user or your code changes the value of a standard item property (such as `Subject` or `To`). Here's the syntax:

```
Item_PropertyChange(ByVal Name)
```

    Name   The name of the property.

The `Read` event fires when the user displays the item for editing in an Inspector or displays the item in a view that allows in-cell editing. This event fires before the `Open` event.

22

The Reply event fires when the user replies to the item or when your code invokes the Reply method. Here's the syntax:

```
Item_Reply(ByVal Response)
```

     Response   The new reply item.

The ReplyAll event fires when the user replies to all or when your code invokes the ReplyAll method. Here's the syntax:

```
Item_ReplyAll(ByVal Response)
```

     Response   The new reply item.

The Send event fires when the user sends the item or when your code invokes the Send method.

The Write event fires when the user saves the item or when your code invokes the Save or SaveAs method.

Working with Controls (Custom Properties)

As you've seen, working with an item's standard properties is straightforward. You can either return or set the Item object's properties, or you can trap changes to the standard properties by writing a handler for the PropertyChange event. (For the latter, the event handler passes the name of the property, so you could set up a series of If...Then statements or even a Select Case structure to handle the various possibilities.)

However, you can also define custom properties for an item. These properties are, generally, non-field controls—such as text boxes and check boxes—that you add to the form using the Control Toolbox. To define the control as a custom property of the form, follow these steps:

1. Click on the control and select Form | Properties.
2. In the Properties dialog box that appears, activate the Value tab.
3. Click New to display the New Field dialog box.
4. Use the Name text box to enter a name for the custom property.
5. Use the Type and Format lists to select a data type and data format for the property (see Figure 22.3).
6. Click OK to return to the Properties dialog box.
7. If you also want to trap events for the control, activate the Display tab and enter a meaningful name for the control in the Name text box. (Note that this is only the name of the control; the name you entered in Step 4 is the name of the custom property.)
8. Click OK.

Figure 22.3.

Use the New Field dialog box to define the particulars of a custom property.

With the custom property now defined, it becomes a UserProperty object for the item. UserProperties is the collection of all UserProperty objects in an item, and you use this collection to reference a specific custom property, like so:

```
Item.UserProperties.Item("Name")
```

Here, *Name* is the name you specified for the custom property (in Step 4, above).

For example, the following statement returns the value of the ReadCounter custom property:

```
Item.UserProperties.Item("ReadCounter").Value
```

Recall, as well, that you can trap a change to any custom property by setting up a handler for the Item object's CustomPropertyChange event. Again, the event handler passes the name of the property so your code can test for different properties.

Finally, you can also trap certain events for custom controls. If you add a command button or a check box, for example, you can trap the Click event. To do this, create a stub procedure with the following structure:

```
Sub ControlName_Event()

End Sub
```

Here, *ControlName* is the name of the control (see Step 7 in the preceding procedure) and *Event* is the event you want to trap. The following example traps the Click event for a command button:

```
Sub CommandButton1_Click()
    [event handler code goes here]
End Sub
```

Summary

This hour shows you various methods for setting up groupware and e-mail applications with Outlook. After a brief introduction to Outlook and its programmable features, I turned your attention to programming Outlook. We began with a look at the Outlook object model and how to access it via Automation. In particular, we took a close look at the MailItem object and how to use it to read and send e-mail messages.

I finished with a look at how to create dynamic Outlook forms by adding VBScript event handlers and procedures.

Q&A

Q Just what are VBA and VBScript, and why is my head spinning?

A We saved the hardest hour until just about the end of the book, so you can relax now. As for the first part of the question, VBA is Visual Basic for Applications, a subset of Visual Basic. VBA is used specifically with Microsoft Office applications. VBScript is a subset of VBA, mostly used for embedded script code in active Web pages. As you saw this hour, Outlook can use VBScript as well.

Q I thought VBA could only program Microsoft Excel macros. Did this change?

A Yes, it did. With the introduction of Microsoft Office 97, all the "Big Four" Office programs (Word, Excel, PowerPoint, and Access) use VBA. This allows for greater integration between the programs. Any future Office-compatible programs will also use VBA for this kind of customization.

Hour 23

It Takes a Licking...

When we were kids, how many times did we look at Dick Tracy's watch communicator and go, "Ooooo"? Or drool with envy over Mr. Spock's tricorder? Fancy stuff, from fanciful shows.

Today, reality has begun to overtake fiction. Portable TVs are almost as small as watches, and cellular phones are nearly identical to the communicators used (the old flip-open ones, not the chest pins). Digital personal assistants, once the size of an old calculator, can now be worn on your wrist.

Introducing the Timex Data Link® Watch

In this hour, you will learn how to use Outlook with this latest bit of technology: the Timex Data Link® watch. This watch allows you to take information you have entered in Outlook anywhere you go with this watch—all without any wires.

After You Open the Box

The Timex Data Link® watch works directly with Microsoft Outlook. You do not need to install the Timex Data Link® software that comes with the watch, but we do recommend that you familiarize yourself with the features.

The Timex Data Link® watch has some specific hardware requirements that must be met in order for you to download data into it. Your computer has to be running some version of Windows (3.1 to NT 4.0). At this time, the Timex Data Link® watch does not work with Apple computers. Also, another stringent requirement is that you must have a CRT monitor, VGA or above. For laptop displays, such as passive scan and active matrix, an optional Notebook adapter is required.

This is because the data from your computer is read visually by your watch. Set your watch down in front of you. See that circle above the display? Looks like a lens, doesn't it? That's exactly what it is. When set to receive, this lens reads a series of white-on-black barcodes that flash across your screen, or reads the flashing LED on the optional Notebook adapter.

TIME SAVER

If you do travel a lot, download all the pertinent data you need or even think you'll need before you leave. However, keep a current version of your Outlook folders on your laptop, just in case.

Notice that you do not need to have Outlook (or its predecessor Schedule+) to use this watch. That's because Timex ships basic scheduling and information management software with the watch. It's pretty functional, but since you're a big Outlook fan anyway, why switch?

Installing the Data Link Software

Okay, the first thing to do is get the software installed. This is not too hard, although there's an initial tutorial that will assist you in setting up your watch.

TIME SAVER

This may seem silly, but before you install the Data Link software, make sure your computer's set for the correct date and time. The watch can be set from the computer's system clock, and a lot of people do not always take the time to check the accuracy of their computer's clock.

23

Want a really accurate time and date for your watch? How about getting the time from one of the world's atomic clocks—the most accurate timepieces on the planet? Surf the Web to `http://www.zdnet.com`, and enter the site's Software Library. Use the search tool and look for the program called AccuSet.

If you download this shareware product and install it, it will dial up a calibration number to any one of a number of atomic clocks and automatically reset your computer to match. Then, if you use the Data Link system to set your watch's time, it will display very accurate time.

I strongly recommend registering this great piece of software!

Let's get this show on the road and install the Data Link software:

1. To start the installation process, run `Setup.exe` on the floppy disk.

2. After you read the Welcome screen, click Continue to proceed through the install program.

3. The install program will ask you to exit all other running programs. Once you have done this, click Continue.

4. The next dialog displays the directory the Data Link software will be installed into. If you agree with the default, click OK. If not, change the directory, then click OK.

5. After a lengthy installation, the Data Link software will request that you restart Windows. You should do so. Click the Restart Windows button.

6. Once Windows has restarted, start the Data Link program by double-clicking its program icon. Initially, your screen will go dark, except for a message that informs you that your screen is being calibrated.

7. When the Auto calibration is complete! message box appears, click OK.

8. The first time the Data Link software is run, the tutorial begins (see Figure 23.1). This tutorial should be used all the way through, so you can get a feel as to where you need to physically place your watch to have it download data.

   Once the tutorial is finished, the main screen of the Data Link program is displayed (see Figure 23.2).

Eight categories of data can be sent to your watch. Table 23.1 describes them. Those categories marked in bold can also be downloaded from Outlook.

Figure 23.1.

The Data Link software tutorial.

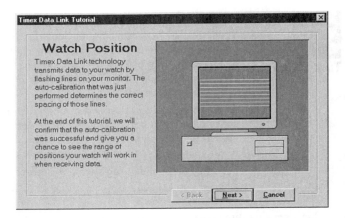

Figure 23.2.

The main Data Link software screen.

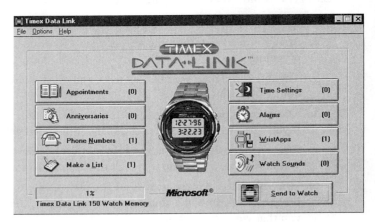

Table 23.1. Talking to your Data Link Watch.

Data Category	Description
Appointments	Appointments and meetings (even recurring) can be transferred.
Anniversaries	Recurring events can be transferred. A special icon in the watch informs the wearer one week before an anniversary or event, and flashes on the day of the event as a final reminder.
Phone Numbers	Contact names and phone numbers can be transferred.
Make a List	Tasks can be transferred.
Time Settings	Time and date for two time zones can be entered.
Alarms	Up to five daily alarms can be transferred.
WristApps™	Specialized watch functions can be loaded one at time.
Watch Sounds	Sound schemes for the watch.

23

As you can see from Table 23.1, Data Link software still has a lot of functionality of its own, despite the overlap with Outlook, so I wouldn't abandon it altogether. The WristApps™ applets alone make it worth it.

Before we learn how to use Outlook and the Data Link watch, let's learn how to download information from the Data Link program, so you can see the differences.

Using the Data Link Program

Because setting the time is something you'll want to do early on, let's walk through this part of the Data Link program now:

1. Click the Time Settings button in the Data Link software.

2. In the Time Settings dialog (see Figure 23.3), you can set your computer's current time and the times and dates for two time zones. Configure the settings to how you want them.

JUST A MINUTE

> If you do not wish to set your watch for more than one time zone, just make sure the information in the time zone sections is identical.

Figure 23.3.

The Time Settings dialog.

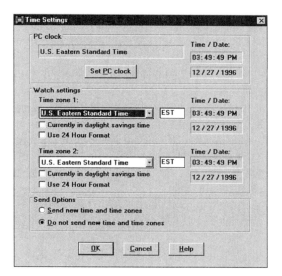

3. In the Send to section, click the Send New Time and Time Zones radio button.
4. Click OK.

5. In the main screen, you will see that a "2" appears next to the Time Settings label. This is because you are ready to upload two time zones' worth of information.

   Also, in the lower-left corner of the main screen is a percentage bar that indicates the percentage of the watch's memory that will be used when the download occurs. Keep an eye on this because you will not be allowed to overflow the watch.

JUST A MINUTE

The WristApps™ features can only be downloaded one at a time. The memory requirements for them are already built into the watch, and therefore downloading a WristApps™ feature does not affect the watch's storage capacity.

6. Click the Send to Watch button.

7. Prepare your watch as the Data Link software tutorial showed you. The Get Ready dialog (see Figure 23.4) appears to remind you of this.

Figure 23.4.

The Get Ready dialog.

8. When your watch is ready and in position, click the OK button in the Get Ready dialog.

9. When the download transmission is complete, a message dialog (see Figure 23.5) appears to confirm you heard no warning alarms from your watch indicating faulty transmission. If you did, click Retry. If you did not, click OK.

Figure 23.5.

Was the transmission complete?

Now that you have seen how the Timex Data Link's software does its thing, it's time to see how Outlook can be used to transmit data to the watch.

23

Outlook and Data Link

As you read in Table 23.1, only three folders of data can be transferred from Outlook to the watch: Calendar, Tasks, and Contacts. This may seem limited, but these are very useful folders, and you can't e-mail with your watch (yet), anyway.

To prepare Outlook to download its data, you must first install the Data Link system add-on. This add-on is an executable Wizard located on your Office 97 CD-ROM, as part of the ValuPack. To install the Wizard, run valupack\timex\timexwiz.exe. A confirming message dialog appears (see Figure 23.6). When you click yes, the Wizard will be added into Outlook.

23

Figure 23.6.
Confirming Wizard installation.

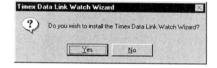

JUST A MINUTE

If you are running Windows NT, run the timexnt.exe file in the same directory instead.

After the wizard is installed, you can now send data from Outlook to the watch using Outlook's exporting functions:

1. In Outlook, click the File | Import and Export menu command.
2. In the first screen of the Import and Export Wizard, select the Export to Timex Data Link Watch option (see Figure 23.7), then click Next.

Figure 23.7.
Starting the exporting process.

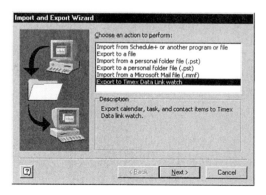

3. The second screen of the Wizard, shown in Figure 23.8, lets you select which types of data from Outlook you want to download into the watch. Check and uncheck the options as desired. When you are finished, click Next.

Figure 23.8.

Choosing the data to send to the watch.

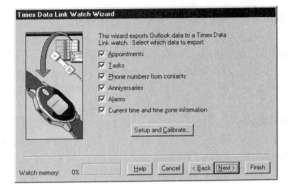

JUST A MINUTE

The remaining screens in the Wizard display if the associated data category was checked in the second screen. In other words, the Tasks screen of the Wizard will not appear if the Tasks option was unchecked.

The remainder of these steps assume that all options were checked. If, at any time, you want to stop configuring the download to the watch, click the Finish button.

4. The third screen lets you specify how much appointment data you want to transmit (see Figure 23.9). Keep an eye on the watch memory bar at the bottom of the Wizard—the more data you download, the more memory will be used. Click Next when finished.

Figure 23.9.

The Appointment configuration screen.

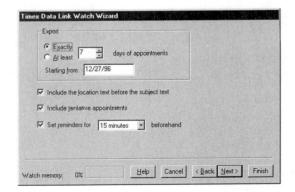

5. The fourth screen is for configuring which tasks you want to download into the watch (see Figure 23.10). Notice that Task priority is a factor, not just the chronology of the Task. Click Next when finished.

Figure 23.10.

The Tasks configuration screen.

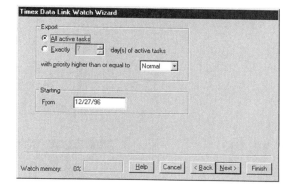

6. The fifth screen, shown in Figure 23.11, lets you select whose phone number will be downloaded to the watch. Remember, keep an eye on the watch's memory box so you don't overload the watch. Click Next when finished.

Figure 23.11.

The Phone Number configuration screen.

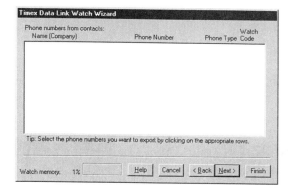

7. In the sixth screen, you select the anniversaries, birthdays, or any other annual event you have in Calendar that will get downloaded into the watch (see Figure 23.12). Click Next when finished.

8. The Data Link watch can have up to five preset alarms set for it on a daily, weekly, monthly, or yearly basis, and the seventh screen (see Figure 23.13) sets these alarms. If an alarm is set with one of the latter three intervals, a date field will appear in that alarm row. Click Next when finished.

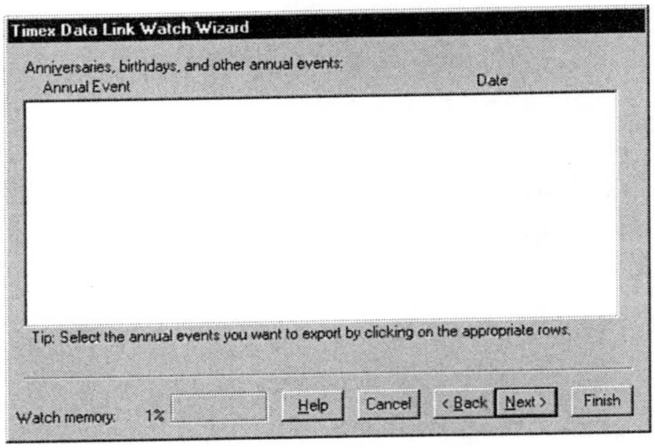

Figure 23.12.

The Annual Events configuration screen.

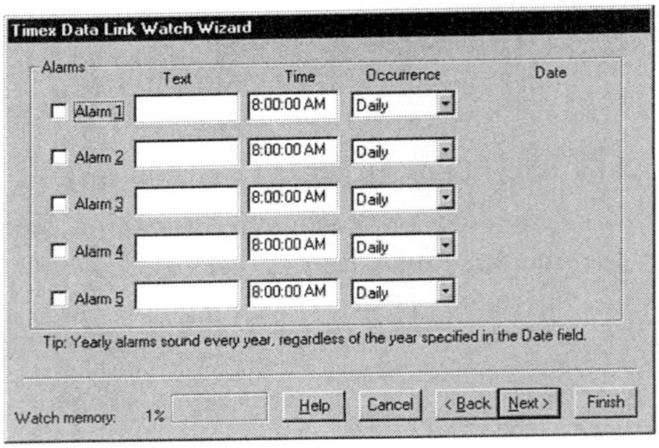

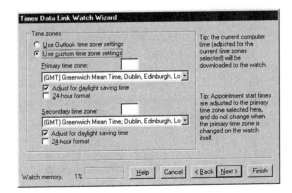

Figure 23.13.

The Alarms configuration screen.

9. The eighth screen sets the time zone information for the watch. Compare what's shown in Figure 23.14 to the Timex Data Link watch Time Settings dialog, shown in Figure 23.3. Click Next when finished.

Figure 23.14.

The Time Zone configuration screen.

10. In the ninth screen, you will briefly see a display similar to the main screen of the Data Link software, which will quickly be covered by the Export to Watch dialog (see Figure 23.15). When your watch is ready as the dialog specifies, click OK.

Figure 23.15.

The Export to Watch dialog.

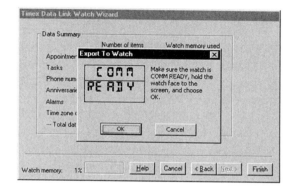

11. When the download transmission is complete, a message dialog (see Figure 23.16) will appear to confirm you heard no warning alarms from your watch indicating faulty transmission. If you did, click No. The Wizard will recycle the transmission sequence. If you did not hear warning alarms, click Yes.

Figure 23.16.

Confirming the transmission.

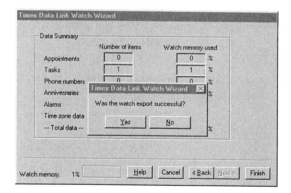

Congratulations, you have entered the world of the truly connected. Some would say the world of the geek, but pay them no mind. You have the world at your fingertips. Or at your wrist, whatever.

Summary

Now that you have learned how to use the Timex Data Link watch, you will be able to take your Outlook information basically anywhere. It's even water-resistant to 30 meters in case you want to take it to the beach.

JUST A MINUTE

> If you really insist on licking the watch, clean it off before downloading data. Smudges tend to goof up the transmission.

In the next hour, you will learn how to use one more nifty bit of Office 97 technology: the IntelliMouse.

Q&A

Q I can't get the watch to download properly. Is there some trick?

A This is why you should go through the Timex Data Link watch tutorial. It will help you get the angle and position right. Basically, if the watch is reading correctly, it will emit a steady stream of beeps. Run through the calibration sequences available in the Data Link software or on the second page of the Import and Export wizard until you find the right place. Make sure your room is well-lit, and the screen is fairly bright. Also, try taking the watch off and holding it in your hand. That may make it more steady.

Q I have been using an older model of the Timex Data Link watch. Can I use it with Outlook?

A Not very well. The Wizard is geared for the Model 150 watch and cannot be told to adjust for the lack of functionality the earlier model has. You can use the Data Link software, however. It can be adjusted by clicking on the File | Advanced menu command.

23

Hour **24**

Using the IntelliMouse with Outlook

Microsoft has developed a new mouse, called the IntelliMouse, that makes it easier to navigate your way through applications. The mouse has a wheel that resides between the two buttons. Mainly, the wheel replaces the need to use the scrollbars in any window, but it has a few more bells and whistles, too.

There are four basic moves that differentiate the IntelliMouse and a regular two-button mouse:

- [ ] Rotating the wheel—This operation helps you scroll up and down documents or windows without having to click on the scrollbars on the edges of a box.

- [ ] Holding the Shift key while rotating the wheel—This combination can do a number of things, depending on where you are using it. Sometimes it toggles between views, and other times it expands and collapses folders.

- [ ] Holding the Ctrl key while rotating the wheel—This combination can be used to zoom in and out in a document window, such as a Word document.

☐ Holding down the wheel while moving the mouse—This operation can be performed to quickly scan through a document or a window. The cursor appears as four arrows and allows the user to scan sideways or up and down by moving the mouse.

How the IntelliMouse Works in Outlook 97

Because the IntelliMouse works differently with each program that recognizes it, this chapter focuses on the ways that the mouse can be used in Outlook.

Using the IntelliMouse to Scroll

The most common way to use the mouse wheel is to scroll through documents (such as e-mail messages) or scroll up and down windows (such as the Inbox window). By rolling the wheel with your finger, you can scroll through a document or a list in a table view. Examples of table views are the Messages view in Inbox, the Events view in Calendar, and the Phone List view in Contacts.

In the Contacts module, rotating the wheel in an Address Card view allows you to scroll through the list of contacts. By rotating the wheel, you can scroll sideways through the cards.

If you want to scroll through a list sideways, hold down the wheel while you move the mouse to the left or right. (If you have done it correctly, the cursor will turn into four arrows.)

If you use Microsoft Word as your e-mail editor, you can simply click the wheel button once in an open e-mail message to have it AutoScroll through the message. Take your hand off the mouse and read; the document will slowly scroll down automatically.

Using the IntelliMouse to Change Views

Using the Shift key while you rotate the wheel allows you to switch views in some of the Outlook views, such as a Timeline view. For instance, if you change the Inbox view to Message Timeline, you can hold the Shift key down while you rotate the wheel to change the time being viewed. If you rotate the wheel, you can switch between viewing a few hours' worth of messages to a day's worth of messages to a few days' worth of messages.

In the Day, Week, and Month views in the Calendar module, you can add the Shift key while you rotate the wheel to toggle between the Day view, Week view, and Month view.

24

Using the IntelliMouse to Expand and Collapse Groups or Folders

If you have folders and subfolders in Outlook, such as folders within your Inbox folder, you can expand and collapse them by placing the cursor over the plus (+) or minus (−) sign and holding the Shift key while rotating the wheel up or down.

In some view formats in which fields group the items, you can place the cursor over the plus (+) or minus (−) sign, hold the Shift key, and rotate the wheel up or down to expand and collapse the groups. A couple of examples of views with grouped items are the By Category view in the Inbox and the Events view in Calendar.

Using the IntelliMouse to Adjust the Width of Columns

Whenever you have selected a Card view in the Contacts folder, just hold down the Shift key and rotate the wheel to lengthen or shorten the columns.

Summary

This chapter discusses the IntelliMouse from Microsoft. You learned how to use the wheel and the mouse buttons to scroll, zoom, and scan through items in Outlook.

Q&A

Q How can you pan through the body of an e-mail message, using the IntelliMouse?

A Hold down the wheel while moving the mouse until arrows appear in place of your cursor. Moving the mouse up and down or sideways allows you to pan through the document.

Q If you want to scroll slowly through the body of an e-mail message, how can you use the IntelliMouse?

A Rotating the wheel allows you to scroll up and down the body of the message.

Q If you are in Calendar, how can you use the IntelliMouse to switch between views?

A Hold down the Shift key while you rotate the wheel to toggle between the Month, Day, and Week views.

24

INDEX

listing 393

MACMILLAN COMPUTER PUBLISHING USA

A VIACOM COMPANY

Technical Support:

If you need assistance with the information in this book or with a CD/Disk
accompanying the book, please access the Knowledge Base on our Web
site at **http://www.superlibrary.com/general/support**. Our most
Frequently Asked Questions are answered there. If you do not find the
answer to your questions on our Web site, you may contact Macmillan
Technical Support at **(317) 581-3833** or e-mail us at **support@mcp.com**.

Visual Basic for Applications Unleashed

—Paul McFedries

Combining both power and ease of use, Visual Basic for Applications (VBA) is the common language for developing macros and applications across all Microsoft Office components. Using the format of the best-selling *Unleashed* series, this book enables users to master the intricacies of this popular language and exploit the full power of VBA. It covers user interface design, database programming, networking programming, Internet programming, and standalone application creation.

CD-ROM is packed with author's sample code, sample spreadsheets, databases, projects, templates, utilities, and evaluation copies of third-party tools and applications.

$49.99 USA/$70.95 CDN   *User Level: Accomplished–Expert*
ISBN: 0-672-31046-5   *800 pages*

Teach Yourself Microsoft Office 97 in 24 Hours

—Greg Perry

An estimated 22 million people use Microsoft Office, and with the new features of Office 97, much of that market will want the upgrade. To address that market, Sams has published a mass-market version of its best-selling *Teach Yourself* series. *Teach Yourself Microsoft Office 97 in 24 Hours* shows readers how to use the most widely requested features of Office. This entry-level title includes many illustrations, screen shots, and a step-by-step plan to learning Office 97.

Teaches how to use each Office product and how to use them together. Readers learn how to create documents in Word that include hypertext links to files created with other Office products.

$19.99 USA/$28.95 CDN   *User Level: New–Casual–Accomplished*
ISBN: 0-672-31009-0   *450 pages*

Microsoft Office 97 Unleashed, Second Edition

—Paul McFedries

Microsoft has brought the Web to their Office suite of products. Hyperlinking, Office Assistants, and Active Document Support let users publish documents to the Web or an intranet site. They also completely integrate with Microsoft FrontPage, making it possible to point-and-click a Web page into existence. This book details each of the Office products—Excel, Access, Powerpoint, Word, and Outlook—and shows the estimated 22 million registered users how to create presentations and Web documents.

Shows how to extend Office to work on a network. Describes the various Office Solution Kits and how to use them. CD-ROM includes powerful utilities and two best-selling books in HTML format.

$39.99 USA/$56.95 CDN   *User Level: Accomplished–Expert*
ISBN: 0-672-31010-4   *1,200 pages*

Teach Yourself Microsoft FrontPage 97 in a Week

—Donald Doherty & John Jung

FrontPage is the number one Web site creation program in the market, and this book explains how to use it. Everything from adding Office 97 documents to a Web site to using Java, HTML, wizards, Visual Basic Script, and JavaScript in a Web page is covered. With this book, readers will learn all the nuances of Web design and will create, through the included step-by-step examples, an entire Web site using FrontPage 97.

CD-ROM includes Microsoft Internet Explorer 3.0, ActiveX and HTML development tools, plus additional ready-to-use templates, graphics, scripts, Java applets, and more.

$29.99 USA/$42.95 CDN　　　　*User Level: New–Casual*
ISBN: 1-57521-225-0　　　　　*500 pages*

Laura Lemay's Web Workshop: Microsoft FrontPage 97

—Laura Lemay & Denise Tyler

The latest release of Microsoft's FrontPage not only integrates completely with the Microsoft Office suite of products, but also allows a Web author to develop and manage an entire Web site. This allows Excel spreadsheets and Word documents to be added easily to a Web page or site. The previous version only allowed single page development and did not work with Office. This book shows readers how to exploit those new features on their Web or intranet site and teaches basic design principles, link creation, and HTML editing.

CD-ROM contains the entire book in HTML format, templates, graphics, borders, scripts, and some of the best Web publishing tools available.

$39.99 USA/$56.95 CDN　　　　*User Level: Casual–Accomplished*
ISBN: 1-57521-223-4　　　　　*650 pages*

Teach Yourself HTML 3.2 in 24 Hours

—Dick Oliver

In just 24 one-hour lessons, users will learn everything they need to know to create effective, eye-catching Web pages—from learning HTML basics, formatting text, and working with graphics to using an HTML editor, publishing to a Web server, and adding interactivity to Web pages.

A support site will be set up on the Sams Web site, providing links to sites mentioned in the book, easy access to Web publishing shareware products, and continuously updated material. Covers HTML 3.2.

$19.99 USA/$28.95 CDN　　　　*User Level: New–Casual*
ISBN: 1-57521-235-8　　　　　*300 pages*

Teach Yourself the Internet in 24 Hours

—Noel Estabrook

This book is the quickest way for users to learn everything they really need to know about the Internet, in just 24 one-hour lessons! Provides extensive coverage of finding access, browsing the Web, e-mail, newsgroups, real-time communication, locating interesting information, and more for Windows and Macintosh.

A support site for the book will be set up on the Sams Web site, providing links to sites mentioned in the book, easy access to Internet shareware products, and updated material.

$19.99 USA/$28.95 CDN
ISBN: 1-57521-236-6

User Level: New–Casual
300 pages

Teach Yourself Windows 95 in 24 hours, Second Edition

—Greg Perry

With learning broken down into 24 one-hour lessons, this easy-to-follow tutorial can be used by individuals as well as in seminars, training sessions, and classrooms. Whether users are just starting out or are migrating from previous versions of Windows, this is a must-have resource to get them up and running quickly and easily.

Loaded with "quick-start" chapters, "Do and Don't" tips, Question & Answer sections, quizzes, and exercises to help users master the concepts with ease. Covers Windows 95.

$19.99 USA/$28.95 CDN
ISBN: 0-672-31006-6

User Level: New–Casual
550 pages

Add to Your Sams Library Today with the Best Books for Programming, Operating Systems, and New Technologies

The easiest way to order is to pick up the phone and call

1-800-428-5331

between 9:00 a.m. and 5:00 p.m. EST.

For faster service please have your credit card available.

ISBN	Quantity	Description of Item	Unit Cost	Total Cost
0-672-31046-5		Visual Basic for Applications Unleashed (Book/CD-ROM)	$49.99	
0-672-31009-0		Teach Yourself Microsoft Office 97 in 24 Hours	$19.99	
0-672-31010-4		Microsoft Office 97 Unleashed, Second Edition (Book/CD-ROM)	$39.99	
1-57521-225-0		Teach Yourself Microsoft FrontPage 97 in a Week (Book/CD-ROM)	$29.99	
1-57521-223-4		Laura Lemay's Web Workshop: Microsoft FrontPage 97 (Book/CD-ROM)	$39.99	
1-57521-235-8		Teach Yourself HTML 3.2 in 24 Hours	$19.99	
1-57521-236-6		Teach Yourself the Internet in 24 Hours	$19.99	
0-672-31006-6		Teach Yourself Windows 95 in 24 Hours, Second Edition	$19.99	
❏ 3 ½" Disk		Shipping and Handling: See information below.		
❏ 5 ¼" Disk		TOTAL		

Shipping and Handling: $4.00 for the first book, and $1.75 for each additional book. Floppy disk: add $1.75 for shipping and handling. If you need to have it NOW, we can ship product to you in 24 hours for an additional charge of approximately $18.00, and you will receive your item overnight or in two days. Overseas shipping and handling adds $2.00 per book and $8.00 for up to three disks. Prices subject to change. Call for availability and pricing information on latest editions.

201 W. 103rd Street, Indianapolis, Indiana 46290

1-800-428-5331 — Orders   1-800-835-3202 — FAX   1-800-858-7674 — Customer Service

Book ISBN 0-672-31044-9